W. G. Sebald's Postsecular Redemption

W. G. Sebald's Postsecular Redemption

Catastrophe with Spectator

Russell J. A. Kilbourn

NORTHWESTERN UNIVERSITY PRESS
EVANSTON, ILLINOIS

Northwestern University Press
www.nupress.northwestern.edu

Printed in the United States of America

10 9 8 7 6 5 4 3 2 1

Library of Congress Cataloging-in-Publication Data

Names: Kilbourn, Russell J. A. (Russell James Angus), 1964– author.
Title: W.G. Sebald's postsecular redemption : catastrophe with spectator /
    Russell J. A. Kilbourn.
Description: Evanston, Illinois : Northwestern University Press, 2018. |
    Includes bibliographical references and index.
Identifiers: LCCN 2018023770| ISBN 9780810138087 (pbk. : alk. paper) |
    ISBN 9780810138100 (cloth : alk. paper) | ISBN 9780810138117 (ebook)
Subjects: LCSH: Sebald, W. G. (Winfried Georg), 1944–2001—Criticism and
    interpretation. | Redemption in literature.
Classification: LCC PT2681.E18 Z658 2018 | DDC 833.914—dc23
LC record available at https://lccn.loc.gov/2018023770

For my father, who was my best reader.

CONTENTS

ACKNOWLEDGMENTS

This book is the result of years of reading and rereading Sebald's prose narratives, in the course of which I had the opportunity to meet and share my thoughts with a good many scholars from all over the world, my fellow Sebaldians, some of whom are the best friends I never get to see. This book was helped into existence by a graduate seminar I began teaching a few years ago at Wilfrid Laurier University on "Memory and Affect in Film and Fiction," featuring (on the literary side) Sebald, Nabokov, and Munro. But it would never have seen the light of day had my colleague Eleanor Ty not suggested this project in the first place. I must also extend my gratitude to my editor, Trevor Perri, and to the rest of the editorial team at Northwestern University Press for their steadfast support, and to the anonymous readers, who went above and beyond in their feedback on the original manuscript. Finally, I wish to thank Sandra and Francesca for never letting me forget what really matters, and of course all our Venetian friends, who give life to the most beautiful city in the world, where the first draft of this book came to fruition.

I gratefully acknowledge that the financial support for the research for this book was received from a grant funded partly by Wilfrid Laurier University operating funds and partly by the SSHRC Institutional Grant awarded to Wilfrid Laurier University.

W. G. Sebald's Postsecular Redemption

Sebaldian Ironies

From Postmodern Metafiction to Postsecular Redemption

> For the time being, our cities still shine through the night, and the fires still spread.
>
> —W. G. Sebald, *The Rings of Saturn*

> This is Electra speaking. In the heart of darkness. Under the sun of torture. To the capitals of the world. In the name of the victims.
>
> —Heiner Müller, *Hamletmachine*

In this book I trace the red thread of redemption across the four prose works of German author W. G. Sebald: *Vertigo* (1999 [*Schwindel: Gefühle*, 1990]), *The Emigrants* (1996 [*Die Ausgewanderten*, 1992]), *The Rings of Saturn* (1998 [*Die Ringe des Saturn*, 1995), and *Austerlitz* (2001). I seek to amplify and extend certain key themes, questions, and preoccupations already present in Sebald scholarship, recontextualizing them in a new conceptual framework conditioned by current thinking around the "postsecular" nature of twenty-first-century culture and Sebald's position within it. In the process I hope to stake new ground in a crowded field that is guided by certain critical ortho-doxies, certain of which I productively exploit and others I either counter or avoid. My critical approach, therefore, is as hybrid as its subject, combining a comparative literary method, focusing on intermedial analysis informed by close attention to Sebald's status as *bricoleur extraordinaire*. At the same time, in my readings I invoke various distinct critical-theoretical approaches, such as those of the Frankfurt school, postcolonial and poststructuralist theories, and Mikhail Bakhtin's theory of the novel. In more than one chapter as well I employ an archival methodology based in research conducted at the Sebald archive. My approach, in short, is manifold, based in my conviction that the critical legacy of the various poststructuralisms is far from played out and that contemporary anti- or posttheoretical trends have too quickly abandoned a repertoire of concepts and rhetorical tools whose long-term significance for the history of ideas is only now becoming apparent. I begin my examination of Sebald, therefore, from a position predicated upon a concatenation of the major theoretical models of the later twentieth century, now relegated to the various critical and fictional "posts" (which are by no means equivalent or of the same order): postmodernism, postcolonialism, posthumanism but also, even more specifically for Sebald, the postmemorial, the postapocalyptic, and especially the postsecular. In the process I engage here with certain recent movements or trends, both positively, as with queer theory, negatively, as with new materialism, and more equivocally, with certain versions of affect theory. And while my ultimate recuperative aim is to explore the degree in which affect inflects the intertextual and intermedial dimension of Sebald's texts, for me, everything—gender, sexuality, affect, materiality—is subordinate to the latter.

My attitude toward the new materialism, whether under a posthumanist rubric or not, is informed by my training in the 1990s in poststructuralist theory. As will become clear over the course of this book, however, my method is to privilege what appears to be Sebald's relationship with such theoretical models, their significance—or lack thereof—for his prose works. What are the implications of the new materialism for received conceptualizations of agency, selfhood, and autonomy? To what extent do contemporary literary or other narratives critique even as they appear to sustain the new materialism? The primary binary dissolved by the new materialism's antimetaphysical stance is that of the literal versus the metaphorical, in that the new and elastic notion of "matter" includes virtual and intangible—"dematerialized"—forms of matter alongside the more traditional embodied and immanent materialities currently accorded such privileged status.[1] But this scenario conceals certain ironies, the first of which is that this very antimetaphysicality was made possible by the deconstructive turn of poststructuralist thought, which, beginning in the mid-1960s, paved the way for the latest florescence of post-Marxist, postconstructivist, posthumanist and yet "materialist" theories of the human. In short, what the new materialism conceals is the ongoing quest to define the human in terms other than the old, tainted binaries of subject-object, self-other, and so on. Instead, we have the contemporary valorization of affect and other radically negatively defined quanta, naming aspects of human being grounded in the body, in its basic materiality, including the brain. The "internal materialism" of the neuro- and cognitive sciences opposes itself to an "external" materialism remaining from a more traditional hierarchy. The challenge here would seem to be to define the human without recourse to conventional notions of subjectivity, consigned by the dominant contemporary critical theories to the dustbin of history.[2] What forms, if any, do these (largely theoretical) struggles take, in contemporary literature? What kinds of responses do writers offer to these questions, particularly when some kind of subject, discursive, grammatical, or structural, remains fundamental to literary narrative? Sebald's prose texts embody a very particular set of answers to these questions.

Intermediality and Genre

But first, how to explain Sebald's enduring fascination among readers of both German and English? In Susan Sontag's view, Sebald's work is "one of the few answers available to English-speaking readers" to the question of the possibility of "literary greatness" in contemporary terms. This despite the fact that all his books appeared first in German and were quickly translated into English by translators with whom Sebald worked closely. (Since this is an English-language book, all quotations from the German are offered here in translation; therefore I tacitly foreground the question of translation when addressing an Anglophone reader.) Sebald's highly intertextual prose narratives, interlarded with photographs and other visual imagery, reveal a post-novelistic intermediality that has yet to be fully accounted for. It is therefore inevitable that this book addresses the seemingly outdated question of the postmodern in this specific context, making a case for Sebald's peculiar—and perhaps exemplary—aesthetic and ethical postmodernity. This depends of course on an expanded and inclusive understanding of modernity and, by extension, modernism. I stress once again that, although the term "postmodern" (and all its variations) has lost its critical vogue in the new postmillennial paradigm, I feel justified in invoking it in relation to Sebald because of the late 1980s–90s period in which he wrote his prose narratives, culminating in *Austerlitz* in 2001, but also because this terminology had been applied in the very first critical studies.[3]

Also, Sebald's productive engagement with other media forms justifies the sustained attention to intermediality his works encourage. This presupposes the older question of intertextuality, which is invoked here in the broadest post-Kristevan sense as another name for a materialized cultural memory, a collective cultural frame of reference, never completely determined by authorial agency, without forgetting that "intertextuality" is Kristeva's translation of Bakhtin's "dialogism."[4] Contemporary cultural theory has by and large bought into a distortion of what Bakhtin meant by "speech," "word," or "discourse" at the root of every utterance (Stam 2000, 201)—the discursive practices of a specific national, cultural, or other collectivity and the aesthetic stylization of these practices by the novelist or other artist.[5] Although intertextuality in itself may not exhaust Sebald's poetics, or rather prosaics, it remains unavoidable in any consideration of Sebald's contribution to genre.[6] According to David Duff (2000, 16–17), "It is probable . . . that the concept of genre will continue to be put in question by more open-ended models of textuality," including "those that emphasize the potentially unlimited scope of intertextuality (genre is, in effect, a restrictive model of intertextuality)." For Ann Pearson (2008, 262), Sebald's prose is essentially the product of a learned and complex intertextuality, one that is "neither misappropriation nor literary exhibitionism but a fertile engagement with earlier texts that contributes to

the historical layering of his narratives." While careful to parse out the intertextual and semantic differences among the various discursive layers typical
of the prose works, Pearson also queries

> the broader significance of Sebald's intertextual practice. Is it, as
> [Stewart] Martin suggests, ultimately conservative—in the mode of
> Eliot's "fragments shored against [the] ruins"—a form of homage to
> models and predecessors that inserts Sebald's own writing within a
> chosen tradition or lineage? Or is Sebald engaging in [what Manfred
> Pfister calls] "playgiarism" . . . that recognizes the inescapability of
> repetition in an era saturated with texts "in which originality will
> only survive in the form of sophisticated games with extant texts and
> traditional structures"? (262)

Pearson acknowledges that "the answer to these questions may depend in
part on which of [Sebald's] books is under consideration" (262) and suggests,
more positively than other critics, that "paradoxically, it is perhaps in this
intertextual polyphony that the true originality of Sebald's writing is to be
found—his extraordinary ability to create something unmistakably his own
out of the fragments he borrows from other writers and reworks in a context
always productive of new meaning even as it draws attention to the continuing resonance of the past" (277). At the same time, as Jonathan Long (2007,
7) points out, Sebald's postmodern intertextuality takes the special, second-
order form of "an allusiveness aimed at academics and designed to ensure the
works' canonicity," a point related to what I argue elsewhere is their status as
works of aestheticized genre theory.[7]
    I would qualify Long's (2007, 7) categorical claim that "intertextuality
is the final major field of Sebald research" by adding that, in some of the
prose works, Sebald's intertextual embedding or appropriation amounts to a
work of *adaptation* or remediation of the source text. What often goes unacknowledged in intertextual studies is that any consideration of a given text's
intertextual dimension leads inevitably to the quasi-synonymous question of
adaptation and, outward from there, toward the world.[8] To predicate our
approach to adaptation upon a dialogic intertextuality (as opposed, e.g., to
one based in the trope of fidelity) "explicitly places the adaptation into its
larger cultural-historical context, taking into account its reception by specific
or general audience(s) (readers, viewers), as well as the broader political-
ethical-ideological implications of a given instance of adaptation" (Naremore
2000, 46). In the poetry collection *Unrecounted*, Sebald writes of a painting
by Jan Peter Tripp: "Time lost, the pain of remembering and the figure of
death have there been assembled in a memorial shrine as quotations from
the painter's own life. Remembrance, after all . . . is nothing other than a
quotation. And the quotation incorporated in a text (or painting) by montage
compels us . . . to probe our knowledge of other texts and pictures and our

knowledge of the world. This, in turn, takes time. By spending it, we enter into time recounted and into the time of culture" (2005, 90). For Sebald, in short, the "unrecounted" [*unerzählt*] only awaits recounting—although this may bring neither closure nor redemption.[9] Worse still, it may not happen at all. In this view, then, adaptation or remediation can be seen as a vital contemporary modality of prosthetic memory: "Remembrance . . . is nothing other than a quotation." In Sebald, memory never avoids an acute self-awareness of its own limitations, not least those produced by modern memory's irreducible reliance upon preexisting cultural forms and technologies of meaning production, including genre, which Bakhtin describes as a mode of thinking (Morson and Emerson 1990, 280).

According to the editors of an early critical collection,

> It goes without saying that Sebald is far removed from the kind of ludic textual experimentation associated with certain strands of post-modernism[10] . . . On the contrary, Sebald's works are informed by a profound ethical and political seriousness. They evince an almost encyclopaedic knowledge of European cultural, social and political history—particularly the history of colonialism—and an enduring concern with what is arguably the defining historical event of recent times: the Holocaust. (Long and Whitehead 2004, 4)

Long and Whitehead identify two of the salient features of Sebald's prose: its extraordinary intertextuality and its deeply ethical and self-conscious approach to the representation of the historical past via fictional narrative. James Chandler frames Sebald's self-reflexive approach to the representation of history in terms of the problem faced by André Hilary, Austerlitz's teacher: "If history is necessary to the purposes of human memory, and history needs a form, and if its forms have degenerated into cliché, then the forms of historiography as we know it must be revitalized by rhetorical genre crossing" (2003, 258).[11] Complicating Lilian R. Furst's (actually James E. Lang's) notion of the "postmodern historical novel," Lynn Wolff (2009, 319) argues that "Sebald's texts trouble the fundamental distinction between the historian or historiographer and the poet, as famously described by Aristotle in book nine of his *Poetics* . . . 'The poet and the historian differ not by writing in verse or in prose . . . The true difference is that one relates what has happened, the other what may happen.'" Unaccounted for in this ancient binary is the fact that Sebald, like any postmemorial writer, also relates what *may have* happened.

As will become clear in the following chapters, one cannot understand the significance of the theme or trope of redemption for Sebald without considering its relation to memory, in both its collective-institutional and personal-affective dimensions. Memory is at the heart of Sebald's postsecular narrative. Through close analysis of Sebald's copies of Nietzsche's "Vom Nutzen und Nachtheil der Historie für das Leben" and *Zur Genealogie der*

Moral, Ben Hutchinson (2009a, 325) deepens our understanding of Sebald's engagement with the central questions of modernity by showing that his poetics of memory is dependent upon "the importance—and paradoxically the impossibility—of forgetting" and that his famous melancholy is therefore in large part the product of the failure of the desire to forget. This reading complements Long's (2007, 162) point that a character like Austerlitz is a representative instance of the modern "archival subject": one who "compensate[s] for his lack of memory by substituting the archive for interiority." In place of repressed memories of being sent as a small child from Prague to England to escape the Holocaust, Austerlitz fills his mind with the history of the outsized architecture of nineteenth-century colonialist Europe. This feature of his character proves to be fundamental not only to who he is by the narrative's mid-1990s present but also, as a function of this, to his complete failure to "find" his parents, in particular his mother, by the book's end. His fascination with specific architectural forms and literal built spaces converges with the imaginative memory work in which he engages late in life, especially once he stumbles upon the fact that he had been sent from Prague in 1939 into quasi-permanent geographic and psychological exile (Sebald 2001, 141). This process eventuates in a particular form of chronotope in which not time but more specifically memory complements the spatial dimension, producing what I would call a postmodern infernal subjectivity.

Metafictionality and (Ironic) Redemption

Before considering Sebald in relation to a postsecular project of transmediating the persistent tropes of a modernist paradigm—redemption foremost among them—it is necessary to clarify and complicate his status as a *post*-modernist writer in the most meaningful sense of one who comes after as the knowing heir to a rich critical literary tradition, as well as one who self-consciously attempts to forge something new and meaningful in the face of an ever-expanding mass of (often ephemeral) cultural material. In the latter sense, then, I read Sebald as creatively extending the metafictional narrative tradition much in vogue in the 1980s, which was a major inspiration for theories of the postmodern in literary fiction in this period.[12] In this view all four of Sebald's prose texts are inventive examples of the kind of

> fictional writing which self-consciously and systematically draws attention to its status as an artifact in order to pose questions about the relationship between fiction and reality. In providing a critique of their own methods of construction, such writings not only examine the fundamental structures of narrative fiction, they also explore the possible fictionality of the world outside the literary fictional text . . . What connects . . . all the very different writers whom one could refer

to broadly as 'metafictional', is that they all explore a *theory* of fiction through the *practice* of writing fiction. (Waugh 1996, 2)

In what I see as a productive contradiction, there is thus always an implicitly ethical-political edge to Sebald's texts, even when they appear to be engaged solely with aesthetic innovation and philosophical inquiry, the relation of "reality" to its representations: "If our knowledge of [the 'real'] world is now seen to be mediated through language, then literary fiction (worlds constructed entirely of language) becomes a useful model for learning about the construction of 'reality' itself" (Waugh 1996, 3). Although Sebald always insisted that his prose texts should not be categorized as novels, they may nevertheless be included in the more expansive category of metafictional narrative. The history of the novel, after all, has always been about the novel's self-interrogation as literary narrative form. Bakhtin's (1981, 3) formulation (of 1941) serves as a baseline definition of the modern novel as "the sole genre that continues to develop, that is as yet uncompleted. The forces that define it as a genre are at work before our very eyes: the birth and development of the novel as a genre takes place in the full light of the historical day. The generic skeleton of the novel is still far from having hardened, and we cannot foresee all of its plastic possibilities." However one categorizes Sebald's texts, Bakhtin's ideas remain significant for their relation to genre: "Novel is the name Bakhtin gives to whatever force is at work within a given literary system to reveal the limits, the artificial constraints, of that system" (xxxi). On a broader cultural level, Bakhtin's historical account of the novel is deeply relevant to Sebald in terms of the critique, central to his work, of what Richard Sheppard (2011, 201) calls "the multi-dimensional sea-change" that is modernity.[13]

As is always the case in the most trenchant discussions from the heyday of postmodernist theory,[14] the postmodern historically addresses the intersection of the aesthetic and epistemological axes of life under mid to late twentieth-century neoliberal capitalism. In this respect the postmodern as a meaningful appellation escapes its most vocal detractors and is shown to be applicable to a writer and former academic, such as Sebald, for whom the critical-theoretical debates in question were likely of only peripheral interest. It is useful to recall here the foundations of the literary postmodern as the aesthetic exploration of crucial philosophical questions: "Language is an independent, self-contained system which generates its own 'meanings.' Its relationship to the phenomenal world is highly complex, problematic and regulated by convention" (Waugh 1996, 3). Metafictions "therefore . . . explore the relationship between this arbitrary linguistic system and the world to which it apparently refers"; they "explore the relationship between the world *of* the fiction and the world *outside* the fiction" (3). There is therefore at once an *epistemological* and an *ontological* dimension to such metafictions, a distinction that is crucial to a basic understanding of Sebald's literary project, insofar as each of his prose texts is concerned with both levels at once: the critical investigation of the

limits of literary representation and the critical appraisal of contemporary
society within a historically inflected perspective. The simultaneously "formalist" and "realist" tendencies in Sebald mark him as both typical of his postwar
generation of writers and yet also in certain ways unique. As a writer, Sebald
is consummately postmodern in that his discourse adheres assiduously to the
fine line between saying something cogent about the world and the identities
of those who inhabit it (realism) and performing an autocritical investigation of its formal properties (formalism) and how these structures are always
already in some sense commensurate with the structures underpinning these
identities and the knowledge to which they give access. Each of Sebald's prose
works finds intratextual resolution, on its own terms, as an individual text,
as well as intertextually and intermedially in terms of the author's complex,
intensive, and, in some ways, obsessive engagement with a cultural heritage
or referential framework that, for many contemporary readers, is itself a thing
of the past.

My other major focus here considers the ironic persistence of redemption or
salvation as theme or formal feature of many contemporary popular narratives but also of more authoritative cultural narratives—including those of
"History." My aim in this respect is to clarify Sebald's position on the two-
sided question of cultural redemption in a supposedly secular world.[15] As I
(Kilbourn 2010, 29) note elsewhere, "the meaning and significance of the
term 'modern'—and therefore the status of 'the modern project'—continues
to turn on this crucial issue of a kind of reflexive, avowedly secular 'faith'
in a repertoire of metaphysical structures that constitute the ironically theological basis of contemporary Western culture." Can culture save us from
the catastrophe of history, and how can we save our culture in the process?
Furthermore: who is the "we" here, and what do "we" mean by "culture"?
As Sebald's texts repeatedly imply (and as I explore in chapters 1, 4, and 5),
the primary questions of a classic postcolonial critique retain their relevance
in this context. More specifically, though, I refer to what Julia Hell (2004,
363) identifies as the prevailing condition in Germany after World War II,
when "the belief in redemption, or in the redemptive potential of violence and
revolution," could no longer be sustained. Sebald is of course precisely of this
generation, born in 1944 at the end of the war. On the formal level, though,
this investigation also circles back to an inquiry into the status of the novel,
or rather the long prose narrative, as eminently writerly object in a visually
hegemonic culture.

It could be said that the model of redemption with which Sebald is working is decidedly modernist, which is to say secular, and predicated upon the
assumption that since the eighteenth century we have been living in an always
already "fallen" world, that we are as it were "congenitally" postlapsarian.
This means, in other words, that the Christological myth of the Fall has a
lingering and tenacious value for art and literature in a modernity that sees

itself on the far side of the Copernican emancipation from theological tyranny. This secular construct rejects for modernity not only the guilt and regret of the loss of an original unity of human and divine but also the hope of a future return to this state through a redemptive transcendence—the promise of a restorative act of grace from "on high" that effaces the stigma of the initial error by which "man" got himself catapulted into time, suffering, and death. Such "fallenness" therefore must be considered in the present context in its revalued form as an unmoored theological metaphor. According to this line, the human condition in modernity is an irredeemably fallen one, with the promise of only an approximate or metaphorical redemption, figured as a return to or restoration or restitution of a place, time, or condition, whether literal or metaphorical, which, however seemingly unchanged, is never the same—home, childhood, a happy relationship, or some more nebulous affective state.

Catastrophe with Spectator

As my title indicates, this book's other principal objective is to consider Sebald's four prose texts in the context of what theorists working at the intersection of literature, film, theology, religious studies, and many other disciplines call the postsecular.[16] This examination is focused in relation to Sebald's abiding preoccupation with redemption, or rather with what comes after or replaces the mechanism of redemption—and all it represents or signifies—in a later modern or postmodern world in which such metaphysical structures persist only as literary, filmic, or other cultural tropes. In Sebald's texts, in fact—and in this respect they are truly *post*modernist—redemption persists negatively, as a thematic and structural absence, in its impossibility or untenability as a source of hope. In this very negativity, however, it continues to signify and produce meanings, albeit of a generally ironic kind. The question begged here, especially in the purportedly secularist legacy of modernism, is redemption from *what*? The answer must likewise be considered from a vantage point beyond such a restrictive binary formation of secular versus nonsecular.

The general answer to this question is addressed in this book's subtitle, "Catastrophe with Spectator," which is borrowed from the German title of Andrea Köhler's 1997 interview with Sebald, "Katastrophe mit Zuschauer," which in turn alludes to German philosopher Hans Blumenberg's 1979 text *Schiffbruch mit Zuschauer* (Shipwreck with spectator), an analysis of one of the most pervasive "paradigm[s] of a metaphor for existence," in Blumenberg's phrase, of modern, which is to say post-Kantian, Western literature and art. More generally, though, the phrase draws attention to the complex centrality to Sebald's narrative project of visual images and visuality per se, a project that might be summed up, to paraphrase Walter Benjamin's essay on "The Work of Art in the Age of Its Technological Reproducibility," as a variegated meditation on late twentieth-century humanity's paying witness to its own slow-motion destruction under late capitalism.[17] This witnessing, I would note, manifests in the form of a singular and specific masculine subject, recurring across all four prose narratives. In this respect I am cognizant throughout this book of Sebald's abiding debt to the Frankfurt school's critique of bourgeois capitalist modernity. At the same time, I look beyond this older model to frame an image of Sebald as a quietly but powerfully political writer whose fictions are charged with an awareness of the contradictions of postcolonial culture and an acute attention to the pitfalls of presumed historical knowledge. In short, I read Sebald as a cartographer of the terra incognita of late modernist subjectivity, writing from a position of anxious ethical self-awareness, the position that permits the postmemorial appropriation of others' voices and viewpoints just as it foregrounds the author's—and narrating subject's—ethical accountability. This is precisely the thrust of each text's metafictional dimension, which means that it is aware of its own fictionality, as it is aware of its own textuality, even as it maintains an ethical relation to the world outside, which is the most radical political gesture a text can make.

The Persistence of the Subject

It is necessary to clarify how I use the term "subject" in this predominantly literary context. Outside a programmatically narratological discourse, the category of the "subject" in literary analysis potentially invokes its philosophical, semiotic, psychoanalytic, or other avatars. For that matter, one of poststructuralism's key insights is the suspicion that every invocation of the subject, narratological or otherwise, conceals the metaphysical subject. "As Deleuze reminds us . . . the question of the subject is a metaphysical question, the question of modern metaphysics, namely, that in order to understand what it means for entities to be, we have to begin with the subject as the principle or ground of philosophy" (Critchley and Dews 1996, 17). In Simon Critchley's words, the "question of the subject" is "what makes modern metaphysics modern" (21). To speak of the subject as inescapably metaphysical is to hearken back to the original Aristotelian sense of subject as *hupokeimenon*: foundation, ground, or substratum; the *subjectum* as "that which is thrown under," "as a prior support or more fundamental stratum upon which other qualities, such as predicates, accidents and attributes, may be based" (13). In Heidegger's account, it was not until the advent of modern philosophy with Descartes that the subject-object relation was inverted and the "metaphysical foundation [was] no longer claimed to reside in a form, substance, or deity outside of the human intellect but is rather found in the human being understood as a subject" (Critchley and Dews 1996, 5). A sentence such as "the subject is the subject of metaphysics" thus conveys both senses of "subject," modern and premodern, as both figure and ground of philosophy, so to speak.[18] But what of the subject of narrative fiction? What of the modern(ist), postmodernist, postcolonialist, queer or postsecular, or other manifestation of the subject relevant to Sebald? What relation does this subject bear to the subject discussed by philosophers or literary theorists, even in a posthuman age? What is its contemporary or abiding political or philosophical significance? It should be recalled that the subject of philosophy is itself tropologically determined, insofar as that preeminent aspect of modern subjectivity as Cartesian *cogito*, as "thinking thing" (*res cogitans*), its *self*-consciousness (Critchley and Dews 1996, 15), is precisely the one attribute of which it remains loath to divest itself. Likewise the subject of modern narrative fiction is characterized in its various stages by different attributes, the most persistent of which are voice and visuality. And it is in the modernist period that a significant negotiation is seen between these metaphorical poles, where it is revealed that what is at stake is the very representability of the subject in the first place—a question as ethical in its import as it is ontological and aesthetic. Hence, again, my invocation of metafiction in the opening section above.

Modernity is the general context most relevant for Sebald, as noted; that period, itself already historical, that includes within its horizon of concerns a preoccupation with or need for a subject—even one that is decentered, deterritorialized, or deconstructed. Ostensibly, the discursive avatars of this subject are met with in the pages of modern novelistic fiction, and insofar as this subject always stands in some relation to others (to the world "within" the text; to the Other), the playing out of self-other relations from a variety of perspectives is allowed for. As a figuration of or substitute for consciousness, as a "self," this subject is *itself* subject to a set of narrative exigencies and contingencies, intertextually recurrent structures and themes, whether ironized or not, since Homer and the Old Testament: love, loss, desire, exile, death, redemption. I adhere therefore to a conception of modern literature that sees itself as firmly, if not always consciously, tied to its past, its history, and yet always, at least in formal or technical terms, striving to push ahead to something new.

In sum, as my title suggests, this book is intended to amplify certain recurrent ideas scattered across much earlier work on Sebald: his abiding preoccupation with subjectivity, and therefore gender, and especially masculinity, in late modernity (but also sexuality and sexual orientation, giving rise to a certain queer sensibility); the fundamental ethical outlook informing all his work (not unconnected from the latter); the irreducibly intertextual or intermedial nature of his writings as extraordinarily complex palimpsestic adaptations or remediations of other, preexisting texts, both verbal and visual; the often neglected political, even postcolonial, dimension of Sebald's texts, all too often overlooked out of an irrational (but unsurprising) critical emphasis upon a supposed metaphysical or transcendent dimension. The latter is one of the ways of reading his texts against which I militate here, in one of the major critical through lines linking the chapters across this book. Sebald is a postsecular writer in the most meaningfully immanent sense, the realist effects of his prose inextricable from the texts' intermediality, the typical Sebaldian subject a postapocalyptic "posthuman" *avant la lettre*, echoing Foucault's "death of man" in *The Order of Things*.[19] According to Rosi Braidotti (2013, 1),

> After the postmodern, the post-colonial, the post-industrial, the post-communist, and even the much-contested feminist conditions, we seem to have entered the post-human predicament. Far from being the nth variation in a sequence of prefixes that may appear both endless and somehow arbitrary, the posthuman introduces a qualitative shift in our thinking about what is the basic unit of common reference for our species, our polity and our relationship to the other inhabitants of this planet.

Citing Jürgen Habermas, Braidotti notes that "the posthuman provokes elation but also anxiety . . . about the possibility of a serious de-centering of 'Man', the former measure of all things. There is widespread concern about the loss of relevance and mastery suffered by the dominant vision of the human subject and by the field of scholarship centered on it, the Humanities" (2). Braidotti cites John Gray's indictment, written two years after Sebald's death, of Humanism as the product of the Christian story of "sin and redemption": "Humanism is the transformation of this Christian doctrine of salvation into a project of universal human emancipation. The idea of progress is a secular version of the Christian belief in providence" (Gray 2003, xiii). On this basis Braidotti (2013, 31), aligning herself with Habermas, concludes, "It is not surprising, therefore, that one of the side effects of the decline of Humanism is the rise of the post-secular condition."[20] It is the framing assumption of this book that Sebald is one of the most important late twentieth-century writers to mount a sustained critique of Humanism as the secularized Christian faith in salvation Gray describes. At the same time, Sebald's work evinces a consistent skepticism toward modernity's all-too-hasty faith in its own secular nature. It is all the more remarkable that he does so from a position informed by the most valuable Humanist cultural legacy. His body of work therefore embodies the fundamental contradictions of a so-called secular Humanism[21]—often lost on Humanism's more enthusiastic critics—as the source of both the worst of occidental culture and of its most likely alternatives. According to Braidotti, the "double challenge of linking political subjectivity to religious agency and of disengaging both from oppositional consciousness, and from critique defined as negativity, is one of the main issues raised by the posthumanist condition" (34). This is also, as it happens, the very challenge Sebald addresses in various ways, throughout his prose texts, albeit from a philosophical perspective thoroughly grounded in the Humanist tradition. Sebald also goes beyond Braidotti's formulation in that his texts evince a sophisticated awareness of the fact that it is not critical "negativity" that is the problem but the ethically negative sense in which "negativity" is defined in this context, as the oppositional term in a positive-negative binary. Negativity's function in a deeper historical and theological perspective is not moralistically Manichaean, however, but logical. And, as Sebald repeatedly shows, in the right (ironic) hands this latter kind of negativity is both critically and creatively productive.

From the Posthuman to the Nonhuman

In John Gray's (2003, xiii) pessimistic view, science, even more than religion, has sown the seeds of future catastrophe:

> Belief in progress has another source. In science, the growth of knowledge is cumulative. But human life as a whole is not a cumulative activity; what is gained in one generation may be lost in the next. In science, knowledge is an unmixed good . . . Science increases human power, and magnifies the flaws in human nature. It enables us to live longer and have higher standards than in the past. At the same time it allows us to wreak destruction—on each other and on the Earth—on a larger scale than ever before.

The "dark side" of the posthuman leads inexorably to what theorists call the nonhuman, which is meant to recognize the vast world of animals, plants, objects, and other nonhuman things that have been underacknowledged or unacknowledged until now. At its most extreme, the nonhuman names a world without humans, which leads to a constellation of epistemological, aesthetic, and above all ethical contradictions. How does narrative cope with the possibility of a world devoid of human subjects capable of witnessing such a world?[22] Eugene Thacker (2010, xv) juxtaposes the concept of the "world-in-itself," by which he means the post-Kantian world free of human observers, with the "world-without-us," a world not only free of human observation but also free of humans entirely. As Anders Bergstrom (2016) points out, where the "world-in-itself" addresses the relationship between human and nonhuman experiences of the world, the "world-without-us" follows the logic of the impossible gaze of Lacanian fantasy, which, as Slavoj Žižek (2010, 84) explains (echoing Benjamin's conclusion to the "Work of Art" essay), is "the gaze by means of which the subject is already present at the scene of its own absence." Therefore in *The Rings of Saturn* Sebald, like Lars von Trier in the 2011 film *Melancholia*, invokes "human annihilation as a metaphor for the impossibility of imagining post-capitalist configurations" (Bergstrom 2016, 95). Sebald narratively exploits the notion of the "world-in-itself," the world free of human observation, to adumbrate the future possibility of a world literally free of humans. This, and not some metaphysical afterlife, is the ultimate inverse of whatever positive humanist traces linger in Sebald's vision.

Book Overview

This book approaches Sebald's four prose narratives as exemplary expressions of a complexly ironic postsecular sensibility. I seek to investigate the idea, implicit in Sebald's prose narratives, that the confusion in late capitalist modernity of the subject-object relation, constitutive of the rational Cartesian space of modern visuality, is a key factor in the breakdown of a stable notion of realism as historically specific aesthetic ideology. In the new model thereby implied, the viewer is at once *within* the (increasingly catastrophic) spectacle, a figure in a landscape, while remaining outside, looking on. Sebald's narrator-protagonists are well-read melancholic wanderers who *seem* to exist well outside an ocularcentric society of the spectacle characterized by increasing surveillance and modes of consumption driven by constant retinal stimulation. In this respect these books do not engage with what Gilles Deleuze (1992) calls the "society of control"; Sebald's worldview is too firmly grounded in a critical postwar optic influenced by certain Frankfurt school thinkers, as well as Foucault and Barthes, among other mid to late twentieth-century theorists.[23] Indeed, Sebald never engages directly with that other strain of antipsychoanalytic poststructuralist theory epitomized by Deleuze.[24] There are good reasons for his retention of both a general Freudian paradigm and the lingering traces of a Marxist political economic critique, aspects of Sebald's intellectual vision that become clear when one considers, as many do, the centrality of memory and trauma, both individual and collective, to his poetics and to his evident horror at the world wrought by capitalism.

A visual culture textbook[25] that appeared soon after the publication of *Austerlitz* in 2001 captures the millennial culture's awareness of the centrality to its identity of the visual image: "We live in a world of the image. The very idea of the self, the ways in which we make sense of the world, the means by which we communicate, have all become invested in, and developed through, the visual. In many ways images have replaced words as the defining aspect of cultural identity" (Fuery and Fuery 2003). One does not have to feel a Romantic nostalgia for a predigital, precinematic, or prephotographic cultural reality to question this assertion about the relation of words and images to cultural identity—even in the acknowledgment that contemporary global culture is a visually hegemonic one. But then one might add, as many have, that this is nothing new in itself, and that the technologies of mechanical reproduction and digital production have only amplified a long-standing—some would say hardwired—cultural bias, going back to Descartes and, ultimately, to the Greeks (Jay 1994): the triumph of vision as "the noblest of the senses." Even though the story isn't that simple, literary studies are now being carried out within a complex postliterate cultural environment in which things such as narrative and visuality combine in a nexus that is unique in human history—unique not only because of its unprecedented technological facilitation but also because of this culture's profound self-awareness coupled with a comparably profound unwillingness to acknowledge its own precarious predicament.

Sebald's prose works are deeply invested in a critique of the visually constituted spaces of the post-Cartesian world, where one can no longer rely upon a clear distinction between "real" and "virtual." After all, the virtual today is overwhelmingly visual, at the expense of the other senses, and also possesses an undeniable materiality, in that the virtual often has dire effects in the real world, effacing any clear distinction. Sebald's books provide a unique perspective on this set of transformations in late modern identity and reality alike by enacting as well as describing the tension between visuality and memory in a pre- or postvisual sense. Sebald critiques certain aspects of modernity determined by reason, commerce, and above all *time*—the modernity of capitalism, driven by the twin engines of combustion and consumption. To this "production of destruction" on the grandest scale—what he terms the natural history of destruction—Sebald opposes a theory and practice of memory as *productive* destruction, by means of which the historical traces of destruction remain visible in the face of our best efforts to efface them. These traces—of events such as war and genocide, natural disaster, and personal trauma— legible in themselves, become much more difficult to interpret when taken together in their complex interconnectivity whose reflected patterns are the raw materials of Sebald's fictions. It is from this point of departure that I launch my interrelated analyses of the four prose texts.

Chapter 1 anticipates the reading of *The Emigrants* in chapter 4 within an overt consideration of the book's engagement with the history of technologies of visual representation and the resulting impact upon social reality and identity. I examine two aspects of Sebald's prose narratives that at once shore up and complicate this categorization. First, Sebald's model of history as "catastrophe" that is inseparable from questions of representation or representability, staged as it is within the author's idiosyncratic critique of capitalism and the modernity it has made possible. Second, I investigate the status of the Sebaldian subject as an extension of a post-Enlightenment and specifically *modernist* subjectivity, defined by its lack of self-presence, its noncoincidence with itself, and the consequent lack of coherent identity. Central to this chapter, therefore, is Sebald's incorporation of aspects of Joseph Conrad's work, another modernist writer whose most famous novel, *Heart of Darkness* (1902), is a key intertext for *The Rings of Saturn*. The narrator-protagonist is an avatar, however, of a postmodern(ist) subjectivity constituted, ironically, in the wake of its deconstruction as positive ground for anything: being, knowledge, itself—a subject that therefore seeks to represent itself (or be represented) via radically empty, "unpeopled" settings within which its own absence is a necessary corollary of ways of seeing and being determined along the rational lines of Cartesian space-time. In each of Sebald's four prose narratives, the narrator-character confronts questions of power, knowledge, and identity within narrative economies that deny redemptive closure and the metaphysical worldview perpetuated under late capitalism. Sebald's engagement with history, subjectivity, or "reality" must be qualified, however, as all such categories converge in his works on the terrain of a visually inflected intra- and intertextuality, the latter construed as cultural memory par excellence.

Chapter 2 begins from the premise that what distinguishes Sebald's third prose work from other contemporary first-person accounts of living in an increasingly globalized postmodern world is the thematic constellation of death, mourning, and memory, materialized in a series of meditations on funerary practices across time and cultural space. With *The Rings of Saturn* as point of departure, this chapter focuses on Sebald's ongoing preoccupation with what he calls those "networks [whose] complexity . . . goes far beyond the power of any one individual to imagine" (Sebald 1998, 91). Sebald weaves his own complex network of literary, historical, and cultural associations whose relations become apparent only gradually in this text's oblique approach to narrative. The narrative as such has as its organizing principle a walking tour of County Suffolk, in the course of which the various intertextual strands arise, intersect, and diverge in the narrator's ambulatory consciousness. From this mundane and very local point of departure Sebald's narrative spins outward to encounter the "global tides of information," flowing "without cease," like the waves of seawater whose relentless battering on England's southern coast have in a few short centuries undermined the human settlements that once flourished there. In a very meaningful sense, *The Rings of Saturn* is a vast, multifaceted memento mori, constructed under the sign of an anti-Cartesian scopic regime, at its center a melancholic modern subject—the figure in which aspects of the baroque and even the medieval combine with the premillennial modern—lamenting the erosion of rituals of mourning in a culture for which death does not signify. What is hidden in the text in full view, *anamorphically*, is the question of redemption within a secular model of history as catastrophe. "Catastrophe" is preeminently an imaginative and therefore productive trope in Sebald; a "paradigm of a metaphor for existence," in Blumenberg's phrase. But, for all the visual-perspectival nature of this metaphor, it remains an extended rhetorical trope, a bitterly ironic intertextual allegory whose ultimate twentieth-century referent is the Holocaust, whose interpretative paradigm continues to be determined less by Adorno's dictum about lyric poetry after Auschwitz than by Wittgenstein's Proposition 7: *Wovon man nicht sprechen kann, darüber muss man schweigen* (Of that which one cannot speak, one must remain silent; *Tractatus Logico-Philosophicus*). This is a point that must be stressed in any consideration of Sebald's fictional semantics—more a *prosaics* than a poetics, or even a species of neobaroque *emblematics*. The complexly dialogic *visuality* invoked by this term affords greater weight to the analysis of Sebald's peculiar brand of realism: the production of meaning out of a visual-verbal dynamic or dialectic that recognizes the inescapably *visual* texture of contemporary life. Here the narrative text operates in relation with the discursive codes of painting, photography, and cinema—even as it evinces a profound ambivalence toward or distrust of the image and a concomitant, albeit self-conscious, nostalgia for the word.

The richly intertextual or intermedial nature of Sebald's prose works manifests in the text of *Vertigo*, his first prose narrative, for which Franz Kafka is a primary literary antecedent. Beginning from Sebald's own Kafka scholarship, chapter 3 analyzes Kafka's "Hunter Gracchus" story (1917), as well as specific entries in Kafka's *Diaries*, as a parable of the crossing of chance with "fate" in an ironically temporized Jewish messianism, here filtered through the Wagnerian treatment of the quintessentially modern Flying Dutchman myth—what Heinrich Heine, another intertextual antecedent, calls "the Wandering Jew of the Ocean." In *Vertigo*, messiah and subject of experience are identified in the figure of the Hunter, in the typical Kafkan conflation of extremes of self and other in the protagonist. Kafka's Hunter Gracchus functions obliquely in *Vertigo* as an intertextual avatar for the Kafkan subject, forever doomed not to death as such but to a living death of endless waiting, an eternity spent ceaselessly traveling over the world's seas after a second accident sent his ship off course (the first accident being the fall from the cliff that inaugurated the journey to the land of the dead now gone awry). Neither properly alive nor properly dead, now permanently erroneous, the Hunter figure appears in several forms across Sebald's first prose narrative, providing not a thematic or formal focus but rather a sort of vertiginously ironic justification for Sebald's quasi-autobiographical narrator's circuitous wanderings through a space that is variously one of history, memory, and imagination.

Chapter 4 explores the manner in which Sebald goes beyond an ironically metafictional Nabokovian resolution by offering a deeply ethical fictional response to the untenable but persistent messianic and Christological paradigms in a contemporary literary-cultural context. Continuing the intertextual approach, this chapter treats the butterfly/moth motif in Vladimir Nabokov's *Speak, Memory* (1967) as an ironic allegory for a Christological paradigm of salvation turned inside out in a typical Nabokovian metafictional aporia—a paradox concealed only by what many critics prefer to read as Nabokov's metaphorical staging of the possibility of redemption. The quasi-allegorical Nabokovian "butterfly man" therefore represents in *The Emigrants* (Sebald's second prose narrative) the always-imminent promise, if not the immanent reality, of redemption; a metonymy of an ever-deferred salvific principle that is nevertheless paradoxically "present" in this seemingly heavy-handed intertextual homage. This chapter charts Sebald's use of these explicit and well-documented Nabokovian elements in order to analyze *The Emigrants* on the basis of Sebald's establishment of an attitude toward the problematic conjunction in fictional narrative of the theme of redemption and the principle of chance—an attitude that can only now be called Sebaldian, at once comprehensive and consistent and yet manifesting itself in significantly different ways in the two early prose narratives because of the radical differences in the Nabokov and Kafka source texts. At issue is the fictional—and, ultimately, literal—status of death: the reality principle that even the most glibly post-modernist narrative fails to subvert, and by subverting negate, hence the per-haps ironic persistence of redemption as a literary theme and formal fulcrum. Sebald's prose texts extend in their different ways Kafka's and Nabokov's separate critiques of the persistence of a naively conceived redemptive poten-tial—a conception generally affirmed in the work of generations of Nabokov and Kafka scholars alike.

The final three chapters go beyond existing research on the intertextual or intermedial dimension of Sebald's texts, especially in terms of his relation to other literatures, including contemporary Italian and Canadian. The latter two of these chapters compare Sebald's *Austerlitz* with Nabokov's *Speak, Memory* and Alice Munro's 2006 short-story cycle *The View from Castle Rock*, respec-tively, within different critical-theoretical contexts. The other chapter is on Sebald, Kafka, and Italian writer Claudio Magris, focusing on Magris's 2008 novel *Blindly*.[26] As disparate as these writers are—Sebald, Magris, Munro—they are united, and their juxtaposition here is justified, by their common artistic and critical investment in the literary interrogation of the intersection of memory and "History" in specific cultural and geographical-spatial con-texts, as well as by their mutual standing as exemplarily innovative writers as famous outside their respective national literary contexts as within them. At the heart of each is a deeply ethical concern for the literary mediation of the subject—not as a universal but as a specific and contingent cultural construct upon which the reader is nevertheless ironically tempted to ground her/his shaky conception of selfhood. In sum, Magris and Munro offer examples of postmodern writers who, in their different ways, take Sebald's arguments on history and eschatology a step further from his liminal position between modernism and postmodernism.

Chapter 5 traces Sebald's intertextual appropriation in *Vertigo* of Kafka's travels through northern Italy in 1913 in order to illuminate the contempo-rary German writer's relation to his fellow "border crosser" Italian Claudio Magris. *Vertigo*'s fictional world intersects with that of Magris's *Blindly* in a scene, set in Trieste, involving an angelic visitation whose original is in a dreamlike passage in Kafka's *Diaries*. This angel in turn stands in signifi-cant relation to Walter Benjamin's angel of catastrophic history in the "Ninth Thesis on the Concept of History," famously inspired by Paul Klee's painting *Angelus Novus*. But where Kafka's and Benjamin's angels convey a pecu-liarly modern sense of ironic eschatological "hope"—for potential salvation indefinitely deferred, for the more immediate "salvation" of writing—Sebald's reimagining of Kafka's time in Italy presents us with a highly idiosyncratic figure as an emissary of an even more contemporary allegory of destruction both general and imminent.

Chapter 6 picks up on the argument broached in chapter 3, in which Nabokov is described as the "tutelary deity" of Sebald's *The Emigrants*. In subsequent works, such as *The Rings of Saturn* and *Austerlitz*, Sebald extends and complicates his intertextual relation to Nabokov. This chapter therefore elaborates upon Sebald's deliberate incorporation of specific passages and images from Nabokov's *Speak, Memory* within the narrative of his last and most "novelistic" prose narrative, *Austerlitz* (2001), focusing primarily on the protagonist's attempts to recuperate mnemic representations of the mother he cannot remember knowing. In this chapter I draw on research carried out at the Sebald archive in Marbach, Germany, where, in Sebald's copy of Nabokov's autobiography one can see marginal notations and other indications of the manner in which he adapted or translated certain scenes or elements into his own version of a *fictional* biography. As in *The Emigrants*, Sebald's tendency in transposing Nabokov is to resignify the latter's "redemption" of temporal exile, emphasizing the contradictory and unresolvable dimension of personal memory. From this empirical basis I extend my reading of Nabokov's central significance for Sebald and the latter's contribution to an oblique "redemption" of the exiled Russian author's reputation.

In chapter 7 I compare the two earlier texts with Canadian author Alice Munro's 2006 short-story cycle. This comparison uncovers less-visible dimensions of the other two memoirs, most notably their markedly gender-specific approaches to the literary treatment of memory as either torture or salvation—as postsecular "hell" or "heaven"—while also revealing Munro's more broadly significant contribution to the emergent subgenre of quasi-fictional autobiography. Finally, Munro's reimagining of her ancestors' journey from Scotland to what is now southern Ontario in the early nineteenth century both complements and complicates the themes of exile and subjective extraterritoriality already linking *Speak, Memory* and *Austerlitz* and running throughout Sebald's body of work. In *The View from Castle Rock*, Munro offers an alternative vision of the intersection of time and space in what Bakhtin calls the chronotope. Across the twelve interconnected narratives, from her family's reconstructed eighteenth-century past Munro exploits the transition from the subjectively grounded fabulations of her Scottish ancestors to ever more factually grounded narratives of uprooting, emigration, and the establishment of new lives in a new land. Within the space of five generations of her father's side of her family tree, Munro's stories track the shift from a culturally specific worldview based in fairy tales and the popular culture they inform to one based in an increasingly objective and rational understanding of history, opening out, in the final stories, into a radically expansive postobjective—or "posthuman"—vision of history understood in terms of geological time, an account of her emergence as a unique mid-twentieth-century subject against this grand sweeping backdrop of the history of the land in which these stories unfold.

Chapter 1

Catastrophe with Spectator

Remediating the Modernist Subject in *The Rings of Saturn*

Destruction . . . alone gives men the room to make themselves
eternal.

The dead are beyond the reach of catastrophe.
—Hans Blumenberg, *Shipwreck with Spectator*

This chapter considers Sebald in the context of the "long modernism,"
between 1900 and 1950, that I construe in terms of the European and Anglo-
American literature, culture, and theory of this period. The initial subject here
is the subject or *subjectivities*[1] in specific examples of modernist prose fiction:
Joseph Conrad's *Heart of Darkness* (1902), Franz Kafka's "The Metamorphosis" (1913), and Samuel Beckett's novel trilogy *Molloy* (1955), *Malone
Dies* (1956), and *The Unnamable* (1959). There is a reason for this particular constellation of texts, which are as different as they are spread out in
time, representing anything but a unitary literary modernism. Conrad looks
back to the just-finished nineteenth century, as much as Beckett (called the
last modernist in Anthony Cronin's 1997 biography) heralds key aspects of
what would be called the postmodern. (In general literary terms I invoke
"postmodern" to qualify the novel's development since World War II as late
capitalist narrative mode, implying, among other stylistic features, an amplified self-reflexivity through the privileging of intertextual remediation over
literary mimesis.[2] Substantively, this mode is characterized by the presentation
of narrative subjects constituted in relation to technologies of cultural production and reproduction, prosthetic "organs" of cultural memory, including
genre.) *Heart of Darkness* marks a significant moment in the history of the
novel, on the level of both content and form, heralding its transformation into
something as radical as Beckett's trilogy; after this (ca. 1950) the novel and its
social function undergo significant change, if only because the whole culture
changes around it. In this respect Kafka is famously singular (as Borges once
said, Kafka created his own precedents [Said 1994, 259]) even as his work is
now recognized as strangely proleptic of the later twentieth century whose
subjectivities it uncannily anticipates. Kafka's significance for modernist literature is explored in chapters 3 and 5. The early twentieth century is also

already named by Walter Benjamin (2002b) in 1936 "the age of technological reproducibility," emerging directly out of the nineteenth-century inventions of cinema and photography and ultimately the printing press in the fifteenth century. In other words, this is also the period of the emergence of the society of the spectacle, which Guy Debord (1994) traces back to the early twentieth century, in the Weimar Republic.

Sebald's third prose narrative, *The Rings of Saturn* (1995), exemplifies the status and function in Sebald's work of *visuality* construed in the highly inclusive terms of turn-of-the-millennium visual cultural studies—beyond the interplay of text and photo for which Sebald is known. *The Rings of Saturn* also offers the clearest instance of Sebald's oblique critique of late capitalism—of the legacy of the Enlightenment and the nineteenth century, of colonialism and imperialism, of Progress and its twin engines of combustion and consumption. My point of departure here is as follows: the confusion in late modernity of the subject-object relation, constitutive of the Cartesian space of *modern* visuality or modern culture per se, is a key factor in the breakdown of a stable notion of realism as a historically specific aesthetic ideology[3]—and Sebald's prose works provide a unique perspective on this key transformation by *enacting* as well as describing it. As mentioned, my focus in this chapter is the modern or *modernist* subject, whose formations and movements Sebald traces through the catastrophes of recent history, from a late twentieth-century vantage point. This is a historically, epistemologically, and literarily (or narratologically) constituted subject, as evidenced in the texts of Conrad, Kafka, and Beckett, all three meaningfully referenced in *The Rings of Saturn*. The complex intertextuality of Sebald's narratives, and the more general intermediality this mirrors, offers a powerful critical framework within which to compare these representations of modern(ist) subjectivity. In fact we can begin to see the degree to which Sebald is himself a kind of belated *modernist*, even as he reveals the self-conscious, self-critical qualities emerging or already manifest in Conrad, Kafka, and Beckett. For *The Rings of Saturn* thematizes the problems inherent in fiction, autobiography, and historiography alike, in the writing and reading of history, like memory, as a necessary privileging of one frame of reference, and therefore one narrative, over others.

Shipwreck with Spectator

The intertextual convergence of subject and object in *The Rings of Saturn* occurs within the visual-spatial and epistemological coordinates of modern catastrophe.[4] "Catastrophe" in Sebald is an imaginative trope, a "paradigm of a metaphor for existence," in Hans Blumenberg's phrase. As noted in the introduction, this chapter's—and this book's—title is borrowed from the German title of Andrea Köhler's 1997 interview with Sebald, "Catastrophe with Spectator" (Katastrophe mit Zuschauer), itself an allusion to Blumenberg's

1979 text. *The Rings of Saturn*, like Sebald's other prose narratives, is a contemporary culmination of a century-long process, rooted in his understanding of the modernist preoccupation with identity. Not only can he be said to have radically revised the novel form for late or postmodernity (whether he acknowledges this terminology or not) but also Sebald makes a significant contribution to a long-standing countertradition of word and image as complementary, mutually influential means of narrative representation. Tying the two together are specific practices of looking, of perspective, voyeurism and visual mastery—ironically balanced by their complementary structures: paranoia, surveillance, subjection. Such a broad intertextual analysis is perhaps *demanded* by the very nature of the Sebaldian text; this approach throws into relief the irony of the return to the "real" represented by much of the literary scholarship under the rubric of twenty-first century cultural studies, a legacy of 1990s New Historicism as much as the impact of the social sciences. This begins to clarify Sebald's intertextual subject, in terms of the narrator's voice and point of view, metaphors from two different registers,[5] but also epistemologically, in relation to the status of the subject in later modernity.[6] The microcosmic text of *The Rings of Saturn* gestures outward, in Sebald's words, toward those "networks of a complexity that goes far beyond the power of any one individual to imagine . . . through which the global tides of information flow without cease" (Sebald 1998, 91) while reminding us repeatedly "how little we know about our species, our purpose and our end" (91). Walter Benjamin is perhaps our best guide here, in his conclusion to "The Work of Art in the Age of Its Technological Reproducibility," in which he claims that, already by the early twentieth century, "mankind" has become "an object of contemplation for itself. Its self-alienation has reached such a degree that it can experience its own destruction as an aesthetic pleasure of the first order" (Benjamin 2002b, 122).[7] I should add that a parallel but rather different revaluation of the subject-object relation takes place within postcolonial critical discourse—in Edward Said's reading of Conrad, for instance.[8] My perspective here is filtered through that of Sebald, however, whose approach to capitalism, imperialism, or modernity in general is conditioned by his reading of a rather different critical and philosophical tradition—that is, *not* postcolonial theory per se, although his works share the same basic sensibility. Besides, "catastrophe" here implies far more than any single historical event.[9]

As Blumenberg (1979, 29) contends, one of "the fundamental ideas of the Enlightenment [is] that shipwreck is the price that must be paid in order to avoid that complete calming of the sea winds that would make all worldly commerce impossible." Therefore one of the ironies of later modernity is the ongoing price of commerce (*Verkehr*): progress itself, in this light, is the perpetual possibility of disaster, paradoxically disguised as the pursuit of a good life. Blumenberg's book *Shipwreck with Spectator* is a genealogy of a visually or perspectively constituted subject that, over time, has become conflated with the role of *theorist* as onlooker, even if that theorist is operating within the theatricalized space of a fictional narrative.[10] As Blumenberg demonstrates, the intermedial topos of the spectator-subject gazing upon a shipwreck runs through the Western literary, philosophical, and, I would add, art historical traditions, reaching its apogee in the nineteenth century. While Blumenberg tracks this trope to the threshold of the twentieth century, its fate thereafter is left to others to record,[11] as shipwreck becomes thoroughly tropological in the life world of the modern urban dweller. The basic structure persists, though, of a generalized catastrophe or other misfortune,[12] whether cataclysmic or gradual, collective or personal, human made or natural,[13] Sebald's usage encompassing equally war, deluge, or acts of various gods, all falling within what he calls "the natural history of disaster," which of course is "natural" only with respect to what some used to refer to as human nature.[14] What Blumenberg's account suggests is that, despite its visual-perspectival basis, this metaphor is also always an extended *rhetorical* trope whose ultimate twentieth-century referent for Sebald is the Holocaust—in spite, or perhaps in fulfillment, of the Adornian prohibition on certain forms of representation after Auschwitz. Perhaps the only possible measure of catastrophe is the possibility of representability, where we would take Adorno at his word and write no more lyric poetry. But that thing that, arguably, we continue to understand *least* well— the self in all its otherness—has not ceased to be a central preoccupation through the last century of literary and artistic endeavor, in Western Europe, North America, Latin America, the Middle East, and elsewhere, despite the caesura of 1933 to 1944. Rather than the question of post-Holocaust response or reaction, however, my concern is to read certain texts *through* Sebald to consider how the ground was laid in the Euro-American modernist period for representing the unrepresentable—even when representability is seen to be itself a culturally determined condition, where *un*representability may have ontological implications for that object or event that falls *outside* every discourse.

For Amir Eshel (2003), "Sebald's catastrophe is not epiphanic. Informed by . . . Blumenberg's notion of catastrophe as a topos of the human imagination, his catastrophe is no longer a sign of the eschatological, of divine fulfillment" (91). I cannot agree, however, with Eshel's assertion that "Sebald's interest is focused on modern, man-made catastrophes marked by their 'paradigmatic senselessness', by the fact that any attempt to distill sense from them would result in questionable mythological narratives" (91)—unless this is to say that even the many natural disasters recounted in the narrative are subsumed within the cultural, that *every* catastrophe in Sebald is cultural, whether "man-made" or not. Catastrophe is preeminently an imaginative trope in Sebald, a "paradigm of a metaphor for existence," in Blumenberg's phrase. Every catastrophe has both a human and a trans- or nonhuman cost; this is an ethical point reiterated across the prose texts. What Blumenberg's account shows is that, for all the visual-perspectival nature of this metaphor, "Catastrophe with Spectator," it remains an extended rhetorical trope, a kind of intertextual allegory, if that is not a contradiction in terms. This trope's ultimate twentieth-century referent is the Holocaust, whose interpretative paradigm, as suggested, continues to be determined less by Adorno's dictum about lyric poetry after Auschwitz than by Wittgenstein's precept about remaining silent in the face of the unspeakable.[15] This is a point that must be stressed in any consideration of Sebald's fictional semantics—more a *prosaics* than a *poetics*, properly speaking—or even an *emblematics*.[16] For Julia Hell (2003, 29), "Sebald's lectures on *Air War and Literature* can be read as his poetics." It is my contention here that Sebald the polemicist and Sebald the author are not to be conflated; that his arguments in the Zurich lectures are not necessarily put into practice in the novels—that in fact they are in some cases directly contradicted.

The Baroque, that is to say Benjaminian, connotations in Sebald's books have been noted by many critics. For example, in her final book on photography, Susan Sontag refers to his prose works as "lamentation narratives."[17] There is an obvious echo in this phrase of the Baroque German *Trauerspiel* (mourning play), not least because of the impossibility, after Adorno, of a "postcatastrophic poetics." The dialogic interplay of visual and textual invoked by the term "emblematics" affords greater weight to the analysis of Sebald's peculiar brand of realism: the production of meaning out of a visual-verbal dynamic or dialectic that recognizes the inescapably *visual* texture of contemporary life and where the narrative text operates in relation with the discursive codes of painting, photography, and cinema—even as it evinces a profound ambivalence toward or distrust of the image. This is because, for Sebald, images *destroy* as readily as they trigger memory and therefore a certain conception of history by interposing a visual representation between the viewing subject and the "authentic" past. By the same token, to opt for the opposite, forgetting or outright oblivion, whether willful or not, is to risk complicity with the historical forces that guarantee the eternal return of the same.

As observed, *The Rings of Saturn* as a certain kind of self-reflexive text emerges out of the "emptiness" resulting from the completion of another work (Sebald 1998, 3); *this* is where it begins: in "the deserted, soundless month of August" (181). And this emptiness is clearly connected with "the paralysing horror" that overcomes the narrator "at various times when confronted with the *traces of destruction* [*Spuren der Zerstörung*], reaching far back into the past, that were evident even in that remote place" (3; emphasis added).[18] Literal physical emptiness connects in the narrative with the existential emptiness and "paralysing horror" that overcomes the narrator at various times when confronted with the traces of a destructive event or events that in effect still lie ahead, in the future. The narrator's "horror" is thus not simply at the prospect of nothingness but at these "traces of destruction" that are *always* discernible in the midst of the most profound desolation.

The Rings of Saturn weaves a network of literary, historical, and cultural associations whose relations become apparent only gradually in the text's

ultimately recursive narrative.[19] The organizing principle is a walking tour of
County Suffolk (which Sebald did undertake in the early 1990s), in the course
of which the various strands arise, intersect, and diverge in what constitutes an
irreducibly intermedial staging of the narrator's ambulatory consciousness.[20]
From this mundane and local point of departure the narrative spins outward,
far beyond the narrator's subjectivity, to encounter what he calls the "global
tides of information," flowing "without cease" (Sebald 1998, 92), like the
waves whose relentless battering on England's southern coast have in a few
centuries undermined the settlements that once flourished there (155–59).[21]
If Adorno (quoted in Crary 2013a, 11n10) correctly assesses modern life
under the scopic regime of bourgeois capitalism as a reality *perceived* as one
of "objects and hence basically of commodities,"[22] it becomes possible to see
how Sebald's frequently desolate spaces—paradigmatically in *The Rings of
Saturn*—signify less as realistic or naturalistic renderings of a specific landscape or architectural structure than as a kind of *allegory* for this melancholic
(masculine) subject,[23] wandering through the evacuated landscape that is the
end product of modernity's transformation of the natural environment and
built spaces of previous eras, and of their now-defunct forms of social life
(Sebald 1998, 263)—not all of which, needless to say, deserve to be mourned.
Among the former, ironically, traditions of *mourning*, and the significance of
death itself, receive particularly close attention in this text (e.g., 188, 296),
in the face of a culture that has forgotten how to remember. This is one way
in which the Sebaldian subject is post-Freudian: the object of its mourning
is no single thing or individual person, making it very hard to discern from
melancholy in terms of Freud's distinction in his essay "Mourning and Melancholy" (1917) (Freud 1973, 243–45). To put it another way, mourning in *The
Rings of Saturn* is on one level a lamentation for the loss of social rituals and
signifiers of mourning, itself a kind of allegorical critique of the compensatory
mechanism of commodity fetishism.

In part 8 Sebald presents the former top-secret Cold War military base at
Orfordness as "the extraterritorial ruined space that is also the space of the
imagination" (Ward 2004, 61). The narrator describes his experience of the
"godforsaken loneliness of that outpost in the middle of nowhere" (Sebald
1998, 234): "It was as if I were passing through an undiscovered country,
and I still remember that I felt, at the same time, both utterly liberated and
deeply despondent. I had not a single thought in my head. With each step that
I took, the emptiness within and the emptiness without grew ever greater and
the silence more profound" (234).[24] Invoking Browne's *Urne Buriall*, the narrator concedes that "the closer I came to these ruins, the more any notion of a
mysterious isle of the dead receded, and the more I imagined myself amidst the
remains of our own civilization after its extinction in some future catastrophe"
(Sebald 1998, 235–37). This imaginary postapocalyptic space is a concretization of an epistemological condition clearly anticipated in Sebald's description
of the final image of post-Brechtian East German playwright Heiner Müller's

Landscape with Argonauts: for Sebald, this peculiar prospect depends on the concomitant negation of the author as "representative of a species" that is as he says "relentlessly" destroying its own habitat. This is a concretization of the epistemological condition clearly anticipated in Carl Weber's description of Müller's play, which ends with "the extermination of the voyager [colonizer] who turns into a landscape, the landscape of his death" (Müller 1984, 125; see also 135). The narrator's "horror" is thus not simply at the prospect of nothingness but at these "traces of destruction" that are always discernible in the midst of the most profound desolation. This setting is not altogether devoid of life but is rather populated by what might be called a species of the posthuman as critical allegory by way of Kafka. The depiction of his near paralysis and hospitalization explicitly appropriates the chronotope of Gregor Samsa's transformed consciousness in "The Metamorphosis": Sebald's narrator in his helplessness and immobility compares himself in the hospital to Samsa as giant bug in order to capture his new sense of alienation from a familiar environment. He recalls the scene in which

> Samsa, his little legs trembling, climbs the armchair and looks out of his room, no longer remembering (so Kafka's narrative goes) the sense of liberation that gazing out of the window had formerly given him. And just as Gregor's dimmed eyes failed to recognize the quiet street where he and his family had lived for years, taking Charlotten-straße for a grey wasteland, so I too found the familiar city, extending from the hospital courtyards to the far horizon, an utterly alien place. (Sebald 1998, 5)[25]

As the reader is soon reminded, however, *The Rings of Saturn*'s opening scene is also a memory work: the narrator-writer is "assembling his notes," self-consciously recollecting his actual hospitalization one year after it happened, one year to the day he began his walking tour of Suffolk in August 1992 (3). Thus the subject of the narrative is also the narrating subject—the point of view seems conventionally retrospective—yet (as in a novel like *Tristram Shandy*) one gets no sense at the end that the narrator-protagonist has changed or evolved or gained in self-knowledge. Rather, this "failure" as such is precisely the point. At the conclusion as at the start his subjectivity amounts to a fundamental lack of self-understanding; he occupies a kind of epistemological blind spot represented through intertextual points of contact with other representations of comparable subjective unknowing, a lack of objective certainty, perspective, or detachment, the impossibility of even a figurative transcendence.

Like a lens shifting in and out of focus, the narrative point of view in the text oscillates continuously between partiality and visual mastery. The hospital room chronotope of the protagonist's gazing out a window conforms structurally to another recurrent trope in Sebald's work: what he termed in a

1996 essay on Nabokov "the synoptic view"—whether across space, as a way of looking at and understanding the world, or across time, as a way of gazing "across the barrier of death" (Sebald 2004a, 114).[26] The subject is positioned as spectator repeatedly in all of Sebald's texts: In part 5 of *Rings of Saturn*, for example, Sebald imagines Joseph Conrad (under his original Polish name) arriving in Brussels in 1890 to be interviewed for his African commission: "Korzeniowski . . . now saw the capital of the Kingdom of Belgium, with its evermore bombastic buildings, as a sepulchral monument erected over a hecatomb of black bodies, and all the passers-by in the streets seemed to him to bear that dark Congolese secret within them" (Sebald 1998, 122). The narrator thereupon travels to Belgium and buys

> a ticket for the Waterloo Panorama, housed in an immense domed rotunda, where from a raised platform in the middle one can view the battle—a favourite subject with panorama artists—in every direction. It is like being at the centre of events . . . Across this horrific three-dimensional scene, on which the cold dust of time has settled, one's gaze is drawn to the horizon, to the enormous mural . . . This, then, I thought, as I looked round about me, is the representation of history. It requires a falsification of perspective. We, the survivors, see everything from above, see everything at once, and still we do not know how it was . . . Whatever became of the corpses and mortal remains? Are they buried under the memorial? Are we standing on a mountain of death? Is that our ultimate vantage point? Does one really have the much-vaunted historical overview from such a position? (124–25)

The present, late- or postmodern moment is built upon an ever-growing pile, the material detritus of ceaseless destruction and death that affords this historical overview: a viewpoint whose very objectivity prevents it absolutely from providing authentic knowledge of the past. One is reminded of Benjamin's (1969) angel of history, in the "Ninth Thesis on the Philosophy of History," but there are significant differences. In Sebald, only the godlike surveyor (the "monarch-of-all-I-survey," in Mary Louise Pratt's phrase of 1992 [2008]) can take in the whole at one glance, a form of retrospectivity that *should* be the viewpoint of the subject of knowledge. Only the subject of experience, down on the ground, unable to see the whole except in parts, piecemeal, is in a position to gain this kind of authentic knowledge—but such a radically subjective position ironically forestalls an understanding of this knowledge; only the historical overview affords the position from which this understanding is theoretically *possible*—and so on. Quasi-omniscient objectivity in Sebald leads inevitably to a kind of epistemological seasickness or vertigo, as the visual mastery such a perspective implies can never be sustained.[27] Nor is the privileged retroperspective of an autobiographical narrative tradition available to

the narrator, recounting his wanderings three years later (294): he ends where
he began, without having transcended his status as narrative subject, a protagonist in search of greater understanding—of the world, of history, of himself.

Sebald and Modernist Realism

The subject-as-spectator is a well-documented trope in Sebald's work. As in
the encyclopedic novels of Claudio Magris (discussed in chapter 5), in *The
Rings of Saturn* Sebald combines a complex meditation on the intersection of
perception, memory, and representation with a density of specific, concrete
historical detail, as if to offer a stylized narrative antidote to the ultimate
impossibility of objective historical knowledge via recuperative historioscopic
restaging.[28] In addition to *Heart of Darkness* (1902), Sebald weaves Joseph
Conrad's early life and seafaring career into the narrative of *The Rings of
Saturn* by imagining a probable visit to the town of Lowestoft, on the Suffolk
coast—justified by the Lowestoft harbor register of 1878, which the narrator
consults at the start of his walking tour (Sebald 1998, 113). Part 5 of *The
Rings of Saturn* is taken up with a recounting of specific events in Conrad's
Congo Diary, his letters, and *Heart of Darkness*. Sebald is especially concerned to foreground in the narrative of Conrad's life his meeting in 1890 with
Roger Casement, at the time British consul in Africa, and the first European to
make public the "nature and extent of the crimes committed against the native
peoples in the course of opening up the Congo" (Sebald 1998, 127).[29] Needless to say, in *Heart of Darkness* the catastrophe is colonialism in Africa at the
end of the nineteenth century, specifically "an even more general consequence
of the colonial situation: the fact that [in Ian Watt's words] the individual
colonist's power, combined with the lack of any effective control, was an open
invitation to every kind of cruelty and abuse" (1979, 143). For Sebald, "in
the entire history of colonialism, most of it not yet written, there is scarcely a
darker chapter than the one termed *The Opening of the Congo*" (Sebald 1998,
118). These passages at once bolster and complicate Bianca Theisen's (2006,
572) argument that one of Sebald's "dominant concerns" is for "the enslaved,
victimized, persecuted, marginalized, and perishing."[30] Ironically, as a source
for this section the narrator cites a BBC television documentary—"an account
of [Roger] Casement's meeting with . . . Joseph Conrad in the Congo"—that
he ends up *not* watching but sleeping through, so that he has to reconstruct
the story from *other* sources (Sebald 1998, 103–4). These include the so-called
"Black Diary, a kind of chronicle of the accused's homosexual relations,"
which the narrator concludes must be authentic. "We may draw from this
the conclusion that it is precisely Casement's homosexuality that sensitized
him to the continuing oppression, exploitation, enslavement and destruction,
across the borders of social class and race, of those who were furthest from
the centres of power" (131–34). Casement, an Irish national, was executed

by the British government in 1916 for "high treason" (127; 103). During his own sojourn in the Congo, as Sebald emphasizes, Casement "was increasingly preoccupied with the nature and origins of power and the imperialist mentality that resulted from it." Accordingly, "in the years leading up to the First World War, when the Irish question was becoming acute, Casement espoused the cause of 'the white Indians of Ireland'" (129). In Kurtz's succinct phrase, which Marlow reads in his report to "The International Society for the Suppression of Savage Customs," the answer is to "Exterminate all the brutes" (Conrad 2003, 125): total annihilation of a culture through the liquidation of its people; a cleansing violence to redeem the uncivilized violence of the non-Western other.[31] Here we see an acknowledgment of the modernist collapsing of the subject-object distinction in Conrad's choice to explore certain historical events through the novel's representation of Marlow's subjectivity and to represent these events through the exploration of that perspective. The two processes are inextricable, which is why any reduction of *Heart of Darkness* to a "racist" work is always problematic, overlooking as it must Conrad's interrogation of the meaning of realism and the very possibility of representing the interiority of a self.[32] In Sebald's appropriation of Conrad's experiences—already self-remediated in *Heart of Darkness*—an explicit critique of Belgian colonialism, in the person of King Leopold II, is reinscribed in what Watt considers Conrad's "universal" condemnation of imperialism. In Conrad's novel Leopold is never mentioned by name, a courtesy Sebald revokes (Watt 1979, 158).

Sebald's approach has its own, complex temporality, couched as it is in a fictional narrative in which the narrator's persistent and close attention to the past places him in an effectively critical but highly artificial position from which he views present and future alike. Nonetheless, Sebald's fictive staging of the unavoidably subjective quality of any truly objective perspective performs a kind of metacritique of the contemporary disavowal of critical objectivity in certain fields. Moreover, as noted, "catastrophe" for Sebald implies far more than any single historical event. In what is in effect his reclamation of *Heart of Darkness* from postcolonial criticism, Sebald reilluminates the most significant aspect of the book for the modernist critique of colonialism—an inevitably ambiguous, irreducibly contradictory critique.[33] The emphasis on surface, antirealism, and intertextual subjectivity found in more radically modernist writers such as Kafka has its anticipatory corollary in Conrad's peculiar self-reflexivity.

In the end, just as Marlow's perspective on and account of Kurtz takes precedence over Kurtz himself, the novel's primary narrator in turn takes precedence over Marlow, and therefore vision, and visuality, give way before voice: but not Kurtz's vaunted voice, barely heard, apart from his famous last words, or even Marlow's, which takes up the lion's share of the narrative. The voice of authority in *Heart of Darkness*, if there is one, is that of the auditor rather than the speaker, the one whose final insight is granted to the reader in the novel's closing as he raises his head on that other boat, anchored in the Thames estuary outside London: "The offing was barred by a black bank of clouds, and the tranquil waterway leading to the utmost ends of the earth flowed sombre under an overcast sky—seemed to lead into the heart of an immense darkness" (Conrad 2003, 158). This darkness, metaphorically speaking, is not just the darkness at the heart of a Europe struggling with its own colonialist guilt nor that in the so-called heart of the individual, like Kurtz, who succumbs to his own barbaric nature—the barbarism of the civilized: "Exterminate all the brutes!" This darkness rather is Conrad's way of representing a subjective seeking for self-knowledge and the projection of that failed quest, that catastrophe, onto the surface of a world whose self-transformation has come at the cost of millions of non-European lives. It is the darkness that, in Sebald's historioscopic intertextualization, continues to cloud the eyes of those who seek above all to understand themselves, at the cost of the other.

Conrad, Kafka, Sebald

Alongside Nabokov and Austrian novelist Thomas Bernhard, among others, Kafka is one of the most significant of Sebald's recurrent intertexts. Surprisingly, little or no critical work has been done on the connections between Conrad and Kafka (although John Zilcosky [2003] does include the "Hunter Gracchus" story with *Heart of Darkness* in a "literary tradition of deconstructing European colonialism from within" [182]). One might for instance compare Kurtz on his bier, being borne to his death, and Kafka's Hunter Gracchus, in which the Hunter's "terrible fate" is to take a wrong turn and miss out forever on his "proper" fate, which would have been the same as everyone else's: the shipwreck that is death (Kafka 1971, 228). In *Heart of Darkness*, by contrast, the *possibility* of redemption is represented, even through Marlow's "white lie" to Kurtz's "Intended" at the end, where he tells her that Kurtz's last words were not "The horror! The horror!" but her name, which is never revealed to the reader. Since the "Hunter Gracchus" story is even more relevant for Sebald's first prose work, *Vertigo*, I focus here on the links between "The Metamorphosis" and Conrad's novel, since they are implied in Sebald's intertextual reframing of elements from either text. As discussed in chapter 3, in *Vertigo* Sebald redefines modern narrative subjectivity through extensive use of Kafka's biographical writings (letters and diaries). He reimagines Kafka's actual travels, as limited as they were, folding them into specific scenes from the fiction, occasionally merging this peculiarly enigmatic subjectivity with that of his own narrator-protagonist. Sebald's use of Kafka in both prose texts not only grants the narrative an extraordinary degree of intertextual complexity but also throws fresh light on Kafka's engagement with the formal parameters of literary representation.

To understand Kafka as a strange kind of postcolonial writer is to better understand Sebald, insofar as the former is one of his key influences. An excellent source for this approach to Kafka is Zilcosky's *Kafka's Travels: Exoticism, Colonialism, and the Traffic of Writing* (2003), where one encounters the phrase "postcolonial Kafka," in reference not only to the story "In the Penal Colony" (1914), set on a tropical island, or to his first novel, *The Man Who Disappeared* (1914),[34] set in an imaginary America, but also to the story "The Metamorphosis" (Gregor is after all a traveling salesman as well as a giant bug) (Zilcosky 2003, 145). Zilcosky convincingly demonstrates Kafka's interest in (the literature of) nineteenth- and early twentieth-century exoticism, in relation to his own abiding, typically modernist, preoccupations: alienation, the impossibility of communication, the representation of subjective interiority, the uncanniness of everyday life. As Zilcosky's subtitle suggests, these themes can be placed right alongside deterritorialization, expropriation, and diaspora, which in Kafka are always reducible to the situation and perspective of the writer writing; Kafka, like many modernists, has the lens turned not directly on the world but on the human subject's relation to that world. Subjectivity, in Kafka at least, is ultimately inseparable from the discourse in which it is expressed. But a far from stable subject it is—and this is where Zilcosky's cultural studies–influenced approach justifies itself. Zilcosky shows how Kafka, who never traveled outside Europe, was nonetheless fascinated by travel literature and popular adventure series set in exotic locales. Having read a great many of these works, Kafka was conversant with the recurrent colonialist and orientalist tropes, particularly the recurrent representation of a way of seeing the exotic from a viewpoint of mastery, which he actively sought to invert or turn inside out in order to view the exotic in the familiar and everyday, as if through the wrong end of the colonialist telescope. According to Zilcosky,

> In many traditional exotic narratives, the narrator climbs to the top of a faraway . . . tower, minaret, or mountain and looks down on the foreign landscape, in order to better survey, demarcate, and map South America, Africa, or Asia. Such a strategy provides the traveler with what Mary Louise Pratt has termed the "monarch-of-all-I-survey" view. This view . . . affirms the traveler's power over the foreign world in two ways: it allows him to delineate the exotic lands' borders and, more important for a discussion of literary innovation, to bolster the singularity of his perspective. Through this view from above, the traveler can gain a better sense of the land's specificities, his own point-of-view, and, finally, his "self." (27)

Kafka employs what Zilcosky calls perspectival dispersion to break down the neatly balanced Cartesian binaries and "to estrange the traveler [or reader] from his own subjectivity" (27) in a manner that anticipates Brecht's *Verfrem-*

dungseffekt. The displacements implied by colonialism become figures for a more radical, but also radically depoliticized, "internal displacement," like that of Gregor Samsa, the traveling-salesman-turned-insect (78).

In "The Metamorphosis" Kafka raises his own stakes; the reader is faced with at least two, inextricably connected tasks: on the one hand, she/he must account for this story as an eminent example of Kafka's capacity for a kind of literary realism,[35] implying the representation of psychology as the "truth" of the self's "inner life."[36] On the other hand, at the same time (in the same chronotopic space) the insect's relative unrepresentability must somehow be borne in mind: that it can be portrayed only in this manner, by verbal means, in the text of this story—and thus translation becomes even more problematic.[37] Famously, Kafka requested that the title page art of the first edition of "The Metamorphosis" *not* depict the insect: "It struck me [he wrote the publisher] that [the] illustrator . . . might want to draw the insect itself. Not that, please not that! . . . The insect itself cannot be depicted. It cannot even be shown from a distance" ([1915] 1977, 141). In a gesture more radical than René Magritte's painting of the pipe that is not a pipe,[38] Kafka foregrounds the insect's unrepresentability, in a strange prohibition of literalized visual representation and in denial of the insect's ostensible metaphoricity.[39] In this light the question is not what *kind* of insect but *why* an insect at all? Elias Canetti argues that for Kafka his room, in which he does his writing, *is* his "outer body," his "forebody," like an outer shell or carapace, the external (but not by any means thick or impermeable) layer protecting him from the world outside, from all potential threats, real or imagined: food, drink, medicine, the air itself.[40] But above all, it protects him from the proximity of other people, such as the members of his family, whom Kafka could never give up, at least not until he was on the verge of death. And especially women: this "carapace"—his very selfhood—is a surefire sexual deterrent.[41] The latter, that is to say sex, is just one of a set of connotations conveyed in the German word *Verkehr*: intercourse, exchange, traffic, commerce. Generally, *Verkehr* signifies for Kafka everything he's missing out on: the unending flow of life, particularly relationships, marriage, and sexual intimacy. *Verkehr* also signifies the formal transactions of business, of which he did for a time partake and which took time away from his writing. There is an obvious emphasis, overall, on the sense of *Verkehr* as synonym for communication, verbal intercourse, exchange, or transaction. At the same time, there is the acute (and growing) consciousness on Kafka's part of the potential impossibility or futility of the latter form of *Verkehr*, of the failure or breakdown of communication at a distance: "telecommunications" (including, most notably, letter writing). In a sense, then, *Verkehr* becomes for Kafka the other of writing, where writing is the impossibility of this kind of communication. But by the same token writing (in the form of fiction) offers at least the possibility of dramatizing this impossibility—the failure of the exchange, of the transaction, of the transmission of a semantic content.

In "The Metamorphosis" Samsa wakes up to find his "inner self" expressed externally, in the form of an insectile carapace presumably resistant to any visualization but the one in the reader's mind. This insistence on the literal primacy of the word, of the narrative voice over visual structures, is to be seen at work as well in *Heart of Darkness*—in spite of its much-vaunted emphasis on vision and visuality, on those aspects of what has been called Conrad's impressionistic realism.[42] This is clearly indicated in the novel's self-conscious prologue, the primary narrative frame, set on a boat anchored in the Thames estuary outside London (Conrad 2003, 67n1). As any number of critics have noted, Conrad's unnamed primary narrator offers what appears to be a key to interpreting Marlow's narrative and therefore perhaps the entire text: "The yarns of seamen have a direct simplicity, the whole meaning of which lies within the shell of a cracked nut. But Marlow was not typical (if his propensity to spin yarns be excepted), and to him the meaning of an episode was not *inside* like a kernel but *outside*, enveloping the tale which brought it out only as a glow brings out a haze, in the likeness of one of these misty halos that sometimes are made visible by the spectral illumination of moonshine" (70; emphasis added). I contrast this to received readings of Conrad as impressionist-realist, or as tacit proponent of nineteenth-century colonialism, which also demands some recourse to realism, even if it is justified by the requirements of a contextualized ideological critique. I read this passage absolutely literally, taking the narrator at his word, locating the "meaning" or the "truth" of the narrative *not* inside, in Marlow's story of visiting Belgium and then traveling to the Congo to take up his commission, to find himself drawn inexorably and uncomprehendingly toward Kurtz, the mad European at the Central Station who has arrogated to himself the powers of a quasi-divine tribal ruler. In Marlow's account, Kurtz has become an "object" idolatrously worshipped by natives—not so much "God" as fetish-object, where the "real thing" here is at a double (or greater) remove from view, on the way to being, in Baudrillard's estimation, the simulacrum of simulacra. If this is the feature of Kurtz that makes him so monstrous—the unspeakable rites that Marlow doesn't quite witness, the implied human sacrifice, "which . . . were offered up to him—do you understand? To Mr. Kurtz himself" (124)—this is also what makes him so fascinating to Marlow, which he doesn't articulate because he cannot fully understand it. But the prologue on the other boat gives us a clue: in an infamous passage, Marlow admits to a kind of justification for colonization: "The conquest of the earth, which mostly means the taking it away from those who have a different complexion or slightly flatter noses than ourselves, is not a pretty thing when you look into it too much. What redeems it is the idea only. An idea at the back of it . . . an unselfish belief in the idea—something you can set up, and bow down before, and offer a sacrifice to . . ." (72). He breaks off. But the connection is clear enough: Kurtz is guilty of taking to its literal extreme the logic of the brutal economics of colonialism, creating a sort of parody of Western European society under bourgeois capitalism that amounts to a parable of Marx's analysis of the commodity fetish. The meaning of Conrad's novel does *not* lie "within" the so-called heart of darkness, which after all does *not* describe the heart of the African continent, which by this time had been explored and charted, the map's interior no longer blank and white but filled in according to the color spectrum of nineteenth-century colonialism (76).[43] Rather, the novel's meaning as such is contiguous with the *surface* of the narrative, in accordance with Conrad's Nietzschean rejection of a received metaphysics of inside over outside, depth over surface, objectivity over subjectivity—even if he does not or cannot refuse *every* aspect of what Abdul JanMohamed calls the "manichean allegory" of colonialism (quoted in Conrad 1988, 15). In his own "aesthetics of description"[44] Sebald extends Conrad's questioning or outright inversion of the various colonialist binaries—"white and black, good and evil, salvation and damnation, civilization and savagery, superiority and inferiority, intelligence and emotion, self and the other, subject and object" (15). The meaning must lie on the outside, since there is no "inside"—or rather, as Marlow makes clear, were such an interiority to exist it would be inaccessible. This is perhaps the darkest irony of the book's title: there is no "heart," only hollow Europeans, mere aggregates of physical idiosyncrasies, and masklike natives. What "inside" there may be goes unshown and unseen, unrepresentable and therefore unthinkable. This is the true horror at the book's core.

Sebald's Copernican Vision

Whether transmutated in the prose texts or treated more straightforwardly in a series of critical essays of the 1970s, Kafka's ironically messianic eschatology remains an abiding interest of Sebald's: a negative or antieschatology, not about the "end" but rather its deferral or impossibility. And for Sebald, too, the macroscopic is writ small, on the level of individual subjectivity. The reader's difficulty in the face of the text is analogous to the seemingly inescapable gap or blind spot in consciousness represented there, focused in terms of either visual perception or the metaphorical perspective of memory. The nexus is precisely the represented *body* of the subject in the narrative's represented spaces: the body that falls, and in falling also links—albeit negatively—the otherwise disparate realms of matter and mind, or the physical and metaphysical. *The Rings of Saturn* economically metaphorizes, *translates*, Sebald's Copernican vision (after Hans Blumenberg): "man" is not (or is no longer) in any literal sense at the center of the universe. And yet—or therefore—subjectivity for Sebald remains the crucial problem at this stage of history: the subject defined by its awareness of its status as an agent determined by preexistent structures and forces. Even the narrator's discursively represented "body" in *The Rings of Saturn* is the objectified locus of an intra- and intertextual subjectivity.

Sebald's representation of subjectivity merges the modern and scientific with the premodern and so to speak irrational; a spherical and a flat earth; astronomy with astrology; and so on.[45] This is nowhere more economically and enigmatically represented than in the book's title, *The Rings of Saturn*, the setting of the narrator's pilgrimage "in August 1992 . . . under the sign of the Dog Star" (Sebald 1998, 3), and in the frequent references to a pre-Freudian, Saturnine melancholia characteristic of an epigonal modern masculine subject. For Sebald, the macro- and microcosmic, the celestial and terrestrial, the cosmological and epistemological converge in this subject. In *The Rings of Saturn* and similarly in *Vertigo* the physical law of gravity becomes a metaphor for the metaphysical law of death: the inevitable fall of bodies, the inexorable force that drags all bodies downward. In the rational, scientific view, these are immutable laws, gravity as much as death; in the non-Newtonian, non-Euclidean—dare I say Sebaldian—logic of fiction, these laws can be bent and broken. Therefore Sebald is on the one hand modern, Copernican, in the spirit of Enlightenment rationalism, and, on the other, "postmodern" in the sense of a return of certain *pre*modern motifs and themes but *not* in the sense of a return to Aristotelianism. He is *not* "neo-Ptolemaic" as much as acutely aware of the stubborn centrality of a melancholic, epigonal subjectivity, ultimately exteriorized in *The Rings of Saturn* (and elsewhere) as empty landscape or cityscape. In this reading (again invocative of Müller's *Landscape with Argonauts*) the landscape and observer are closely, uncannily, identified—the exteriorization of an interior—and the "story" in question, as in Samuel Beckett's novel trilogy, for instance, is always the *meta*story of the narrating subject.[46]

Beckett and Sebald: Voice over Vision

It is by no means the case that in *The Rings of Saturn* Sebald is "merely" extending a Conradian modernist realism into a critique of the nonspaces of the postmodern subject. It is essential to also consider Sebald's debt to another, more formally radical, modernist tradition. In Beckett, and, less directly, in Beckett's influence upon Sebald, we see the culmination of a modernist apotheosis of voice over vision, even as the metaphor of "voice" reveals itself as inadequate to the trilogy's ironically apophatic discourse. In *The Unnamable*, in particular, Beckett attempts to reduce the representation of interiority to the irreducible datum of a voice, speaking, in the absence of any conventional elements of novelistic realism or subjectivity—like a body in a space. In Beckett's trilogy ontological give way completely to epistemological concerns, which in turn give way before the ceaselessly babbling voice.

Beckett's novels are all "about" voice, and yet—like Kafka's, but differently—they are manifestly *written*. Beckett, like Kafka, Nabokov, and every other novelist since Cervantes, is separated from his thinking, speaking, writing predecessors by the fact that he is working in a genre (the novel) within a tradition that is younger than, and has been determined by, the book as fetish-object, mass-produced consumer product, or tool. This is Bakhtin's point: there is no such thing as an oral novel, in terms of the novel as Bakhtin takes great pains to define it (e.g., 1981, 3). Determined by language's spoken forms ("speech genres") but intended to be read silently, the novel is therefore irreducibly written. The voice or voices in Beckett's novels are not so much peculiar as utterly exemplary of the conjunction of speech and writing in what Bakhtin calls the novelistic voice-image. Thus Blanchot's question is entirely apt: "*Who* is doing the talking in Samuel Beckett's novels?" (Gontarski 1986, 141; emphasis added).

Of the various exemplars of literary modernism singled out here, the Irish author's impact upon Sebald is the least overt, pervading the prose texts with a peculiarly Beckettian disposition at the level of the narrative subject in its ambiguous bifurcation into narrator and protagonist—really a sort of *continuum* of subjectivity, without clear division. More specifically, the narrator's problem at the outset of *The Rings of Saturn* is equivalent to that of Beckett's novelistic protagonists: an epistemological *malaise* manifest on the level of *mobility*—a problem derived in part from Dante-pilgrim, at the start of the *Commedia* wandering in a dark wood (*una selva oscura*), constrained by the moral geometry of the afterlife to travel always in the same direction, his bodily self regulating the process of purgation that is "fated" (for Dante) to end in redemption. As explored further in chapter 2, in their prose works Beckett and now Sebald are the heirs to the letter, if not the spirit, of Dante, in terms of a *planar* model of time and memory in which the only possible movement is on the horizontal, around in circles. The subtitle of *The Rings of Saturn*, not incidentally, is *An English Pilgrimage*.[47] Lacking recourse to the logical alternatives available to the protagonist of a realist novel, Sebald's narrator's subjectivity is born of the asymptotic limits of an ambulatory consciousness trapped in a purgatorial time-space, a kind of macrochronotope,[48] in which any conventional release or "deliverance," like conventional narrative closure, is impossible.

Beckett's (1991, 7) trilogy begins, in *Molloy*, with its own "synoptic view"; it begins, that is, with the narrator, who is and is not Molloy, speaking, saying that he is in his mother's room. He is telling a story, his own, and *this* is his beginning: "here it is," he says, speaking of the text that the reader is reading, in the peculiar tense Sebald also invokes at the start of *The Rings of Saturn*. *Molloy*'s narrator begins to recount what appears to be an anecdote, since it is in the past tense, but soon enough this neat temporal distinction breaks down. The speaker describes himself "perched higher than the road's highest point and flattened what is more against a rock the same colour as myself, that is grey" (10). He crouches in the rock's shadow "like Belaqua"—the protagonist of Beckett's early story collection *More Pricks Than Kicks*.[49] This is Beckett's favorite subject position, ultimately appropriated from canto 5 of Dante's *Purgatorio*: the circle of the late repentant through negligence; in other words, the morally lazy, whose only chance to abbreviate their stay in Purgatory is the intercession of a pure soul's prayers.[50] Belaqua's listless attitude—like that of Marlow's auditor's—is the literalized physical manifestation of his spiritual lassitude.[51] The speaker claims to have witnessed from this vantage point two figures, called A and C, encountering each other on the road.[52] There is no B, apart from the narrator, avatar of Belaqua/Beckett:

> So I saw A and C going slowly towards each other, unconscious of what they were doing. It was on a road remarkably bare . . . The town was not far. It was two men, unmistakably, one small and one tall. They had left the town, first one, then the other, and then the first, weary or remembering a duty, had retraced his steps. The air was sharp for they wore greatcoats. They looked alike, but no more than others do. At first a wide space lay between them. They couldn't have seen each other . . . But the moment came when together they went down into the same trough and in this trough finally met. (8)

Who are A and C? They seem at times to bear attributes of characters not yet met in the narrative, such as Moran, Molloy's uncanny counterpart, or Molloy himself, despite the fact that he appears to be the one looking on. In a sense, it does not matter who they are, which is which, and so on. The sequence is set off from the surrounding narrative, such as it is, by the speaker's device of recounting in a strange mixture of tenses—"I speak in the present tense, it is so easy to speak in the present tense, when speaking of the past" (26)—how he, Belaqua-like, watched the scene unfold from an elevated vantage point. It is as much geometry problem as parable, although the former implies a solution that the latter genre may preclude. For some critics this primal scene of A and C meeting on a country road represents a "succinct summary" of the plot of *Molloy* (Bloom 1988, 100). Others, however, choose to read this story "as a kind of dramatic prologue, a shadow-play summary of the narrative activity to follow"; a story "about two complementary characters whose identities coalesce"—a story that "Molloy then proceeds with Moran to act . . . out" (100–101). This is supportable, although it should not be overlooked that the Molloy and Moran in the larger narrative never actually "meet," whether in the chronotope of the road or in the novel's space-time more generally (see Bakhtin 1981, 243).

Beckett's achievement in the trilogy is the kind of aesthetic cul-de-sac beyond which there is no going further without the book's ceasing to at least *resemble* a novel. As a modernist, Beckett comes late, marking the transition to whatever comes after, via a pronounced premodern intertextual basis. For Beckett, the crisis, the catastrophe, is precisely identity, and the representation of subjectivity—the preeminent modernist preoccupation with "self-expression"—becomes his main theme. His conclusion, though, is one of the most radical ever presented: while a certain kind of "expression" may be possible, the "self" is not. Beckett's aesthetic credo is appropriately apophatic: "Nothing to express, nothing with which to express, no power to express, no desire to express, together with the obligation to express" (1965, 103). This radical crisis of subjectivity is one that Sebald must negotiate, like every writer working at the other end of the twentieth century, in a world transformed by capitalism into an image of itself.

As noted in this book's introduction, I use "visuality" here in the special sense of visual cultural studies, encompassing how we see and interpret not just those things traditionally viewed as visual texts but also everyday life as well as our interior worlds—the "self."[53] I would extend this sense further to include a new kind of narratology that takes into account the impact of cinema, photography, digital production, and other visual technologies upon the scopic and epistemological modalities of contemporary literary discourse. To put it reductively, if the "postmodern" view is from the midst of things, where subject and object are always in danger of becoming hopelessly confused, not really a "perspective" at all, then the "modern" view is on the way to this, with some kind of objectivity or transcendence, based in Cartesian space and linear perspective, remaining a possibility or dream: the modern crisis of the individual self figured in terms of the representation, or construction, of subjectivity. This paradoxical situation is so to speak the result of the anamorphosis implicit in the patterns to be discerned behind the cultural world, of which "nature" is of course a part. From the masterful vantage point of an unreconstructed historiography, one sees a neat and ordered, *rational* world—or at least its potential, in the very representations that provide this visual analogy. In the alternative anamorphic perspective toward which Sebald gestures—a kind of "dialectics of seeing"[54]—a distended, distorted view of things is clarified, takes on meaning. What this requires is an adjustment of perspective, of the angle of perception, on the *representations* of things themselves. This adjustment has an initial effect: it foregrounds the artificiality, the constructedness, of history—the mediation of historical "truth" via conventional or official forms of visual representation, such as the Waterloo panorama in *The Rings of Saturn*, for example. For Sebald, the thrust of this analogy, of this paradox, is that the reading or interpretation of such representations *as* representations, such texts as texts, in context, *intertextually*, is of fundamental importance, since the "thing itself"—a totalized, objective account of history, or of the present moment, and therefore of the self—is otherwise beyond our grasp.

It can be argued that a certain antiocularcentric strain runs through modernist literature to counter and critique this aspect of early twentieth-century life and that this is part of what Sebald finds so compelling in authors as diverse as Kafka, Conrad and Beckett. But the historical roots of this iconophobic or, more accurately, apotropaic counternarrative, run deep, merging in the twentieth century with a more general opposition to commodification and consumer culture, on the one hand, and to colonialism, on the other.

The Disintegrating Image:

Vision?

Chapter 2

"The Extermination of the Voyager Who Turns into a Landscape"

Intermediality and Postsecular Redemption in *The Rings of Saturn*

Conscientia scrupulosa nascitur ex vitio naturali, complexione melancholica [An overscrupulous conscience springs from a natural defect, from a melancholic disposition].
—Robert Burton, *The Anatomy of Melancholy*

W. G. Sebald's academic and nonfictional work on literary and related subjects bespeaks a critically insightful but relatively conservative, modernist-humanist frame of reference, owing a debt to movements and critics as varied as the Frankfurt school (Adorno, Benjamin, Kracauer) and certain poststructuralist and postcolonialist theorists (Barthes, Foucault, Said).[1] Sebald's fictional texts, on the other hand, bear witness on the conceptual and formal levels to a metadiscursive, autocritical tendency that I am calling postmodern in the historically determined sense that they relentlessly interrogate the meaning and significance of the modern. In this chapter I move beyond the previous one, situating Sebald more firmly in the context of literary postmodernism. Using *The Rings of Saturn* as focus, I examine three aspects of Sebald's prose works that both shore up and complicate this categorization. First, building on the previous chapter, I explore Sebald's model of history as "catastrophe," which is inseparable from questions of representation or representability, staged as it is within Sebald's idiosyncratic critique of bourgeois capitalism and the modernity it has made possible.[2] Second, moving beyond the previous chapter, I investigate the status of the Sebaldian subject as an extension of a post-Enlightenment and specifically *modernist* subjectivity, defined by its lack of self-presence, its noncoincidence with itself, and the consequent lack of a coherent identity. This is the subject of the age of mass-mediated reality, never at home, or at one, with itself: a sociocultural construct as archetype. The Sebaldian subject is therefore an avatar of a postmodern(ist) subjectivity that constitutes itself, or becomes constituted, in the wake of its deconstruction as positive ground for anything: being, knowledge, itself—a subject that therefore seeks to represent itself, or be represented, via radically unpeopled settings within which its own absence is a necessary corollary of ways of seeing and being determined along the rational lines of Cartesian space-time. In each of Sebald's four prose texts, the narrator-protagonist confronts questions of power, knowledge, and identity within narrative economies that deny redemptive closure and the metaphysical worldview perpetuated under late capitalism.[3] Sebald's engagement with history, subjectivity, or "reality" must be qualified, however, as all such categories converge in his works on the terrain of a visually inflected intra- and intertextuality/-mediality, construed as cultural memory par excellence.[4] This brings me to the third aspect of Sebald's prose works I want to consider, one that effectively envelopes the first two: his approach to literary realism, which in *The Rings of Saturn* takes the form of what I called in the previous chapter his prosaics or emblematics.

What is often referred to as Sebald's realism remains the evaluative index for book reviewers, if not all academic critics. I consider the peculiar ontology of Sebald's fictional worlds within a contemporary culture dominated by images and expressed in a realism predicated on mimetic iconicity. Sebald's narratives intervene at the intersection of the image and word, visual and verbal text, in a ceaselessly re- and transmediated literary culture, gesturing outward, beyond themselves, toward those "networks of a complexity that goes far beyond the power of any one individual to imagine . . . through which the global tides of information flow without cease" (Sebald 1998, 91). *The Rings of Saturn*, in its own formal complexity, mirrors an overarching vision of these temporal and spatial networks while never failing to remind us "how little we know about our species, our purpose and our end" (91).

The Rings of Saturn: Surveying the Scene of Destruction

From Lowestoft and Dunwich to Orfordness and Suffolk's desolate coastal heaths, quasi-postapocalyptic spaces throughout *The Rings of Saturn* concretize an epistemological condition anticipated in Carl Weber's description of the final image of playwright Heiner Müller's *Verkommenes Ufer Medeamaterial Landschaft mit Argonauten (Despoiled Shore Medeamaterial Landscape with Argonauts)*: "the extermination of the voyager who turns into a landscape, the landscape of his death" (Müller 1984, 125).[5] In her survey of German post-Holocaust authorship, Julia Hell (2003) connects the "reemergence of Holocaust images from the visual cultural archive of East and West Germany" and "German authorship in terms of masculinity and the male narrator's gaze" in relation to what she calls "Sebald's aesthetics of description" (13). Hell's phrase recalls Svetlana Alpers's work on the "art of describing" in Dutch painting of the seventeenth century. Hell (2003, 28) emphasizes that this "new aesthetics," the "poetics of description," is sustained by "the desire to see what cannot be seen"—at once an affirmation and a denial of realism, as if anticipating the visual logic of photography. For Hell, "Sebald is dedicated to an aesthetic of description that freezes into textual images evoking the past in the present"; Sebald's "realism rests on an ontology that assumes a hidden structure producing specific effects . . . This is Sebald's paradox: the desire to write with the wide-open eyes of Benjamin's angel. He wants to write as an eyewitness with immediate visual access to things that have long since disappeared" (29–30). In other words, the anamorphic quality of *The Rings of Saturn*'s text is *both* temporal *and* spatial—or rather, these are one and the same.

In this analogy between Sebald's poetics and seventeenth-century Dutch painting, the scopic regime entailed by Cartesian space is disrupted: "Rather than positing a privileged beholder outside the painting gazing on a theatricalized scene from afar, [seventeenth-century Dutch art] placed the viewer inside the scene as an ambulatory presence" (Jay 1994, 60–61).[6] But all analogies are dangerous: what Sebald is doing in *The Rings of Saturn* is *literally* describing, just as he is *literally* narrating, and it is not clear that these two processes are so easily separated. Worth considering in this context is Alpers's (1983, 229) discussion of the opposition in Dutch art between a realist and an emblematic interpretation: is it not possible that these apparently mutually exclusive theories are both equally valid in aesthetic terms and that this moment in the history of painting in fact marks the emergence of the modern in the transformation of the value of a represented object from emblematic vessel of concealed meaning into empirically "realistic" commodity? This period in Dutch painting, in short, marks a profoundly significant shift in the meaning of realism, to its fully modern, bourgeois sense. Even if this were not true of Dutch art, it seems accurate to say of Sebald that his prose narratives rehearse such a shift as they plot the subsequent peregrinations of the melancholic subject whose alienation is reflected in a landscape whose perpetual emptiness also always signifies in terms of a literal "natural history of disaster."

The narrator's encounter in part 1 of *The Rings of Saturn* with Rembrandt's 1632 painting *The Anatomy Lesson* (Sebald 1998, 12) is a revealing instance of Sebald's engagement with early modern Dutch painting and a telling example of the "art of describing" peculiar to his texts, wherein the narrator's discourse and gaze become those of the art theorist and historian.[7] The narrator claims that, along with Thomas Browne, Descartes himself may have been present at the landmark anatomy lesson (13).[8] For Sebald the scene records a key moment in history: the simultaneous birth of modern medical science (focused on the body) and modern metaphysics (the ego/mind/ thinking "I"/self), Descartes's "philosophical investigations . . . form[ing] one of the principal chapters in the history of subjection" (13).[9] The allusion to Foucault points to one of the historical threads being unraveled here, for, as the narrator points out, if "we stand today before the large canvas . . . we are standing precisely where those present at the dissection . . . stood, and we believe that we see what they saw then": the obliquely foreshortened body of Aris Kindt, petty thief. "Yet it is debatable whether anyone ever really saw that body, since the art of anatomy, then in its infancy, was not least a way of making the reprobate body invisible" (13). At the outset, the body on the dissection table becomes emblematic of the mountain of death upon which a catastrophic history is constructed.[10] As will be seen below, the explicit spatialization of this image is entirely in keeping with Sebald's peculiar "dialectics of seeing."[11] In a strange filiation, the pile of bodies at the end of an English baroque *Trauerspiel* such as *Hamlet*[12] makes its way as image through the backdoor of German postwar avant-garde theater, exemplified by Heiner Müller's work of the 1970s and 1980s, into the long, hybrid prose narrative that is *The Rings of Saturn*.

The theory of realism Sebald offers at the book's outset implies an epistemology predicated on an ethical critique of modernity. The narrative foregrounds the positionality of the spectator-viewer vis-à-vis the text and therefore the reader as a species of the subject-as-spectator. In contemplating the radical reification of an other, the spectator is him-/herself *subjected* by *The Anatomy Lesson*, constrained to view from a site determined by its alignment with the Cartesian coordinates extending outward from the represented visual space. As Sebald reads it, the beginning of modern medical practice is conflated in Rembrandt's painting with the emergence of a new way of seeing. "Realism" in this context names bourgeois capitalist realism, an aesthetic ideology looking back to Renaissance painting through nineteenth-century academic painting, as well as the historical and realist novels, up to and including twentieth- and twenty-first-century media. In this definition, the emphasis "is on an objective reality, a world of material things, which it is the job of representation, whether textual or photographic, to capture. Connected explicitly with the discriminating power of vision, realism is part of a broader ideology of *enlightenment*, defined by rational scientific knowledge and economic liberalism" (O'Brien and Szeman 2004, 74; emphasis in original).[13] This is a realism, in other words, that challenged, and continues to challenge, an older, Neoplatonic or Christian dualist metaphysical model. Under bourgeois capitalism the index for "reality" shifted from the unseen, spiritual, or transcendent to the hard material surface of a world of commodities—or at least this was the dominant model. As Martin Jay and others have argued, "modern ocularcentric culture" is riven by contradiction from its inception in the sixteenth century, disrupted by alternative representational regimes in which the visual held a decidedly different, more ambiguous status and where the "unseen" lingered in plain view in the interstices of dominant culture. For Jay,

> domination did not mean uniformity . . . the modern era emerged with a much more complicated attitude toward vision than is often assumed . . . our previous history is not the petrified block of a singular visual space since, looked at obliquely, it can always be seen to contain its moment of unease . . . That moment was largely perpetuated by the subterranean presence of what can be called the baroque ocular regime as the uncanny double of what we might call

the dominant scientific or "rationalized" visual order (itself . . . not fully homogeneous). (1994, 45)

The two contrasting models of realism—and hence "reality"—continue in a strange coexistence.

Sebald's narrator offers his critique of *The Anatomy Lesson*, in particular the spectacle of the realistically rendered corpse at its center: "Though the body is open to contemplation, it is, in a sense, excluded, and in the same way the much-admired verisimilitude of Rembrandt's picture proves on closer examination to be more apparent than real" (Sebald 1998, 16).[14] The "crass misrepresentation" the narrator identifies in Rembrandt's painting is in fact evidence of the artist's sympathy with the dead and flayed thief, whose body is the object of the lesson, and only in this sense the "subject" of the painting (17).[15] In other words, Rembrandt's "misrepresentation" signals his non-Cartesian gaze upon the dead man: "His gaze alone is free of Cartesian rigidity," where the Renaissance tradition of perspectively determined verisimilitude, and its concomitant metaphysics, is undermined. Rembrandt is thus brought onto the side of death over life, of nonbeing over being,[16] emblematized throughout Sebald's text by the various expanses of emptiness—real and metaphorical, physical and psychological—through which the narrator passes in his "English pilgrimage" (*Eine englische Wallfahrt*), the book's original German subtitle.[17] Sebald suggests that Rembrandt, like the narrator himself, looks upon the dead thief as it were anamorphically and painted him accordingly: out of true with the realist conventions of art practice dominant at the time. In this optical analogy, the angle of view determines what is seen, as in Holbein's 1533 painting *The Ambassadors*, with its anamorphically concealed memento mori.[18] In a very meaningful sense, *The Rings of Saturn* is the novelistic inverse: a vast, multifaceted memento mori constructed under the sign of an anti-Cartesian scopic regime, at its center a melancholic modern subject—the figure in which aspects of the baroque and even the medieval combine with the modern[19]—lamenting the erosion of rituals of mourning in a culture for which death does not signify. What is hidden in the text in full view, anamorphically, is the question of *redemption* within a secular model of history as catastrophe.[20]

With Sebald, to adapt Todd Samuel Presner's reading, the nineteenth-century historical novel's productive relation with photography, and its antecedent visual technologies, with its promise of the verisimilitudinous reproduction of historical reality "as it really happened" (to use Leopold von Ranke's phrase[21]), reaches its apogee and its negation. In one of Sebald's many references to the Napoleonic Wars, the narrator travels to Belgium to visit the Waterloo Panorama, in which one gains an ideal overall perspective on the frozen scene of destruction before one's eyes. One of many comparable passages across his oeuvre (as quoted in the previous chapter),[22] this scene underlines what might be Sebald's fundamental attitude toward history and its representation vis-à-vis the subject as spectator, what James Chandler (2003, 257) labels Sebald's "historical epistemology." In Claudio Magris's 1986 novel *Danube*,[23] the following reflection on history and historiography appears, in a passage invoking an analogous meditation in Stendhal's *The Charterhouse of Parma* (1839):

> History comes into existence a little later, when it is already past, and the general connections, determined and written down years afterwards . . . confer on an event its role and its importance. Speaking of the capitulation of Bulgaria, an event decisive to the outcome of the First World War and therefore to the end of a civilization, Count Karolyi writes that while he was living through it he did not realize its importance, because "at that moment, 'that moment' had not yet become 'that moment.' (Magris 2001, 40)[24]

What follows is underlined in Sebald's copy of the German translation of Magris's novel: "The same is true in fiction for Fabrizio del Dongo, concerning the battle of Waterloo: while he is fighting it, it does not exist. In the pure present, the only dimension, however, in which we live, there is no history." In chapter 3 of *The Charterhouse of Parma*, the protagonist, Fabrizio del Dongo, in the midst of battle cannot tell for sure where the battle is and whether or not it even is a real battle (Magris 2001, 44). As Chandler points out, Sebald's primary Stendhalian intertext in the first section of *Vertigo* (apart from *De l'amour*) is *Vie de Henry Brulard*, composed thirty-five years after the youthful Marie-Henri Beyle participated in the Napoleonic campaign (2003, 244). Sebald employs Stendhal's 1836 memoir to exemplify the incommensurable relation between sensation and cognition, perception and understanding, and how this manifests in representations of historical events and in historiography, figured visually, or what I call historioscopy. "If strong emotion can erase the very impression it generates," remarks Chandler, contradicting Wordsworth,[25] "the images by which we try to revive those impressions can be all the more treacherous for their air of reliability" (244). In Sebald's account Beyle is "severely disappointed" to discover years after the fact that his indelible memory of "the panoramic view of the town of Ivrea" is "nothing but a copy" of an engraving of the *Prospetto d'Ivrea* that he had forgotten having seen and that had, in effect, displaced the actual memory (Sebald 1999, 7–8).[26] Chandler (2003, 245) identifies a paradoxical temporality upon which Sebald puts his own peculiar spin: "Sometimes images displace memories, but displacement is often a form of conservation—a trace that enables someone to track back to something crucial. It is seldom an easy matter in a Sebald narrative to tell whether one is moving in the direction of remembering or of forgetting; one is often doing both, and neither, at once." To be more precise, memory is destroyed in the act of remembering; one no sooner remembers than the "authentic" memory is forever lost. We are far from Proust, at this point.[27]

As suggested in the quoted passage from *Danube*, however, the historioscopic intersection of memory and visuality in Sebald is more complex still:

the Stendhalian intertext is refracted through Magris's late twentieth-century encyclopedic novel of ideas. The passage, highlighted in Sebald's copy of *Danube*,[28] anticipates in language and theme the commentary in *Vertigo* on Stendhal's, or rather Beyle's, own struggle with "the various difficulties entailed in the act of recollection" (Sebald 1999, 5).

In his memoir, in a phrasing that validates Chandler's thesis, Beyle admits that, thirty-five years after the events, "he now has no clear idea whatsoever of the things he found so horrifying then. It seemed to him that his impressions had been erased by the very violence of their impact" (Sebald 1999, 6). As a visual aide-mémoire Beyle created a sketch of a battle scene "by means of which [he] sought to remember how things were" (6). Within the crude drawing (reproduced in *Vertigo*) is an *H* marking Beyle's position: "Yet, of course, when Beyle was in actual fact standing at that spot, he will not have been viewing the scene in this precise way, for in reality, as we know, everything is always quite different" (7). Throughout Sebald's prose works, the inevitable failure of historical memory and historiography alike is rendered in the terms of a failed visual mastery, reflected as well on the level of individual memory.[29] It is worth recalling here Austerlitz's teacher André Hilary's lecture on the Battle of Austerlitz:

> All of us, even when we think we have noted every tiny detail, resort to set pieces which have already been staged often enough by others. We try to reproduce the reality, but the harder we try, the more we find the pictures that make up the stock-in-trade of the spectacle of history forcing themselves upon us . . . Our concern with history, so Hilary's thesis ran, is a concern with preformed images already imprinted on our brains, images at which we keep staring while the truth lies elsewhere, away from it all, somewhere as yet undiscovered. (Sebald 2001, 71–72)

In *The Rings of Saturn*'s intertextualization of Michael Hamburger's memoir of his Berlin childhood, for instance, the same locutions appear in relation to a different historical context: "Whenever a shift in our spiritual life occurs and fragments [of memories] such as these surface, we believe we can remember. But in reality, of course, memory fails us. Too many buildings have fallen down, too much rubble has been heaped up, the moraines and deposits are insuperable" (Sebald 1998, 177).

Voyager as Landscape

What sort of landscape does Sebald's paradoxical historioscopy produce? Toward the end of *The Rings of Saturn* (part 9) the narrator recounts the late eighteenth-century English ruling class practice of constructing vast estates of empty parkland surrounding a manor house:

The object was to enjoy an uninterrupted view from the house over a natural expanse innocent of any human presence . . . The least costly aspect of laying out a landscaped park was planting trees as specimens or in small groups, even if it was not seldom preceded by the felling of tracts of woodland and the burning-off of unsightly thickets and scrub that did not comply with the overall concept. Nowadays, given that only a third of the trees planted at the time are still standing in most parks, and that more are dying each year of old age and many other causes, we will soon be able to envisage once more the Torricelli-like emptiness in which great country seats stood in the late eighteenth century. (Sebald 1998, 262–63)

Premodern natural philosophy was dominated for nearly two millennia by Aristotelian thought, which was then reinterpreted by the Scholastics in accordance with Christian theology. Evangelista Torricelli's 1644 experiment, in which Newton's less-famous fellow scientist proved that nature indeed tolerates a vacuum, was symptomatic of the broader scientific revolution that marked the transition to a modern episteme. As John D. Barrow (2000, 102) explains,

Torricelli's simple experiment led eventually to the acceptance of the radical idea that the Earth was cocooned in an atmosphere that thinned out as one ascended from the Earth's surface and was eventually reduced to an empty expanse that we have come to call simply "space" or, if we keep going a bit further, "outer space." This dramatic background stage for life on Earth provided the beginning for many reassessments of humanity's place and significance in the Universe. Copernicus had published his startling claims that the Earth does not lie at the centre of the solar system about one hundred years before Torricelli's work. The two are closely allied in spirit: Copernicus moves us from a central location in the Universe while Torricelli reveals that we and our local environment are made of a different density of material than the Universe beyond. We are isolated, swimming in a vast *emptiness*. (emphasis added)[30]

Such literal emptiness provides one referent for the metaphorical or allegorical emptiness in *The Rings of Saturn*. This negative space is closely related to the visual-spatial coordinates of modern catastrophe, whose collapsing of subject and object is so succinctly announced in Benjamin's conclusion to "The Work of Art" essay.[31] As Sebald (1988, 8) wrote of 1970s and 1980s German theater, the "prospect in which the subject and object of destruction are one is a central theme of playwriting in Germany today." He cites as an example Müller's *Landschaft mit Argonauten*: "That there is an audience watching the calamitous scene of destruction brings the whole arrangement in line with one of the most pervasive *topoi* of Western literature and art identified by Hans Blumenberg as *Schiffbruch mit Zuschauer*" (Sebald 1988, 8). The "prospect" Sebald identifies depends on the concomitant negation of the author as "representative of a species" that observes itself "relentlessly" destroying its own habitat.

All of Sebald's narratives are characterized by the radical absence of people from their landscapes and cityscapes, a feature I identify as one of their primary *anti*realist characteristics; time and again Sebald conjures what are in mimetic terms highly convincing spaces while undermining their verisimilitude by means of the uncanny absence of humans, animals, or other sentient beings. More than one critic has remarked upon this feature, typically disparagingly: "The depopulated nature of Sebald's landscapes of ruin has been commented on before . . . On the surface, this is a paradox, given the fact that his works are very much about individual human stories. This depopulation is a function of a perspective that views the ruin as a building or buildings . . . without human use or function" (Ward 2004, 59). As Greg Bond declares, "Sebald's method is not realist, but it does not take an inveterate realist to find [Sebald's characteristic invocation of darkness, emptiness, and general gloom] forced" (40). Bond (2004, 40) quotes Alan Bennett's assessment of *The Rings of Saturn* in the *London Review of Books*: "I persevere with Sebald but the contrivance of it, particularly his unpeopling of the landscape, never fails to irritate . . . Sebald seems to stage-manage both the landscape and the weather to suit his (seldom cheerful) mood . . . Once noticed Sebald's technique seems almost comic . . . The fact is, in Sebald nobody is ever about. This may be poetic but it seems to me a short cut to significance." Bennett's assessment is entirely sympathetic to the aesthetic ideology of bourgeois novelistic realism, but Sebald's novels can be fully understood only within a broader cultural-historical and aesthetic context.[32]

Arguably, on the question of Sebald's deserted spaces Bennett does not go far enough: also worth remarking is the related absence in the prose works of all but the quirkiest of commercial commodities.[33] Generally speaking, the flotsam and jetsam of contemporary consumer culture are rarely to be found in Sebald's fictional world. If realism, to update Peter Bürger, is the objectification of the self-understanding of the class of consumers that has come to dominance over the past century, then Sebald's narrators and other characters generally operate in a space on the margins if not outside the society of the spectacle—a feature that also contributes to the *anti*realism that vexed many early reviewers while pleasing many critics.[34] The "spectacle" in *The Rings of Saturn* is not solely that of a world transformed by capitalism into an image of itself; it is a "desert of the real" but not in Baudrillard's sense—Sebald is too much the heir of the Frankfurt school critique of later modernity. It is the dryland shipwreck of *King Lear*,[35] a saturnine intertext that underscores and deepens the nonrealist significance of all the empty, quasi-postapocalyptic landscapes, uncannily devoid of people (e.g., Sebald 1998, 174–75, 189).

SB

How better to represent the potential cost of destruction on this scale—a psychic as much as environmental or social-cultural cost?

As noted, the original German subtitle of *The Rings of Saturn* is *Eine englische Wallfahrt*: an English pilgrimage. As walker-pilgrim the narrator-protagonist is as distinct from a post–World War II consumer-subject as he is from Benjamin's modernist *flâneur*. These last two combine mobility, spectatorship, and historically specific modes of consumption, whether more passive or active in form, whereas Sebald's narrator in all four books remains a particularized outside observer.[36] In a sense, the Sebaldian subject is a desocialized hyperconscious version of Foucault's subjected subject: *self*-surveyed and -surveilled, acutely aware of the attenuated regulatory effect of specific urban and rural spaces, not to speak of the defunct social practices whose traces can still be detected.[37] This is an irreducibly intra- and intertextualized, visually inflected, postmemorial subject that therefore many readers are tempted to identify with the historical Sebald because the latter has granted the former autobiographical attributes in a self-reflexive, so to speak "postmodern," manner evocative of Vladimir Nabokov.[38]

Combustion and Consumption

The Rings of Saturn is both typical and unique as a novel in its combination of micro- and macroperspectives: typical in that it displays a sweeping view of history, from an English to a European to a global context; unique in the manner in which it links this macroview to the singular subjective specificity of its narrator-protagonist. In part 7 Sebald lays bare the twin engines of industrialized civilization: consumption and combustion (Sebald 1998, 169). Environmental destruction is compared implicitly to social-political upheaval and personal trauma. Fire takes the form of either heat or light, guaranteeing survival and enlightenment, or combustion and destruction:

> Whatever was spared by the flames in prehistoric Europe was later felled for construction and ship-building, and to make the charcoal which the smelting of iron required in vast quantities . . . Our spread over the earth was fuelled by reducing the higher species of vegetation to charcoal, by incessantly burning whatever would burn . . . Combustion is the hidden principle behind every artefact we create. The making of a fish-hook, manufacture of a china cup, or production of a television programme, all depend on the same process of combustion. Like our bodies and like our desires, the machines we have devised are possessed of a heart which is slowly reduced to embers. From the earliest times, human civilization has been no more than a strange luminescence growing more and more intense by the hour, of which no one can say when it will begin to wane and when

it will fade away. For the time being, our cities still shine through the
night, and the fires still spread. (170)

In *The Rings of Saturn*, combustion as crucial infrastructural process—making
possible ceaseless consumption—always has the same end product: ashes.

While Sebald's project *cannot* be reduced to a nostalgic reclamation of
territory lost to modernity's ineluctable eroding of a former, ostensibly better
world, there is within it a recurring critique of the relentless expansion of capital—a process directly proportionate to the destruction of any stable position
from which the subject can survey in relative objectivity the scene of its own
striving: "the dissolution," to quote *Austerlitz*, "in line with the inexorable
spread of processed data, of our capacity to remember" (Sebald 2001, 286).
This scene, typically represented in Sebald as a literal rural or urban space, is
therefore unpeopled, radically empty, mirroring its metaphorical counterpart:
the *interior* field of action of a subject radically alone, alienated in a melancholic condition whose pre-Freudian resonance ironically offers one of the
few glimpses in the narrative of something like hope. Therefore this gloomy
or uncanny unpeopling is quite other than some pathetically fallacious post-
Romantic solipsism. This is not merely the exteriorization of an interior state
or the infusing of a landscape with affective content but both at once. Sebald's
emptinesses operate, on one level, to ironically represent certain crucial problems of representation characteristic of modernism that arose even earlier, in
the Baroque period: at the center of Sebald's narrative one meets again and
again the confusion of perspectives, the loss of the distinction between author-
producer and narrator-character, on the one hand, and theorist-critic and
reader-consumer, on the other. This *sounds* like a contradiction of Benjamin's
(Benjamin 2002b, 122) conclusion to the "Work of Art" essay, in which he
claims that humankind had become by the early twentieth century "an object
of contemplation for itself. Its self-alienation has reached the point where it
can experience its own annihilation as a supreme aesthetic pleasure."[39] But
a work like *The Rings of Saturn* actually bears out Benjamin's claim in the
most effective way, by (to invoke a mimetic-realist register) reflecting an ocularcentric world in which Cartesian distinctions between subject and object,
observer and observed, are confused or even collapsed. At the same time the
social role of author-narrator as witness to historical catastrophe acquires a
new urgency in the face of changing technologies of representation (especially
visual), new social practices and ideological formations, and the evolving status of the long prose narrative as a forum for the staging of such witnessing.

The Sebaldian Subject

As noted in the previous chapter, the narrative point of view in *The Rings of
Saturn* oscillates continuously between affective immersion or embeddedness

and distanced visual mastery. The scene of the protagonist gazing out a window conforms structurally to another recurrent trope in Sebald's work, what he termed the synoptic view in a 1996 essay on Vladimir Nabokov, in which he constructs a revealing analogy between a kind of "transcendent" narrative perspective and seventeenth-century Dutch painting:

> [Nabokov's] work contains many passages written from a kind of bird's-eye-view . . . This is to see the world through the eyes of the crane, as the Dutch painters sometimes did in painting scenes like the Flight into Egypt, when they rose above the flat panorama surrounding them down on earth. In the same way, writing, as Nabokov practiced it, is raised on high by the hope that, given sufficient concentration, the landscapes of time that have already sunk below the horizon can be seen once again in a synoptic view. Nabokov also knew, better than most of his fellow writers, that the desire to suspend time can prove its worth only in the most precise re-evocation of things long overtaken by oblivion. (2005, 145)[40]

"The synoptic view," whether across space, as a way of looking at and understanding the world, or across time, as a way of gazing "across the barrier of death" (205)—where death is to life what oblivion is to memory, which makes it sound as though death is therefore "redeemable" in the same sense that things forgotten can be brought back to conscious light. In his own fictions, however, Sebald is just as likely to show that this analogy depends on a second-order oblivion: the necessary disavowal of the knowledge that both death and the past in themselves are irreducibly mediated by representations and that the visually inflected nature of these representations sustains the illusion of the knowability or visibility of what is, in any direct sense (to maintain the visual metaphor), always just beyond the range of apprehension. In *Austerlitz* this theme finds expression in the protagonist's individual subjectivity and the narrator's critique of the culture's ocularcentrism suggested in his attention to "the fixed, inquiring gaze found in certain painters and philosophers who seek to penetrate the darkness that surrounds us purely by means of thinking and looking" (Sebald 2001, 5). *The Rings of Saturn* anticipates *Austerlitz* in its extension of the critique of Enlightenment values pursued, in their different ways, by Adorno, Benjamin, and others. The postsecular dimension of these books, however, emanates as much from their comparable incorporation of premodern intertexts combined with Sebald's peculiar brand of environmentalist ethics.

Conclusion: Dantean Inversions

The ironic variations on a Christian-Neoplatonic model of redemptive transformation throughout *The Rings of Saturn* are evidence of Sebald's oblique, intextualized response to the ongoing prevalence of narratives of redemption in contemporary literary and popular culture, representing a critical engagement with the instrumental and recuperative metaphysics of capitalism underpinning contemporary social reality. Sebald's "natural history of destruction," however, interweaves the subjective experience of immersion in an irrecuperable present and consequent alienation from "History" with a salvific or redemptive historical model that ironically combines Walter Benjamin's modernist messianism with a literary filiation of romantic questing.[41] Habermas (2001, 1751) describes "Benjamin's concept of the *Jetztzeit*, of the present as a moment of revelation; a time in which splinters of a messianic presence are enmeshed." Sebald is also influenced by Ernst Bloch's utopian "Principle of Hope"; in a 1976 essay, subtitled "Authority, Messianism and Exile in *Das Schloß*," Sebald suggests that messianism, as one of the "ways of transcending [K.'s] hopeless situation," has a very problematic presence in *The Castle*. Evoking Bloch, Sebald (1976, 46) claims that "the only invariable and decisive feature [of Jewish messianism in particular] is the concept of hope as the guiding principle in a maze of illusions." In the latter part of *The Rings of Saturn* this principle is filtered through the ironically inverted Christological allegory of the soul's journey through darkness toward the light of salvation.

In part 9, toward the end of the book, the governing motif of catastrophe comes to a head as the narrator laments the "ever more rapid decline in the numbers of trees" in England since the mid-1970s, through virus, drought, and catastrophic storm (Sebald 1998, 264). He describes a freakish hurricane in October 1987: "It seemed as if someone had pulled a curtain to one side to reveal a formless scene that bordered upon the underworld . . . I knew that everything [in the park] had been destroyed" (266). In the hurricane's aftermath, he wanders in disbelief among the masses of felled mature trees, lying in the deep darkness of a power outage: "But the stars had come out, in a display so resplendent as I had seen only over the Alps when I was a child, or over the desert in my dreams . . . The sparkling constellations were spread out . . . Unchanged and, it seemed to me, more magnificent than ever before, they revolved above me" (267).[42] It is tempting to read this as a hopeful recuperation of vision, contrasted with the desolate view from his hospital window at the narrative's outset, when in his state of near paralysis he identifies with the metamorphosed Gregor Samsa. However, just as *Vertigo* stands as one of the best guides to Dante's presence in Kafka,[43] the image of the stars here evokes the last lines of canto 33 in Dante's *Inferno*, in which we read a foreshadowed vision of promised redemption, still concealed in the allegorical aesthetics of *this* world and *this* life. In the *Commedia*'s medieval aspect, Dante adheres to the Ptolemaic concentric-spherical model of the universe, in which the "Sphere of Saturn" is the penultimate frontier, beyond which lies the "Sphere of the Fixed Stars."[44] And in Sebald, so in Dante: this vision is the product of an ironic inversion, when the pilgrim emerges right side up at the end of his sojourn through the underworld. Sebald reinverts this, giving Dante's redemptive irony a further twist: "Now, in the truest sense of the word, everything was turned upside down" (268). The eschatological dimension of this vision of destruction is thoroughly resignified; the redemptive economy of Dante's narrative is negated as it is appropriated to give ironic form to another economy in which destruction—and therefore death—is not recoverable, at least not in metaphysical terms.[45] The final image in this section is one of apocalyptic devastation and emptiness, contradicting, in a bitter irony, the vision of the star-filled sky a page before and bearing out, metaphorically, or emblematically, the Torricellian conclusion that nature does not in the least abhor a vacuum: "The rays of the sun, with nothing left to impede them, destroyed all the shade-loving plants so that it seemed as if we were living on the edge of an infertile plain" (268).[46]

Early modern science dispelled the myth of horror vacui, of nature's intolerance of a vacuum, proving that a radically empty space, void of anything like matter, the absence of "nature" within nature, not only can be created but also readily tolerated by science and nature alike. Rather it is *culture*, in the expansive sense it has today, that does not tolerate a vacuum: the radical absence of anything cultural, construed in terms of the processes and practices of meaning production and of the material, social, and symbolic forms that result—including, ironically, any notion of "nature." No sooner does an opening appear in the cultural landscape but something—not matter but meaning, not energy but power—comes rushing in to fill the gap. Here we see the most disturbing aspect of Sebald's emptinesses: whether the product of apocalyptic devastation or gradual erosion, natural or man-made disaster, their presence foregrounds the absence of spaces in which, to paraphrase *Austerlitz*, a "living connection to the past" can somehow manifest itself (Sebald 2001, 286).

In the *Divine Comedy* Dante-pilgrim learns over the course of his narrative how to read the eschatological allegory of Hell, Purgatory, and Heaven; in *Rings* Sebald's narrator acquires only a *negative* knowledge: how to see, how to look at death and destruction in a way that is predicated *neither* in present identification with the other *nor* on the future redemption of the self. In Julia Hell's (2003, 33) phrase this is Sebald's "ethics of the gaze" in a text that remains deeply suspicious of the image because of the propensity of iconic visual representations to replace what we take to be authentic memories. This suspicion is only complicated by the presence of photographs and other visual images throughout the prose works. This is a formal strategy that throws the ethical weight onto the prose discourse itself, in its dialogic relation with visuality in the work of not merely representing but also *constituting* what I am calling a particular, historically specific, postmodern subjectivity—a subjectivity constituted in the excavatory *work* of reading, writing, and remembering. In part 1 of *The Rings of Saturn* the narrator remarks that his colleague Janine Dakyns, marooned in her paper-flooded office, resembles the figure of *Melencolia* in Dürer's 1514 engraving, surrounded by her "instruments of destruction" (Sebald 1998, 9). "[We] are able to maintain ourselves on this earth," the narrator remarks, "only by being harnessed to the machines we have invented" (283).[47] Here at the end, in what can safely be called a Nabokovian move, Sebald makes overt the metaphorical and literal links among weavers, operators of silk looms in the eighteenth century, and "scholars and writers with whom they have much in common": all three tend "to suffer from melancholy and all the evils associated with it" because their work forces them "to sit bent over, day after day, straining to keep their eye on the complex patterns they created. It is difficult to imagine the depths of despair into which those can be driven who, even after the end of the working day, are engrossed in their intricate designs and who are pursued, into their dreams, by the feeling that they have got hold of the wrong thread" (283).[48] The reader pursues the narrative's "intricate design" across the three-hundred-odd pages of *The Rings of Saturn* (three hundred fifty in the German) until—like the narrator, and like Beckett's novelistic heroes, as heirs to Dante-pilgrim—she/he reaches a point almost identical to that at which the book commenced. The narrative as such is thus revealed to be a purgatorial series of concentric circles, extending indefinitely outward, encompassing a universe of meaning, and yet delimited by the saturnine melancholia of the narrator's hospital-bound psyche.

Like Kafka and Beckett, Sebald displays an aversion to a realism reflective of (in the former's case) a commoditized protoconsumerist reality; that is, he echoes their inward focus while also representing what for him is the catastrophe of capitalism through the traces of destruction it leaves in its wake. He does this while displaying an ambivalently nostalgic attitude toward the object system representative of a pre-1933 European world now forever lost. But Sebald does not limit his subject to the modernist innovations of a Beckett or Kafka; his is never immobilized for long, nor does the body ever disappear altogether. There is an allegiance in his prose narratives to the realist tradition, filtered through writers like Conrad, reaching back to the Baroque in Thomas Browne, repeatedly negotiating the crucial early modern moment of cultural transformation and epistemological inversion to which we can trace our current "posthuman" condition. His is the necessarily embodied, historically implicated, and visually inflected subject of an ocularcentric late modernity, constrained to express itself in the ironically (post)apocalyptic terms of a world on the verge of imminent collapse. In putting itself as it were into the landscape as participant-spectator, Sebald's subject acknowledges the compromised autonomy and sovereignty of its position—within time as well as space.

Chapter 3

Interminable Journeys

Vertigo and Kafka's "Wandering Jew of the Ocean"

> It is a fundamentally insane notion . . . that one is able to
> influence the course of events by a turn of the helm, by will-
> power alone, whereas in fact all is determined by the most
> complex interdependencies.
>
> —W. G. Sebald, *Vertigo*

My readings of Sebald's prose texts are predicated upon their highly intertextual nature[1] and the understanding that Sebald's fictional world is an irreducibly *literary* structure within which the mediated experience of subjectivity
is the primary object of representation. In this chapter I consider Sebald's
bricolagic appropriation and translation in *Vertigo* of Franz Kafka's "Hunter
Gracchus" fragment (1917), as well as Kafka's diaries and letters of 1913.[2] I
seek to examine *how* these diverse intertexts signify within the narrative in the
context of Sebald's abiding interest in the problematic conjunction in fictional
narrative of the aleatory principle—the element of *chance* or coincidence—
and the theme of redemption. Somewhere between is *choice* as a product of
the pattern—call it fate—rather than as an individual act of volition.

At issue, though, is the fictional—and, ultimately, literal—status of *death*:
the reality principle whose cultural valuation in the modern period is always
at odds with the problem of its representation. The "common supposition,"
according to Sebald, is to see in representations of death "a cipher for salvation" (Sebald 1972, 22).[3] More generally, the metaphysical category of
redemption has long since been revalued in the gradual shift to a so-called
secular late modernity, the occidental world's semiconscious disavowal of
its abiding allegiance to categories such as God or an afterlife.[4] As noted in
the introduction, however, it seems more accurate to qualify this episteme as
postsecular, which embraces the possibility that such a disavowal was never
total and that the perspectives and values of the Enlightenment project have
lost whatever hegemonic hold they may have had.

Sebald's prose texts extend in their different ways Kafka's and Nabokov's
divergent critiques of the persistence of a metaphysical worldview that is nevertheless often affirmed by Nabokov and Kafka scholars alike. It says far more
about prevailing literary critical values in the previous century than it does

about the authors under discussion that the question of a *positive* vision of an afterlife or "other-world" has proven particularly tenacious, for both Kafka and Nabokov scholars. I focus here on the subtle relation between *Vertigo's* initially metonymic *identification* of the narrator with Kafka and Kafka's Hunter, Casanova, Stendhal, Dante, and others, historical and fictional,[5] as well as *The Emigrants'* repeated invocation of Nabokov's quasi-allegorical personae. Ultimately, I aim to shed light on Sebald's unique contribution to an erotic-salvific model predicated on a specific relation between a narrative subject and an *other* as embodiment of the promise—or hope—of redemption. What is of interest here is the manner in which Sebald responds to the ironically metafictional Nabokovian "solution," as well as to the interminably open-ended nonsolution adumbrated in Kafka. This response takes place in the larger context of Sebald's abiding concern with the manner in which we— as subjects of late modernity—have yet to come to terms with what we have already left behind.

Informing this comparison is the question of Sebald's position vis-à-vis what Jürgen Habermas famously calls the incomplete project of the Enlightenment in modernity; why it is possible to call Sebald as much *anti-* as *post*modern.[6] As Matei Calinescu remarks in his discussion of the famous Habermas-Lyotard debate on the postmodern, modernity is "premised on a finalistic vision of universal history, and in this sense Christianity (as the story of humanity's final redemption from the original Adamic sin) is constitutively modern. All the major 'stories of emancipation' of modernity are essentially secularized variations on the Christian paradigm" (Calinescu 1987, 274).[7] In this light, the Jewish messianic historical model of exile, wandering, and waiting can be seen as either pre-, post-, or even *anti*modern, depending on one's perspective. It can also be seen as in many ways representative of the contemporary postsecular cultural moment. Insofar as it is interpreted according to a Christological typology, the messianic model is premodern in that it forecasts and foreshadows the coming modern age. But if it is read, and to a certain degree rewritten, in the way it was in the twentieth century, this "messianicity," to use Derrida's term, becomes emblematic of a "postmodern" narrative that is defined by its need to emancipate itself from this very type of totalizing interpretation, reasserting a more open-ended historical model. *Messianicity*, distinct from messianism, is Derrida's name for what might be called the ethical relation of the archive toward not the past but the future. In Derrida's (1993, 36) terms, the question of the archive "is a question of the future, the question of the future itself, the question of a response, or a promise and of a responsibility for tomorrow." This messianicity is a feature of a Jewishness distinct from Judaism, a cultural identity predicated on a form of hope that is an "opening toward the future" whose obverse is memory-as-archive (72–75). What an analysis of Sebald should reveal is the degree to which the meaning and significance of the term "modern"—and therefore the very status of "the modern project"—continue to turn on this crucial issue of a kind of reflexive, avowedly secular *faith* in a repertoire of metaphysical structures that constitute the ironically theological basis of contemporary postsecular Western culture.

"The Wandering Jew of the Ocean": *Vertigo* and Kafka's "Hunter Gracchus"

In a series of critical essays of the 1970s Sebald offers his interpretation of aspects of Kafka's oeuvre, focusing in particular on what might be called Kafka's ironically messianic eschatology: a negative or antieschatology not about the "end" as such but about its deferral or impossibility. In a 1972 essay on "the death motif" in *The Castle* Sebald (after Benjamin and Adorno) ascribes to Kafka the bestowal of "messianic traits" on "his alter-ego K." (Sebald 1972, 29). In recognizing this dimension of Kafka's text, Sebald overlooks K.'s incomprehension of his own motives, thereby implying the presence of a positive hope for some kind of resolution in a novel whose very structure, of unfinished and unfinishable narrative interminability, militates against such a reading. As noted in the previous chapter, in the 1976 essay, subtitled "Authority, Messianism and Exile in *Das Schloß*," Sebald suggests that messianism, as one of the "ways of transcending [K.'s] hopeless situation," has a very problematic presence in *The Castle*. Following Ernst Bloch, Sebald claims that "the only invariable and decisive feature [of Jewish messianism in particular] is the concept of hope as the guiding principle in a maze of illusions" (46). That the Hebrew words for land surveyor (*mashikha*) and messiah (*mashiakh*) differ by only one unwritten vowel Sebald takes as evidence, again, of K.'s secret status as avatar of a Jewish messiah (57).[8] The other interpretation— more plausible from the evidence of Kafka's oeuvre—is that this single-letter difference is the difference between everything and nothing; it is the specific, signifying difference that keeps K. forever on the hither side of messiah-hood. But then Sebald seems to acknowledge this, highlighting Kafka's virtuosic use of the German subjunctive tense, for instance in constructions employing "as if" [*als ob*], as "a token of the desperate disparity between the messianic promise and its actual achievement" (49). Here Sebald lays the ground for much of his subsequent fictional output through a sympathetic combination of Walter Benjamin's modernist messianism[9] and Bloch's (1986) utopian "Principle of Hope." Sebald argues that K. is "a cipher for a future that perpetually retreats ahead of a disheartening reality, a cipher of hope, deeply engrained in privation and never redeemed. Even if this principle is forlorn in its own unreality there remains the desire for its realization" (Sebald 1976, 50).

Sebald openly acknowledges the incommensurability of a messianic impulse and its goal of salvation: "That messianism is doomed to miss the fulfillment of its hopes by a hair's breadth appears to be the mark of its calamitous origin" (52). This origin, he clarifies, is despair, manifesting in K.'s case from his "constitutional, inbred weakness. The origins of messianism in despair are the inherent cause of its unavoidable failure and incongruity" (53). Eventually Sebald comes down on the side of a modern Jewish mysticism as manifest in thinkers such as Bloch and Franz Rosenzweig: "What is important in messianic thought is solely the viability of what Ernst Bloch called *das Prinzip Hoffnung*, 'the Hope Principle', a principle which to Franz Rosenzweig appeared to be *der Stern der Erlösung*, 'the Star of Salvation'" (53). As Sebald makes clear, this is a principle whose "viability" is not threatened in any way by the recognized likelihood that the messiah may always be an impostor, a "fictive and merely assumed" identity (53). Again, in K.'s case—and on this point Sebald's analysis does not tally with that of others, including my own—the messianic figure may not even be aware of his own pseudomessianic status. According to Sebald's reading of Kafka, though, this additional "weakness" on K.'s part only redoubles the paradoxical truth value of a principle of hope "stifled and obscured by an oppressive reality" (53).

A preoccupation with identity, construed in terms of language, homeland, "Jewishness," and so forth, characterizes a certain strain of twentieth-century literature and thought, finding new expression in Sebald's prose works. In this respect, Kafka's oeuvre is an uncannily proleptic paradigm. The question here is how this aspect of Kafka signifies within Sebald's appropriation of the Gracchus story and its idiosyncratic treatment of the theme of salvation through another's intercession: salvation from bachelorhood through his fiancée, Felice Bauer; salvation from Felice, and a stifling bourgeois life-in-death, through the nameless gentile Swiss girl from the Riva trip (Sebald 1999, 157–59). How, finally, he passively opts for neither form of salvation, neither bourgeois respectability nor erotic bliss; how he opts for nothing except the certain denial of any salvation that a life of writing represents. In the broadest sense, Nabokov makes a comparable choice to place literature above everything else—except consciousness itself. Only for Nabokov this is not problematic at all, as it is for Kafka. For Nabokov the literary expression of memory represents the possibility of a genuine aesthetic redemption—which is the only form of redemption available to a consciousness trapped within itself while able to conceive (albeit negatively) of its own self-transcendence (see, e.g., Nabokov 1989, 296–97). For his part, Kafka accedes to the existence of "an infinite amount of hope—but not for us."[10] The first person plural here is ambiguous; again, it comes down to identity, whether personal, collective, or cultural. For both writers, as remediated by Sebald, "salvation" is also always a question of the relative possibility of returning to a home or homeland in a future that signifies only in relation to a golden past (Nabokov) or promises to be no different from the present, barring the only real escape, death—the *Heimat* without return (Kafka).

On the one hand, then, Sebald exploits in *Vertigo* the "Hunter Gracchus" story as a parable of the crossing of the aleatory principle with a notion of "fate," in an ironically temporized, structurally open-ended messianic narra-

tive. Here messiah and subject of experience are identified in the figure of the
Hunter (*der Jäger*), in the typical Kafkan conflation of extremes of self and
other in the protagonist. On the other hand, there is Sebald's appropriation of
the butterfly-hunting motif in *Speak, Memory* and in Nabokov's postemigration life generally, which could be read as evidence of what many critics see
as Nabokov's tacit "faith" in some ontologically autonomous "other world"
or level of being upon which is predicated the possibility of some kind of
deliverance beyond a so-called *aesthetic* redemption.[11]

In *Speak, Memory*, as in his other autobiographical and fictional writings,
Nabokov elaborates a theory of memory as *art*,[12] as a *technique* of redemption through the conscious *divestment* of one's recollections transfigured as
aesthetic objects, transpositions and translations of remembered experience
given away as a gift whose giving—if one takes Nabokov at this word—
benefits the giver as much as the receiver. This is the Nabokovian version of
redemption through art, an aesthetic transfiguration of experience through
the recuperative mnemonic restaging of the past in the temporal equivalent of
the effacing or transcendence of spatial boundaries. Ultimately, for Nabokov,
this *modern* art of memory results in a redemption of the experience of exile
and loss of identity through displacement in time and space. As Nabokov was
fond of pointing out, this kind of highly aestheticized mnemonic reconstitu-
tion allows him to overcome nostalgia for the Russia of his youth—a place
and time beyond any but an imaginative recuperation—since an aestheticized
version of the best parts of that past is always in his possession, his to review
or even to give away at will (e.g., Nabokov 1989, 76–77).[13] For Nabokov,
one of the most celebrated of all literary émigrés, literature and memory are
coterminous image systems (see, e.g., Foster 1993, 183).[14]

The title of *The Emigrants* encourages a cultural-historical perspective on
the reality of a state of exile and emigration that may or may not be one of
homelessness. This is the crux of the book as a whole, in terms of Sebald's
oblique juxtaposing of his various emigrant-characters' states of dispossession
with Nabokov's permanent link to a home that exists only in his memory, yet
which in its artistic, *hypomnesic*, translation constitutes for him not simply
a powerful antidote to the unstructured messiness of life but also a means of
imparting that mess with a meaning it otherwise lacks. Having lost everything,
he lacks for nothing and even feels free to share his eidetic riches across space
and time through the gift of his fictionalized memoirs. For Nabokov, then,
"home" is ultimately a function of identity in its linguistic expression and is
therefore always present, always wherever he is, in a collapsing of space that
is simultaneously memory's "negation of time" (Nabokov 1973, 78)—the
redemption of loss and even death (e.g., Nabokov 1989, 76–77).

For Kafka, on the other hand—that is to say, for the Hunter Gracchus—
identity is defined as a state of permanent alienation from homeland and
language. For Kafka, the ironic messiah of the *impossibility* of redemption,
what Heinrich Heine (1967, 173) calls "the Wandering Jew of the Ocean,"

signifies a collective or cultural identity predicated on a desire for a *Heimat*, whether through assimilation or translation. Next to the legend of "the Wandering Jew,"[16] one of Kafka's most significant intertexts is Richard Wagner's first symphonic opera, *The Flying Dutchman* (*Der fliegende Holländer*, 1841). Interestingly, "[of] all of Wagner's mature operas, with their mythic or legendary subject matter . . . *Der fliegende Holländer* . . . has the shortest prehistory. Indeed, it was as late as the very end of the eighteenth century that the legend of the wandering seafarer achieved literary form, in various English and German versions" (Grey 2000, 25). The myth of the eternal seafarer is thoroughly modern, offering a literary model for a modern subject complementary to that of Faust. "Wagner's chief source" for his opera was not Coleridge's *Ancient Mariner* (1798), as one might imagine, but Heine's 1834 satirical autobiographical fragment *Aus den Memoiren des Herren von Schnabelewopski*.[17] The whole of what would become Wagner's plot is adumbrated in the seventh chapter of Heine's anti-Romantic pseudomemoir. Wagner's Flying Dutchman is emblematic of the other major expression of this particular modern subject: "Wagner's self-identification with the Dutchman . . . focuses on the theme of spiritual, psychological alienation as the lot of the Romantic artist . . . In true Romantic fashion, Wagner yearns for a homeland he has never actually known, a utopian artistic 'space' that is more a state of mind than any real place" (Grey 2000, 10). In the opera his Romantic "longing for [a] German homeland" manifests itself in the Dutchman's longing for a woman, "the redeeming woman" whom he envisions as "the feminine element in general" (10). It is through this anthropomorphism that the longed-for homeland (*Heimat*)—"that is . . . the sensation of being embraced by some intimately familiar community"—promises him "salvation" (10.). In this light, identity, whether personal or cultural, private or public, signifies for Kafka an ongoing anxiety or frustration around the relations at the heart of social life, most significantly the sexual-erotic and matrimonial-domestic realms from which Kafka always felt more or less excluded. As the Romantic-Wagnerian version of the Flying Dutchman makes clear, the desire for a woman on the part of this particular modern subject is equivalent to the longing for the possibility of redemption through the return to a place never seen or visited before, a new "homeland" that, as much as place or community, is about a *positive* relation through memory to the past and therefore to the present.

A model of time structured according to a logic of redemption would seem to preclude any aleatory principle. What I mean here by the element or principle of *chance* is obliquely addressed in *Vertigo*, part 3 ("Dr. K.s Badereise nach Riva," the section based largely on letters Kafka wrote from Italy in 1913 to his erstwhile fiancée, Felice Bauer). In one scene an old general, Dr. K.'s tablemate at the sanatorium and a compulsive reader of Stendhal, observes, "It is a fundamentally insane notion . . . that one is able to influence the course of events by a turn of the helm, by will-power alone, whereas in fact all is determined by the most complex interdependencies" (Sebald 1999,

157). In this view, the course of events—what we might call a certain narrative logic—is determined neither by individual agency nor by some kind of "fate" but by the complex interdependence and interconnectivity of things; in other words, by what is commonly referred to as *chance*, where chance occurrences, coincidences, and all other manner of accidents, when viewed from the proper perspective, can be seen to relate together in fantastically complex but discernibly meaningful configurations. In Kafka's (1971, 228–30) story, for example, the wrong "turn of the helm" is just that: a mistake, not a choice on the part of the helmsman. Further, the apprehension of meaning on this level, in this fashion, is not necessarily connected to or dependent upon any narrative resolution in any conventional sense, or even some more specific *Erlösung*. The connections may make themselves visible at any point, in any order, not necessarily according to a traditional logic of causality and consequence. "Fate," in this context, equals narrative inevitability as an effect of retrospection—a retroperspective.[18] More than a banal observation about certain kinds of novels, this is to underline the centrality of memory as a kind of "technique" in determining the novel's form, as much as that form shapes memory.[19] To put it another way, this inevitability—a dynamic recursivity—becomes the law of a certain kind of narrative, just as it provides the model for what passes for "fate" in everyday life. For Sebald, intermediality is the principal vehicle for the representation of this interconnectively determined meaning. It is by no means coincidental if in the German term (*Erlösung*) we highlight here the narrative sense of solution, resolution, or "closure." Therefore in this aspect every narrative resolution is a *deliverance*, a kind of ironic *redemption*, in the face of an authentic redemptive possibility, which is forever deferred.[20] This general observation about narrative—applicable to many modern novels—does not explain, however, why, for example, the majority of Kafka's longer narratives *fail* to resolve, remain unfinished, fragmentary—but it must be taken into account when considering what kind of effects such narratives produce, or *fail* to produce, when the Kafkan fragment becomes the model. (It should be noted, by contrast, that Nabokov's novels, even when they do not offer conventional narrative closure, are always on the formal level consummately "finished.")

But *chance*, as what might be called a thematized compositional principle, enters into Sebald's narrative much earlier. For instance, in part 1 ("Beyle, or Love Is a Madness Most Discreet"), Marie-Henri Beyle, otherwise known as Stendhal, and one Mme Gherardi, in 1814 journey together into the Italian Alps, to Desenzano and Riva on Lake Garda. The latter they reach by boat, and as they enter the port they see "two boys already sitting on the harbour wall playing dice" (Sebald 1999, 24). This is of course the opening line of Kafka's Gracchus story (1971, 226)—what some might see as a blatant example of authorial intention: allusion as intertextuality. The rest of the scene in *Vertigo* reproduces the Hunter's advent in Riva, to which Kafka traveled in 1913, a key date in the book, and which is also the setting of the Gracchus narrative:

"Two men in dark silver-buttoned tunics were at that moment carrying a bier ashore on which, under a large, frayed, flower-patterned silk cloth, lay what was evidently a human form" (Sebald 1999, 25). Beyle's, and the reader's, "chance" encounter with the Hunter Gracchus does not simply illustrate the ineluctable interpenetration of the aleatory and the predetermined in novel-istic fiction: it enacts it. In Sebald's proleptic image, this "sombre moment in Riva" will in the future cross Mme Gherardi's memory "like a shadow"—just as it crosses and recrosses the narrative's at times turbulent, at others opaquely reflective, surface (25).

In part 2 of *Vertigo* (*"All'estero"*), through a shifting series of identifica-tions with the exiled Dante, the Hunter Gracchus, and other historical and literary figures, the narrator becomes Kafka's shadowy doppelgänger (e.g., Sebald 1999, 151). Trapped in Vienna in 1980 by a kind of creeping paralysis of purpose, the narrator describes how he compulsively follows the same paths each day, literally not knowing "where to turn" (34–35): "If the paths I had followed had been inked in, it would have seemed as though a man had kept trying out new tracks and connections over and over, only to be thwarted each time by the limitations of his reason, imagination or will-power, and obliged to turn back again" (34). The narrator's problem in *Vertigo* is equiv-alent to that of most of Kafka's heroes and (as seen in chapter 1) of Beck-ett's: an epistemological *malaise* manifest on the level of *mobility*—a problem derived in part from Dante-pilgrim, wandering in a dark wood (*una selva oscura*), constrained by the moral geometry of the afterlife always to travel in the same direction, turning the same way, his bodily self regulating the process of purgation that is fated to end in redemption (see Sebald 1999, 35). The nar-ratives of Kafka and Beckett and now Sebald are the heirs to the letter, if not the spirit, of Dante, in terms of a *planar* model of time and memory in which the only possible movement is on the horizontal, around in circles, or from side to side. His narrator's subjectivity is born of the asymptotic limits of a consciousness trapped in a purgatorial time-space in which any conventional release (*Erlösung*), like conventional narrative closure (*Lösung*), is impossible. This is at least in part the function of the narrative's governing conceit of time as not a river but a sea: a vast expanse of water upon which one sails at will or at the mercy of chance rather than upon a unidirectional current rushing inexorably to a predetermined end (see, e.g., Sebald 1999, 37–47). Sebald capitalizes on this image system; *Vertigo* is a tapestry of recurrent patterns of which the nautical is the most significant: water, waves, boats, sailing, mar-iners, and seasickness.[21] Whether literal or figurative, these elements appear to represent a radical epistemological crisis symptomatic of an irreducibly intertextual subjectivity.[22]

Seasickness, of course, is one of the primary manifestations of the "feel-ing of dizziness" named in the book's German title, *Schwindel: Gefühle*. The narrator's bouts of vertiginous giddiness and motion sickness overlap with his rhythms of sleeping and waking—a narrative rhythm also derived from

Dante-pilgrim in his sojourn through Hell. This is also, for lack of a better word, the Hunter Gracchus's life: asleep on the boat, awake when on land—a horizontally oscillating process differing from Dante's vertical spiral in the crucial absence of a terminus. Sebald's narrator is characterized by this oscillation of states of aimless wandering and feeling "at sea" and then of immobility and outright unconsciousness—a hyper-Prufrockian vacillation between indecision and decision whose other intertext, ironically, is the Flying Dutchman and his cycle of restless wandering punctuated every seven years by a chance to marry and be redeemed through love (act 2; Sebald 1999, 124).

As the nautical imagery merges with the depiction of the narrator's nomadic and alienated existence, his subjectivity—his voice and point of view—increasingly overlaps with that of the Hunter Gracchus. This process of identification—ultimately an identification with Kafka's self-presentation[23] but with the conspicuous *absence* of Kafka's ongoing difficulties with women and relationships—is perhaps the point on which Kafka's intertextual presence in *Vertigo* diverges most explicitly from that of Nabokov in *The Emigrants*. More significant, though, in terms of Sebald's ironic invocation of Dantean tropes, is the manner in which Sebald exploits the tension between an allegorically externalized moral stance and a modern secular internalization of an equivalent state of being, in the slippage between the narrator's represented "psychological" and "physical" conditions—an elision effected through the subjunctive evocation of waking up in Venice on All Saints' Day:

> On that first day of November in 1980, preoccupied as I was with my notes and the ever-widening and contracting circles of my thoughts, I became enveloped by a sense of utter emptiness and never once left my room. It seemed to me then that one could well end one's life simply through thinking and retreating into one's mind . . . my limbs were growing progressively colder and stiffer with my lack of movement, so that . . . I felt as if I had already been interred or laid out for burial. (Sebald 1999, 65)

The premodern allegorization of the soul-body division exemplified in Dante is here transformed as if in response to Kafka's postrealist rewriting of this tradition. Sebald's narrator as it were internalizes Kafka's portrayal of the Hunter as a description adequate to his own epistemo-ontological condition—a postsecular approximation of the "poor unredeemed souls" whose day of remembrance (02 November 1980) the narrator spends in this torpid condition, finally "restored" by a set of secular sacraments: "a hot bath, yesterday's sandwiches and red wine" (Sebald 1999, 66) (*die Butterbrote und der Rotwein*). In a sense, the "redemption" at least symbolized by All Saints' and All Souls' Days is a literalization of the kind of metaphorical redemption or "salvation" that Kafka perhaps sought but knew was unavailable to him—a salvation that has its secular-erotic counterpart in the sort of relation with a woman that he seemed virtually incapable of realizing—except, perhaps, for the one time in Riva, with the mysterious "Italian-looking" woman (157). Nor was the alternative—acting on his (ostensible) homosexual urges—available to him. At the same time, as Zilcosky (2003, 105) shows, such redemption or "rebirth" for Sebald's narrator involves the dissolution of "his psychological difficulties," freeing him "from the literary ghosts—Dante, Casanova, Grillparzer, Kafka—that continue to haunt him."[24] For Zilcosky, in fact, Sebald's narrator's "wanderings reveal only that he cannot leave literary history's wellworn path . . . he cannot develop a Romantic situation of writing peculiar to himself: he can only walk/write in the footsteps of Dante, Kafka and Grillparzer" (105–6), "inking in" the paths, tracks, and connections he obsessively traverses each day, only to be "obliged to turn back again" and again (34).

Sebald's most audacious gesture in the Venice section of *Vertigo*, perhaps, is the tacit conflation of aspects of Kafka's biography with the adventures of Casanova, when the latter fell victim to "Venetian justice" (Sebald 1999, 54). Sebald links the two overtly through the word "tribunal" (*Gerichtshof*), which, according to Sebald's account, Casanova used in reference to the morning he was arrested—like Joseph K. in *The Trial*—and summoned to a cell under the roof of the Doge's palace (55).[25] "Tribunal" is the same word Kafka (1976, 293) employs in his diary account of the end of his engagement with Felice Bauer. The general tendency among Kafka scholars has been to read a story such as "The Hunter Gracchus" as an allegory for Kafka's "personal consternation" over whether or not to marry his fiancée (Prager 2006, 115). As Brad Prager (2006, 115) explains, Sebald is merely taking things to a logical conclusion by amplifying the underlying emphasis on sex that is already there in Kafka. Prager deepens this reading, however, by invoking Benjamin and Adorno's different approaches, both authors with whom Sebald was very familiar,[26] especially the latter's linking of Gracchus "to the historical category of the bourgeoisie, which refuses to die despite its utter uselessness" (116). In keeping with the Frankfurt school critique of the fate of the Enlightenment project in the early twentieth century, Adorno connects Gracchus ultimately to "the horror of Auschwitz." In the "Gracchus" tale, "History becomes Hell . . . because the opportunity for salvation was missed. The late bourgeoisie itself brought this about. In the concentration camps, the boundary between life and death was eradicated. A middle ground was created, inhabited by living skeletons and putrefying bodies, victims unable to take their own lives" (Prager 2006, 116). At its most extreme, this Adornian reading of the "Gracchus" story, generally endorsed by Sebald, comes down to the classic critique of mechanical reproduction: "Under conditions of capitalist production the subject turns itself into the very object that it wishes to dominate" (116). This was possible because of the mass-reproduction techniques characteristic of early twentieth-century culture, exemplified in the cinema.

Pace Adorno, Kafka's relation to his bourgeois background is both deeply banal and defined by repression. As recounted in both his letters to Felice

Bauer and Sebald's fabricated version in part 3 of *Vertigo*, "Dr. K. Takes the Waters at Riva," "Dr. K." spends three weeks at "Dr. von Hartungen's hydropathic sanatorium in Riva," where he feels strongly attracted to a mysterious young "Italian looking" woman. But "he is also clearly distracted by his own desires for men. Like Mann's Aschenbach, Dr. K. seems inspired to romance and homosexuality alike by the appearance of Italian waters, and perhaps the guilt from this tryst occasions the reflections that . . . inspired Kafka's 'Gracchus'" (Prager 2006, 117). In part 3 of *Vertigo* Sebald "directly and indirectly illustrates how Kafka links the inability to die with his subject's own self-hatred for having wandering desires" (118).[27] Prager makes the point that while "Dr. K. Takes the Waters at Riva" shares much in common with *Death in Venice* . . . Sebald and [Kafka] refuse their protagonists the easy way out that was given to Mann's Aschenbach: Dr. K. was denied the luxury of a satisfying love-life as Gracchus was denied the possibility of a satisfying death, and the two appear to partake of the same purgatory" (119). The shift in eschatological terminology from Adorno's "History becomes Hell" is noteworthy. According to Prager, for Kafka, Austrian playwright Franz Grillparzer "symbolized the possibility of acting on one's homosexual desires" (118). Thus it is all the more significant that Sebald's narrator in part 2 of *Vertigo*, as he sits on the Riva degli Schiavoni in Venice, reading Grillparzer's *Italian Diary*, adds the detail that when he is traveling he "often feels as Grillparzer did on his journeys" (Sebald 1999, 53). This is explained in terms of the writer's tendency to be disappointed by everything he encounters on a journey, but it should be remarked that it is through this evocation of "the poor hypersensitive" Grillparzer that Sebald is put in mind of one of the most famous "victims of Venetian justice," Giacomo Casanova (54).

In Sebald's account, upon his arrest Casanova dresses himself in "his best shirt and new coat . . . as if he were off to a wedding" (Sebald 1999, 55), in a proleptic echo of one of the stranger details from the "Gracchus" fragment.[28] In Kafka's version, while alive the Hunter had had no fear of death: "'I had been glad to live and I was glad to die. Before I stepped aboard, I joyfully flung away my wretched load of ammunition, my knapsack, my hunting rifle that I had always been proud to carry, and I slipped into my winding sheet like a girl into her marriage dress'" (Sebald 2005, 229). This parodically erotic cliché highlights the Hunter's passive abdication of volition as he throws off the attributes of the hunter, lying down and placing himself willingly in the hands of his "fate," which he expects to be death in its absolute finality (leaving open the possibility of death as genuine transcendence)—a death that is inadvertently circumvented. And it is this unintentional, inadvertent, and ironic *avoidance* of his "proper" end that Salvatore the Bürgermeister of Riva calls "a terrible fate" (229) (*ein schlimmes Schicksal*; *Beschreibung*, 106)—what Sebald (1999, 167) calls "the fate of being unable to depart this life." Sebald thus suggests an uncanny connection between the inscrutable operation of state or civic law and the mysterious threat of conjugal love, marriage, and so on—a connection already present in Kafka's *The Castle*. In his prison-bound deliberations, "Casanova likened a lucid mind to a glass, which does not break of its own accord. Yet how easily it is shattered. One wrong move is all that it takes" (56).[29] Sebald inflects Casanova in order to echo the above-quoted line from "Hunter Gracchus," invoked across the text of *Vertigo*: "It is a fundamentally insane notion . . . that one is able to influence the course of events by a turn of the helm, by will-power alone, whereas in fact all is determined by the most complex interdependencies" (157). Sebald also likens the imprisoned Casanova to K. in *The Trial*, found guilty without being accused of anything, his life thereby transformed into a period of awaiting final judgment. "When the tribunal seized a criminal, it was already convinced of his guilt" (56). In Sebald's version, Venice itself is invested with this tribunal's uncanny power, brought to bear on his avatar in the book's reimagined 1980 journey.

Vertigo's second section owes as much of a debt to Borges as to Casanova, however. Time and again in his subsequent peregrinations the narrator encounters strange figures and places that suggest his own fall is imminent, just around the next turn. He feels he is being followed by a pair of shadowy functionaries who may or may not be murderers, may or may not even be following him: "so ominous [do] these probably quite coincidental encounters" appear to him as he conflates the aleatory and the foreboding (1999, 72). These Borgesian encounters may be proleptic of a murder, but someone else's. Of course a *plot*, once discerned, gives one's life a shape, a narrative meaning, it previously lacked. As the narrator explains to Luciana, the proprietress of the hotel in Limone, the text he is writing "might turn into a crime story, set in upper Italy, in Venice, Verona and Riva. The plot revolves around a series of unsolved murders and the reappearance of a person who had long been missing" (95). As will be seen, a mysterious death *is* foreshadowed here: one that takes place in the narrator's past, revisited in the book's final section. Who is the hunter and who the hunted, who the type and who the shadow, is no longer clear when logical causality has already been problematized on the formal level, and in terms of its relation to a historical model on the one hand and a realist tradition on the other. Nor, it seems, is this the point. *Vertigo* is a "crime story" in the same sense that Kafka's *The Trial* is a story about legal shenanigans, or "The Metamorphosis" about a traveling insurance salesman. Besides, it is easy to forget that the Hunter Gracchus was already dead when his story opens. In Sebald's story, the Hunter dies "for real" at the end, while the narrator succumbs early in part 2 to the death-in-life of Kafka's Hunter Gracchus. The at times almost parodically cloak-and-dagger atmospherics in this section manifest the narrator's hyperbolically paranoid epistemology, now recognizable as the "typical" Sebaldian anxiety around the elision of the ontological and the textual in his rigorous interrogation of the representation of subjectivity within the long prose form.

By part 3 of *Vertigo* it becomes clear that the narrator's movements, far from the result of mysterious forces or even momentary whims, are as it were predetermined by Kafka's movements through northern Italy recorded in letters and diary entries between 1913 and 1917 (just as they had been foreshadowed in parts 1 and 2 by Stendhal's and Casanova's travels in the eighteenth century). The "law" of the narrator's trajectory in part 2 is Kafka's itinerary in northern Italy, just as the novel's overall logic is the illogic or nonlogic of the Hunter Gracchus (Sebald 1999, 85). The nomadic, perpetually "Wandering Jew of the Ocean" has become a type, a subject position that need not be coded as Jewish, as Wagner, Coleridge, and Kafka himself have shown. This is not least because in Kafka's text and elsewhere such a subject has been spliced with the Dantean Christian pilgrim, in the combination of a radically horizontal with an overridingly vertical itinerary, the spatial-temporal coaxial model translated into moral-redemptive narrative terms. But the resulting subject is one that in Sebald, as in Kafka, is always already in exile from the very possibility of return or release—"homeless" (*Heimatlos*) in the most radical sense.

Already in part 2, Kafka, Kafka's Hunter, and Dante and Dante-pilgrim are properly conflated in the narrator's descent into the Desenzano train station *pissoir*. The narrator finds himself wondering "whether Dr. K., travelling from Verona, had also been at this station and found himself contemplating his face in this mirror. It would not have been surprising. And one of the graffiti beside the mirror seemed indeed to suggest as much. *Il cacciatore*, it read, in awkwardly formed letters . . . I added the words *nella selva nera*": "the hunter" in not a dark wood but a "black forest" (*Schwarzwald*) (Sebald 1999, 86–87). Dante's opening setting in the *Inferno* thus merges with the Hunter Gracchus's Bavarian homeland, in a restroom graffito that Kafka, like the narrator, may have read while seeking relief.

In appropriating, transposing, and redistributing fragments of Kafka's "Gracchus" fragment across his own text, Sebald gives us the beginning, the backstory, last. In part 2 he had already structured the narrator's recollection of his own experiences according to the template of Kafka's movements at the time, which the narrator reads as themselves proleptic of the "Gracchus" narrative. In part 3 Sebald imagines the emergence of the story in Kafka's own imagination over the years that follow as he recalls his time in Riva. Sebald reproduces verbatim and at intervals the principal details of the story's opening,[30] ultimately reducing the "meaning of Gracchus the huntsman's ceaseless journey [to] a penitence for a longing for love" (Sebald 1999, 165): "the terrors of love, which for Dr. K stood foremost among all the terrors of the earth" (167). Here Sebald ends by advancing a theory of the generation of this story out of Kafka's own repressed homosexual urges—a somewhat reductive gesture that threatens to obscure Sebald's subtle reimagining of Kafka's falling victim to the vertigo of desire: "How are we to fend off the fate of being unable to depart this life . . . as Gracchus the huntsman does, touching, in a moment of distraction, the knee of the man who was to have been our salvation" (Sebald 1999, 167).

In part 4 of *Vertigo* ("*Il ritorno in patria*"), in which the narrator returns to the southern German village of Wertach im Allgäu (Sebald's hometown), Kafka's Hunter appears in the third person as Hans Schlag: the (Bav)Aryanized Hunter whom the narrator remembers witnessing having sex with Romana the barmaid (238–39), and who subsequently dies under mysterious circumstances, in a fall into a snow-laden gorge (245–49).[31] The description of the dead hunter is only the last of several in the book that reiterate, with slight variations, Kafka's description of the dead Hunter Gracchus (see Sebald 2005, 227). There are salient variations of detail: after he is covered with a blanket the hunter's pocket watch "played a bar or so of the popular song 'Üb immer Treu und Redlichkeit' [Always be faithful and happy]"; on the upper left arm of Sebald's dead hunter is discovered the tattoo of a sailing ship (Sebald 1999, 249). Most significant, perhaps, is the fact that, not counting the "little death" of his tryst with Romana, Sebald's hunter dies once and stays dead. It is as if his death stood in an obliquely redemptive relation to someone *else's* life, an *other* who, ironically, already suffered and suffers Kafka's hunter's fate of a living death without hope of redemption, solution, or closure. This other, it seems, is the narrator, who, in the tradition dating back to Dante and Augustine, splits himself into a narrating and narrated—experiencing—self for the purposes of narrative exigency, only in *Vertigo* the shape of the narrative never replicates Dante's retrospectively ineluctable reconciliation of the subject of memory with the remembering subject.

Sebald's other addition to Kafka's narrative, transposed from a wholly other context, is the presence of the village girl Romana, the narrator's first and unrequited love (Sebald 1999, 234–35), who, in choosing to couple with Hans Schlag, seems to have become the unwitting engine of destruction in the village (see 239). In Romana we see Sebald's utterly un-Wagnerian reinclusion of the erotic-salvific dimension to Kafka's ironic messianic model[32]—an element of generally disastrous significance in Kafka's own life, as exemplified in the Riva episode, in which the nameless Swiss girl plays the role of an anti-Senta, sailing away on a ship forever, leaving nothing but the unwritten memory of their brief love.

The element of Kafka's story in *Vertigo* that links this discussion to Sebald's use of Nabokov in *The Emigrants* is the singular appearance of a butterfly. On the train from London to Italy at the end of part 4—following the enigmatic appearance of the "Winter Queen," the last in a series of beautiful young women readers on trains whom the narrator observes but never addresses (see 104–7), and before the narrator's final dream of traversing an Alpine trail, bordered by "a drop into truly vertiginous depths" (262) (a void then filled with the echo of a passage from Samuel Pepys's apocalyptic account of the Great Fire of London in 1666, prompted by his reading of Pepys's *Diary*)—the narrator recounts his "butterfly memory": "I could hardly believe my eyes, as the train was waiting at a signal, to see a yellow brimstone butterfly [*Zitronenfalter*] flitting about from one purple flower to another, first at the top, then at the bottom, now on the left, constantly moving" (260).[33] The level of factual detail alone puts Sebald in the same camp as Nabokov. Here, though, the immediate intertext is Kafka:

> "I, who asked for nothing better than to live among my mountains, travel after my death through all the lands of the earth."
>
> "And you have no part in the other world?" asked the Burgomaster, knitting his brow.
>
> "I am forever," replied the Hunter, "on the great stair that leads up to it. On that infinitely wide and spacious stair I clamber about, sometimes up, sometimes down, sometimes on the right, sometimes on the left, always in motion. The Hunter has been turned into a butterfly. Do not laugh." (Kafka 1971, 228)

The Hunter's remark invokes entomological metamorphosis as an archetypal metaphor for literal death-in-life: the temporary "death" of the caterpillar in its cocoon, followed by "rebirth" as a butterfly. Clichéd symbol of a fully realized state of being, of the successful transcendence or "translation" from one state into another, in Kafka's story the butterfly still signifies an intermediate, terrestrial state of pointless perpetual motion (105). As hunter-turned-seafarer, Gracchus cannot fulfill the paronomasic potential of his name; there is no possibility of going "as the crow flies."[34] Only in his dreams can the Hunter break out of the terrestrial circuit, making a "supreme flight" (*der größte Aufschwung*) from which he awakens right where he started; his perpetual motion is at the same time a strange immobility (105, 229). At the story's end the Hunter says of his boat that it is "driven by the wind that blows in the undermost regions of death" (230).[35] Either way, whether up or down, the "other world" is utterly beyond his reach, an impossible destination. In Wagner's treatment the eternally wandering sailor's desired *Heimat* had ceased to be an earthly homeland, becoming the state of death in its oblivious finality ("*Ewige Vernichtung*"[36]). In Kafka's radical alteration to this intertext, even this negative consolation is denied the doomed Hunter.

Conclusion: The Modern Subject of Catastrophe

If Sebald's remediation of Conrad in *The Rings of Saturn* results in some of his most overtly "political" pages, his intertextualization of Kafka in both *Vertigo* and the later text complicates the representation of subjectivity by throwing fresh light on Kafka's engagement with the formal parameters of verbal representation. This is a modernist aesthetic project with a deeply epistemological thrust, challenging received notions of what constitutes the "human." Ironically, the last proper noun, if not the very last word, in the last sentence of Kafka's story "The Metamorphosis" is *Körper*, "body." The vivacious body in question is that of Gregor Samsa's sister, Grete, a girl on the verge of womanhood (1935, 130). The difference between the two bodies, Gregor's and his sister's, apart from the number of legs, is that hers is full of promise, of hope for the future—her parents' "new dreams"—whereas his new body from the beginning represents not just the absence of a recognizable "humanness," if not humanity, but the absence of any comparable hope for the future—for recovery, or redemption. Gregor's insect body is the sign of hopelessness in general and specifically for the possibility of not merely recovery or retransformation but also, and perhaps more important, reconciliation or atonement (*Versöhnung*): the meaning of the Jewish *Yom Kippur*, Day of Atonement, reconciliation between father and lost son. At one point Mrs. Samsa refers to the possibility of Gregor's returning to them, invoking the archetype of the Prodigal Son (*wenn er wieder zu uns zurückkommt* [102]). There is every indication that Gregor was anything but a prodigal son, and thus the associations are deeply ironic. In German the emphasis is on straying or being in error, being figuratively lost, but only for a finite period, followed by a literal or figurative return, usually seen as a restorative, conservative action, in accordance with the prevailing socio-politico-economico-cultural and finally theological order, the paternal law.[37]

As Stanley Corngold (2008, 57) points out in his discussion of metaphor and "The Metamorphosis," "The exact sense of [Kafka's] intention is captured in *Ungeziefer*, a word that cannot be fully expressed by the English words 'bug' or 'vermin.' *Ungeziefer* derives (as Kafka probably knew) from the late Middle High German word originally meaning 'the unclean animal not suited for sacrifice.'" Following this line, at the end of *The Trial* Josef K. could be read (ironically, agrammatically) as *Geziefer*, as ritually "clean" and eminently suitable for sacrifice—except his death lacks any traditional sacrificial significance. Between "The Metamorphosis" and *The Trial* there is an as it were regressive shift from a displaced, "nonhuman" victim (Gregor) and thus the operation of an inverse, catachrestic metaphor—to temper Deleuze and Guattari's hyperbole[38]—to a rehumanized victim who is a scapegoat, but in a special sense, because he is *undisplaced*. There is no substitution, as in the Abraham story (or even, in a different sense, as in "The Metamorphosis"), and there seems to be no possibility of such a substitution—by a woman, for instance—because the very ground for redemption is utterly lacking.

At the beginning of *The Rings of Saturn*, as discussed in chapter 2, Sebald explicitly references "The Metamorphosis"—for all its fantastic imagery a radically *written* text, with a very judicious and exacting use of figurative language, typical of Kafka's modernist adaptation of a kind of anti-Pauline aesthetic dispensation suspicious of visual representation. In "The Metamorphosis" Kafka raises his own stakes; the reader is faced with at least two tasks, inextricably connected: on the one hand, she/he must account for this story as an eminent example of Kafka's capacity for literary realism, implying a psychological veracity, the "truth" of subjective interiority. On the other hand, at the same time, in the same space, the insect's relative unrepresentability must somehow be borne in mind: that it can be portrayed only in this manner, discursively, in the text of this story—and thus even translation, a further metamorphosis of the text, becomes problematic.

The original English translation of the scene in "The Metamorphosis" (appropriated by Sebald) of Gregor the insect looking out his bedroom window is as follows:

> [He] nerved himself to the great effort of pushing an armchair to the window, then crawled up over the window sill and, braced against the chair, leaned against the windowpanes, obviously in some recollection of the sense of freedom that looking out of a window always used to give him. For in reality day by day things that were even a little way off were growing dimmer to his sight; the hospital across the street, which he used to execrate for being all too often before his eyes, was now quite beyond his range of vision, and if he had not known that he lived in Charlotte Street, a quiet street but still a city street, he might have believed that his window gave on a desert waste where gray sky and gray land blended indistinguishably into each other. (Kafka 1971, 112–13)

In Sebald's refocalization, the subject is represented as itself a product of modern catastrophic history, in conformity with Blumenberg's master trope of shipwreck with spectator. The passage in *The Rings of Saturn* continues, "I could not believe that anything might still be alive in that maze of buildings down there; rather, it was as if I were looking down from a cliff upon a sea of stone or a field of rubble, from which the tenebrous masses of multitudinous carparks rose up like immense boulders" (Sebald 1998, 5). It is not as much the scene itself as the viewer that has transformed. For Sebald, far more explicitly than in Kafka, the catastrophe of catastrophes is modern civilization as it has evolved under capitalism, whose narrative he calls the natural history of disaster, and there is therefore the greatest urgency, or better *responsibility*, to represent this self in its response to the ongoing crisis, in relation to an other whose resistance to representation is central to Sebald's aesthetic project.[39]

Chapter 4

Metafictional Redemption

The Emigrants and Nabokov's "Butterfly Man"

That in some cases the butterfly symbolizes something (*e.g.*, Psyche) lies utterly outside my area of interest.

—Vladimir Nabokov, *Strong Opinions*

Memory implies a certain act of redemption. What is remembered has been saved from nothingness. What is forgotten has been abandoned.

—John Berger, *About Looking*

Introduction: *The Emigrants* and Nabokov's "Art of Memory"

Beginning from an analysis of Sebald's manipulation in *The Emigrants* of a recurring motif from Vladimir Nabokov's autobiography *Speak, Memory* (1967), this chapter considers how Sebald makes use of the narrative of Nabokov's postemigration life in America and Switzerland—and one key scene from his idyllic European childhood—to lay bare the complex ironies of Sebald's richly intertextual relation to the Russian-American author. It will be seen that memory, in conjunction with representation, becomes in *The Emigrants* a source of redemptive hope for the individual in the face of what appear retrospectively as the inexorable forces of historical "fate."[1]

"I have hunted butterflies in various climes and disguises: as a pretty boy in knickerbockers and sailor cap; as a lanky cosmopolitan expatriate in flannel bags and beret; as a fat hatless old man in shorts" (1989, 125): thus Nabokov describes himself in *Speak, Memory*'s sixth chapter. Nabokov the butterfly hunter, pursuing his prey from the Russia of his beloved childhood across Europe as a young husband and father to his temporary home in America as an expatriate—yet never prey himself to the pitfalls of nostalgic homesickness, equipped as he is with the perpetually restorative powers of memory for which his obsession with butterflies is strangely emblematic (210). Reproduced in *The Emigrants* is the famous picture of Nabokov in full butterfly-hunting gear: the paradigmatic image of one of the twentieth-century's greatest memoirists, Nabokov the hunter of elusive memory. The latter is emblematized in his imaginative world by *Parnassius mnemosyne*, the butterfly species that Nabokov's biographer Brian Boyd calls "a sort of tutelary deity in *Speak, Memory*—which Nabokov would have liked to call *Speak, Mnemosyne*" (1991, 563–64).[3] The butterfly hunter embodies for Sebald the salvific potential of the Nabokovian art of memory, elaborated further in chapter 6, in a bitterly ironic symbolism whose radically negative significance at key points in the narrative underscores the peculiar situation of these characters as not so much subjects *of* as subjected *by* memory.

Nabokov's avatar puts in an appearance at a key moment in each of *The Emigrants*' four parts. In a manner as ironic as it is serious, these intertextual apparitions seem to signal or represent the moment for each of Sebald's protagonists when the burden of memory comes to outweigh its beauty, and the subject of memory must confront the cost of exile in time as well as space. Sebald's use of Nabokov's autobiography reverses the chronology, moving from the elderly butterfly hunter in Switzerland to the little boy on a southern German holiday. After twenty-odd years in America, Nabokov retired in 1961 to Montreux, Switzerland, where he lived with his wife, Vera, in the Palace Hotel until his death in 1977.[4] The specificity of the dates is important because each of the four parts of Sebald's book is in fact stitched to the others along a timeline keyed to the chronology of Nabokov's life. In the first section, "Dr. Henry Selwyn," it turns out that Selwyn has had a youthful sojourn in Switzerland, the story of which justifies the narrator's seemingly incongruous comparison of the slide of the elderly Selwyn in Crete with the photo of Nabokov "in the mountains above Gstaad" (Sebald 1996, 13)[5]—hence the inclusion of the photo of Nabokov mentioned above.

The explicit comparison between Selwyn and Nabokov is ironic: Selwyn is tellingly un-Nabokovian in that his relation to his past, and therefore to the present, is increasingly determined by despair (12). Similarly, in section 2, "Paul Bereyter," there is an explicit reference to the actual book *Speak, Memory*: when Bereyter first meets her in the French Alps in 1971, Lucy Landau is reading "Nabokov's autobiography," which, like Paulo and Francesca's *Galleotto*,[6] brings her together with a stranger, Bereyter himself (43). As with Dante's famous lovers, their story ends unhappily. In an ironic metaphorization of Dante's representation of the "shades" of the damned, Bereyter is already before he dies a soul in hell. Sebald's allusion to Nabokov here is characteristically ironic in that Bereyter's fascination with trains and the railway, and the desirable conjunction of fates, leads him as if inevitably to his suicide on the tracks outside his hometown, whereas Nabokov's comparable preoccupation with the trains and rail journeys of his childhood carries him back into a reconstituted golden past (62).[7] It need hardly be mentioned that Bereyter's obsession with trains and timetables also refers to the infrastructure of the Final Solution (see, e.g., Arthur Williams 1998, 109). This past time, more than simply commensurable with the present, transforms it according to the timelessness of consciousness, whose constitutive faculty is memory in consort with imagination, memory as an image system. "I would say that imagination is a form of memory . . . An image depends on the power of association, and association is supplied and prompted by memory. When we speak of a vivid individual recollection we are paying a compliment not to our capacity of retention but to Mnemosyne's mysterious foresight in having stored up this or that element which creative imagination may want to use when combining it with later recollections and inventions. In this sense, both memory and imagination are a negation of time" (Nabokov 1973, 78).[8]

In part 3 of *The Emigrants*, "Ambros Adelwarth," memory is presented even more explicitly as the potential bearer of both salvation and self-destruction. As the narrator says of his Uncle Ambros, "Telling stories was as much a torment to him as an attempt at self-liberation. He was at once saving himself, in some way, and mercilessly destroying himself" (100). Uncle Ambros, too, is the opposite of the Nabokovian subject in this respect: "The more Adelwarth told his stories, the more desolate he became" (102–3). When "the butterfly man" first makes his appearance in part 3 he is "middle-aged": this takes place in 1952 (103), when Nabokov was, in actuality, the same age as the century— give or take a couple of weeks (104). In the years 1952 to 1953 Nabokov was in Ithaca, teaching at Cornell and writing *Lolita* (Boyd 1991, 210). In other words, where Nabokov is suggested to the narrator in chapter 1 by the slide of Henry Selwyn in Crete (which is not reproduced in the text), entering into the story as it were at two removes, and where in chapter 2 Nabokov enters into the story in the form of his unnamed autobiography, here in part 3 the historical Nabokov enters literally into the book's fictional world as a participant, also unnamed, in the narrator's Aunt Fini's account of Uncle Ambros's last years in the Samaria Sanatorium in upstate New York. The final image of Uncle Ambros is of a man transfigured by a "longing for an extinction as total and irreversible as possible of his capacity to think and remember" (Sebald 1996, 114). From this desire for a radical negation of memory as the negation of consciousness, of self—the desire for the extinction of all desire that owes as much to Beckett as to a certain philosophical tradition—nothing could be further than "the butterfly man" for whom Ambros is passively waiting on the day before the electroshock treatment that finally kills him (113–15).

Finally, in the book's fourth part, "Max Ferber," like Selwyn and Bereyter before him, the artist Ferber ("Aurach" in the German) recounts to the narrator a trip to Switzerland that was itself a repetition of an earlier trip to Geneva and environs thirty years earlier, with his father, who took him climbing in the alps above the lake (174). Like Jacques Austerlitz in Sebald's last work of fiction, Ferber "retraces" this "long-buried" memory when he makes the same journey in the mid-1960s to view Matthias Grünewald's *Isenheim Altarpiece*.[9] (As in 1936 with his father, the adult Ferber stays in the Palace Hotel in Montreux, which is the very hotel in which Nabokov lived out the last years of his life [Boyd 1991, 643–62]). Ferber then recounts how he undertakes the same climb he made with his father thirty years before. The view from the mountaintop is so unchanged from his recollection of it that he is tempted to hurl himself down into the abyss, when suddenly "a man of about sixty . . . appeared before him—like someone who's popped out of the bloody ground. He was carrying a large white gauze butterfly net" and announced "that it was time to be thinking of going down if one were to be in Montreux for dinner" (Sebald 1996, 174). The "butterfly man" reappears here at a crucial moment, as he did for Ambros, and, in a very different manner, for Paul Bereyter and Selwyn. Sebald's evocation of the historical Nabokov is, once again, in accordance with the latter's actual biographical trajectory.

On the level of plot, however, the effect of each appearance differs significantly: Where Nabokov's photo provides for the narrator (and reader) a counterpoint to the quietly despairing Selwyn, and his autobiography plays go-between for Bereyter and Lucy Landau (also a point appreciable by the reader), here in Ferber's reminiscence the butterfly man, whose appearance to Ambros is either a taunt or signal of release, as it were "saves" the adult Ferber from memory's inexorably vertiginous pull. Following this incident he experiences a total and prolonged lapse of memory, thereby failing to retain any recollection of the journey down the mountain and back to England. This is soon followed by a crisis in which he tries and fails to capture in paint the apparition of the "Man with a Butterfly Net," falling into a despair in which he is unable to paint anything at all (174). And if despair, as Sebald notes in his 1976 essay on Kafka, is the "source" of messianism, or at least of a desire for salvation, this never benefits Ferber. It is the reader who must make sense of Ferber's narrative in light of its conclusion with the narrator's reconstruction of Ferber's mother's journal. To paraphrase Kafka, there may be hope, but not for Ferber, nor for the subjects of the book's other three narratives. That is to say, this is not the kind or quality of hope Sebald seeks to represent.

In the latter section of part 4 Ferber gives to the narrator his mother's memoirs, handwritten between 1939 and 1941, when it was no longer possible for her and her husband to emigrate from occupied Germany (192). (In a clear anticipation of one of *Austerlitz*'s central plot points, Max, their son, had already been sent to safety in England.) Employing indirect discourse within the overall narrative, Sebald here embeds a first-person fictional autobiography. Ignoring their present "hopeless situation" Luisa Lanzberg instead recounts her childhood and youth, recalling for example a summer excursion in 1910 with her boyfriend, Fritz, outside Bad Kissingen, in southern Germany. During their walk she sees "two very refined Russian gentlemen" and "a boy of about ten who had been chasing butterflies and had lagged so far behind that they had to wait for him" (213–14). One of Luisa's companions claims that the elder and particularly "majestic" of the two gentlemen was "Muromzev. The president of the first Russian parliament." All these details— the two Russian gentlemen, one described as "majestic," the little boy chasing butterflies, Nabokov's age at the time (eleven), and so forth—are taken almost verbatim from *Speak, Memory*'s sixth chapter,[10] which is devoted to an account of Nabokov's lifelong obsession with butterfly hunting. Sebald here synchronizes the date (1910) of Luisa's excursion with the actual timing of Nabokov's own visit to Bad Kissingen.[11] In Nabokov's account (noted and underlined in Sebald's copy of *Speak, Memory*) the elder gentleman (the other is of course Nabokov's father, a famous liberal) warns Nabokov the younger, "Come with us by all means, but do not chase butterflies, child, it spoils the rhythm of the walk" (1989, 130). Sebald, however, in his first-person rendering of Luisa's account, in her own voice, as it were allows the youthful Nabokov to chase the butterflies, thereby affording Luisa a memory of this occasion that would come back to her three summers later (1913, the same time as Kafka's trip to Riva[12]) when her beloved Fritz proposes to her right "in the middle of a carefully worked out reminiscence of [their] first outing to Bodenlaube" (Sebald 1996, 214)—a memory-within-a-memory. Too overcome to reply, Luisa nods, remarking retrospectively, "and, though everything else around me blurred, I saw that long-forgotten Russian boy as clearly as anything, leaping about the meadows with his butterfly net; I saw him as a messenger of joy, returning from that distant summer day to open his specimen box and release the most beautiful red admirals, peacock butterflies, brimstones and tortoiseshells to signal my final liberation" (214). This last act of releasing the carefully gathered specimens, including the yellow brimstone species the narrator recalls in *Vertigo*, with its overtly metaphorical overtones of redemptive liberation,[13] is a moment of complete fabrication in *The Emigrants*, and not merely because it does not feature in the anecdote Sebald appropriates from *Speak, Memory*.[14] Habitual and unrepentant insecticide aside, Nabokov's autobiographical project, as a kind of microcosmic figuration of his entire fictional output, stands as one of the modern period's most successful attempts to represent the redemptive power of memory as an art in the service of life, while consistently avoiding the trap of a sentimentalizing nostalgia for its own sake. Sebald's embedding of this highly visually detailed moment from Nabokov's autobiography within his recounting of Luisa Lanzberg's recollections of an idyllic Bad Kissingen is like a further giving of the gift already granted in *Speak, Memory*, making of Luisa's recollections a narrative even more poignant than Nabokov's—if such a comparison is possible. This filiation of gift giving is only fitting, it seems, given that Luisa's account is written as a gift for her son, Max Ferber, safe in England at the time of writing. The "liberation" signaled by the butterflies is double-edged: in itself the memory is joyous, but from the reader's perspective it is a bitterly ironic liberation, whose significance must remain metaphorical. In a further irony, the naturalism of Luisa's voice in the reconstituted memoir is inseparable from a vivid description of a September day artfully reconstructed in someone else's autobiography. But this is precisely Sebald's strategy: of all the principal characters—or in this case voices—in *The Emigrants* only Luisa Lanzberg exploits memory, in its conjunction with representation, for its redemptive power. In Sebald's reimagining, she looks back to well before the long shadow of the Holocaust fell across Europe, to the day she agreed to marry the man she loved, who died very soon after—all of this described in the very terms of Nabokov's preemigration childhood. Mark McCulloh (2003) identifies "the value of memory" as "the aesthetic compensation for the ineluctable passage of time"—a description as applicable to Nabokov as to Sebald, perhaps. Unlike Nabokov's, though, Luisa's narrative seems to stand not as compensation but as a kind of *consolation*, as if she, facing the singular fate of millions, could know that Max might someday read of the little Russian boy and the temporal redemption he, as the elder expatriate author composing this scene, has already experienced.

The salient difference between Luisa and Nabokov as memoirists, apart from the fact that her memoirs are Sebald's invention, is that Nabokov's vividly recalled childhood reminiscences merge seamlessly with his subsequent and present-day experiences. For example, the last scene in the final paragraph of *Speak, Memory*'s sixth chapter shows the Nabokov of 1910 stepping out of a Russian marsh into a Rocky Mountain setting some forty years later:

> I confess I do not believe in time. I like to fold my magic carpet, after use, in such a way as to superimpose one part of the pattern upon another. Let visitors trip. And the highest enjoyment of timelessness—in a landscape selected at random—is when I stand among rare butterflies and their food plants. This is ecstasy, and behind the ecstasy is something else, which is hard to explain. It is like a momentary vacuum into which rushes all that I love. A sense of oneness with sun and stone. A thrill of gratitude to whom it may concern—to the contrapuntal genius of human fate or to tender ghosts humoring a lucky mortal. (Nabokov 1989, 139)

To this we can compare the final scene in *The Emigrants*, the narrator's deliberately overdetermined reading of the Genewein photo of the three young carpet weavers in the Litzmannstadt ghetto:

> Behind the perpendicular frame of a loom sit three young women, perhaps aged twenty. The irregular geometrical patterns of the carpet they are knotting, and even its colours, remind me of the settee in our living room at home. Who the young women are I do not know. The light falls on them from the window in the background, so I cannot make out their eyes clearly, but I sense that all three of them are looking across at me, since I am standing on the very spot where Genewein the accountant stood with his camera. The young woman in the middle is blonde and has the air of a bride about her. The weaver to her left has inclined her head a little to one side, whilst the woman on the right is looking at me with so steady and relentless a gaze that I cannot meet it for long. I wonder what the three women's

names were—Rosa, Luisa and Lea, or Nona, Decuma and Morta, the
daughters of night, with spindle, scissors and thread. (237)

The carpets and patterns are undoubtedly coincidental—but then the beauty
of intertextuality is its freedom from intention. It is in fact as a coincidence,
and not as represented objects, that these carpets signify here—unless they
are seen both literally and figuratively as *text*, which is true in either instance.
Nabokov deliberately folds his carpet to expose the malleable texture of time
subject to sovereign consciousness, the indefatigable "I" that does not "believe
in time," superimposing one pattern on another in a concrete imaging of
retrospectively perceived coincidence, whose code names are, variously, "contrapuntal genius" or those "tender ghosts."[16] In contrast to Nabokov's highly
visualized verbal imagery, Sebald's ekphrastic description stands in lieu of the
photo it simultaneously interprets. The three women have stopped their weaving to pose for a photo we cannot see[17]—an image Sebald dares us to read allegorically, in the terms of a premodern, pointedly non-Judaic eschatology—a
wholly other economy of "fate" and coincidence—in which the three young
Jewish women become the Parcae, the three Fates of the Roman pantheon.[18]
In a quasi-Nabokovian move, the passage's blatant literariness throws our
attention back onto the text *as* text, while simultaneously its specific historical context makes us reflect on its reference to a now-vanished world. The
irony in Sebald's gesture of ascribing to these particular women the status
of goddesses of human Fate, sitting in judgment, is terrible and inescapable,
glimpsed as they are in a context in which their destiny is stripped of its gen-
erality, and granted the terrible specificity, and fatality, of a destination.

The "Butterfly Man"

The quasi-allegorical "butterfly man" represents in *The Emigrants* the always-
imminent promise, if not the *immanent* reality, of redemption, a metaphor for
an ever-deferred (secular) salvific principle that is nevertheless paradoxically
present in Sebald's seemingly heavy-handed intertextual homage.[19] Kafka's
Hunter Gracchus, in *Vertigo*, functions more obliquely as an intertextual
avatar for the Kafkan subject, forever doomed not to death as such but to a
sort of purgatorial living "death" of endless waiting, an eternity spent ceaselessly traveling over the world's seas after a second accident sent his ship off
course—the first accident being the fall from the cliff that inaugurated the
journey to the land of the dead now gone awry (Kafka 1971, 228). Neither
properly alive nor properly dead, now permanently errant, the Hunter figure
appears in several forms across Sebald's first prose text, providing neither a
thematic nor a formal focus but rather a sort of vertiginously ironic justification for Sebald's quasi-autobiographical narrator's circuitous wanderings (in
parts 2 and 4 especially) through a fictive space that is variously one of history,

memory, and imagination. In both *Vertigo* and *The Emigrants* Sebald, in his more Kafkan mode, resists the Nabokovian resort to an ironically metafictional solution or resolution. Nevertheless, the latter book offers a subtly but significantly different response to the possibility of redemption held out to the victim of traumatic memory—a possibility embodied in what a Nabokovian fictional poetics presents as memory's collapsing of spatiotemporal depth.[20]

Sebald's presentation of the subject *of* memory subjected *by* memory follows a more radical modernism—a true postmodernism—that goes further than either of these predecessors. Like Nabokov's, Sebald's protagonists move through geographies of memory, history, and imagination whose metaphysical laws are those of consciousness itself. Like Kafka's, the Sebaldian hero must continuously confront the truth that this consciousness is inseparable from the endlessly reiterated narrative patterns of Western literature. This intertextuality, or intermediality—"cultural memory" par excellence—is the only place we can hope to find even the promise of a redemptive mechanism.

Ashes and Silk

As noted in chapter 2, *The Rings of Saturn* weaves a network of literary, historical, and cultural associations whose relations become apparent only gradually in the text's oblique approach to narrative. Blumenberg's shipwreck paradigm is fully transformed into an intertextual trope, structuring Sebald's text. What distinguishes *The Rings of Saturn*, though, from other contemporary first-person accounts of living in an increasingly globalized, late capitalist world, even in such an assiduously rural form, is Sebald's other, no less significant, constellation of themes: death, mourning, and the potentially redemptive power of memory, materialized in a series of meditations on funerary practices across time and cultural space. Hence (to cite *The Emigrants*, 193), the heartbreaking but irresistible effort of "remembering, writing and reading"; the paradoxical task of pursuing through a mediating narrative the empirical traces of destruction—from ashes to the black silk of mourning.

In this context, Thomas Browne's *Hydriotaphia, Urne-Buriall* (1658) emerges as the major early modern intertext for *The Rings of Saturn*, Sebald's often baroque style a self-reflexive emulation of Browne's. While this is present in the German original, it becomes even clearer in Michael Hulse's English translation, accomplished in consultation with Sebald: "It is true that, because of the immense weight of the impediments he is carrying, Browne's writing can be held back by the force of gravitation, but when he does succeed in rising higher and higher through the circles of his spiraling prose, borne aloft like a glider on warm currents of air, even today the reader is overcome by a sense of levitation" (19). "Gravitation" versus "levitation": the gravity of Sebald's prose style is literalized as the force whose law Newton discovers in Browne's time, the mid-seventeenth century;[21] the oscillations of Sebald's prose style manifest textually the contradictory creative and destructive impulses inscribed in the melancholic temperament.[22] In the 1514 engraving *Melencolia I*, Albrecht Dürer "illustrates an imaginative and melancholic artist at the 'unhappy moment when Practice and Art have become separated.'"[23] Sebald links the melancholic temperament with a late modern epistemology grounded in Browne's baroque sensibility.[24] Browne, "the son of a silk merchant" (Sebald 1998, 11), is also the text's first link to the silken thread that zigzags through the book, manifesting at points as Browne's "quincuncial" network, whose pattern recurs "in the seemingly infinite diversity of forms," the "universal" lozenge-shaped structure, found ubiquitously in the natural and man-made worlds alike, epitomized in the structures in which humans house their remains in order to guarantee their immortality (Sebald 1998, 19).[25] For example, in the long disquisition in part 3 on the history of the North Sea herring industry, we learn that the herring nets are traditionally made of "coarse Persian silk . . . dyed black" (56). These nets are a highly revealing instance of the book's many metaphors of networks and interconnectivity: at once a literal quincuncial network and yet ambiguous in significance. The overriding meaning of this particular example, however, is perhaps negative: instruments of capital's inexorable expansion via the exploitation of the ocean's herring stocks, these nets also signify, in a kind of literal structural prolepsis, the ultimate ethical condition of mourning on a global scale of interconnectivity in the face of the inevitable decimation of the herrings' numbers, "the endless destruction wrought in the cycle of life" (57). Sebald's environmental sensitivity here meets his relatively old-fashioned humanist ethics.

In this regard also *The Rings of Saturn* most closely resembles *Urne Buriall*, upon which it is, in a sense, modeled, where the latter is also a quasi-Sternian encyclopedic compendium of things relating to death, funerals, mourning practices, and time's inexorable work of destruction.[26] "There is no antidote, against the opium of time," Browne writes (24), a thought that leads Sebald's narrator to a meditation on the theme of "life after death," instantiated in burial rites throughout history. Browne's account turns to the ancient funerary urns "unearthed in a field near Walsingham" containing cremated human remains and buried with a variety of other objects (25). Here Sebald's narrator brings together the adumbration of *Urne Buriall* and, to use Browne's word, the narrative's central symbol:

> For Browne, things of this kind, unspoiled by the passage of time, are symbols of the indestructibility of the human soul assured by scripture, which the physician, firm though he may be in his Christian faith, perhaps secretly doubts. And since the heaviest stone that melancholy can throw at a man is to tell him he is at the end of his nature, Browne scrutinizes that which escaped annihilation for any sign of the mysterious capacity for transmigration he has so often observed in caterpillars

and moths. That purple piece of silk he refers to, then, in the urn of Patroclus—what does it mean? (Sebald 1998, 26)

As Browne (1958, 24) writes, "in the *Homericall* Urne of *Patroclus*, whatever was the solid Tegument, we finde the immediate covering to be a purple peece of silk." The scrap of purple fabric is the silken thread that weaves its way, anamorphically, through Sebald's narrative; or rather the silken skein that *is* the narrative, thrown over the world in order, depending on one's point of view, to capture, shroud, or save it: the symbol, metaphor, metonymy, or sign "of the mysterious capacity for transmigration [Browne] has so often observed in caterpillars and moths" (Sebald 1998, 26). As a manifestation of Browne the nascent scientist's "Christian faith" in life after death, the eschatological guarantee of continued life in a metaphysical afterworld is prefigured in the physical transformation of specific insect species. We are reminded of Nabokov as the "butterfly man"; Sebald had of course already written *The Emigrants*—the "long stint of work" mentioned at the outset of *The Rings of Saturn*, whose completion in the summer of 1992 precipitated the "emptiness" that, as the narrator says, always takes hold of him at such times (Sebald 1998, 3). The "transmigration of souls" is figured in the moth as translation of *form*; in *The Rings of Saturn* this process is metaphorized in the governing image of silk, produced by silkworms before transforming into moths and then synthesized through human technology into, among other things, the accoutrements of mourning. By the book's last section, the weaver has become contiguous with the reader and writer.[27]

The narrative spirals back to one of its primary imagistic threads: silk production in imperial China and the introduction of sericulture to the West in the sixth century (274): "The silkworm's native habitat seems to include all those Asian countries where the white mulberry trees grow in the wild. There it lived in the open, left to its own devices, until man, having discovered its usefulness, was prompted to foster it" (276). Silk in all its permutations provides the network, connecting otherwise radically disparate people, places, and events. Upon reaching the town of Dunwich, which has gradually eroded into the sea, the narrator is reminded of Victorian poet Algernon Swinburne, who connects the section on China with the narrative's late nineteenth-century historical layer:[28] "Dunwich, with its towers and many thousand souls, has dissolved into water, sand, and thin air. If you look out from the cliff-top across the sea towards where the town must once have been, you can sense the immense power of emptiness" (159). Sebald links the inexorable dissolution of the Suffolk coast to the gradual self-annihilation of the writer: "Only when all hope of dying a hero's death was gone, thanks to his underdeveloped body, did he devote himself unreservedly to literature and thus, perhaps, to a no less radical form of self-destruction"—a trait in which Sebald's narrator would seem to share (163). According to Bianca Theisen (2006), Sebald rejects "the aspect of ascension" germane to the symbolic meaning of insect metamorphosis, expressing "his fascination with the way . . . insects [such as moths and butterflies] 'perish'" (572). This in turn links the poet to the narrative's other principal metonymic image, ashes:[29]

> One of the visitors to [Swinburne's residence at] Putney at the turn of the century wrote that the two old gentlemen put him in mind of strange insects in a Leiden jar. Time and again, looking at Swinburne . . . he was reminded of the ashy grey silkworm, *Bombyx mori,* be it because of how he munched his way through his food bit by bit or be it because, out of the snooze he had slipped into after lunch, he abruptly awoke to new life, convulsed with electric energy, and, flapping his hands flitted about his library, like a startled moth (Sebald 1998, 165)

This passage anticipates an episode in the Welsh section in *Austerlitz*, in which Gerald's uncle Alphonso introduces the boys to the world of moths: "Describing their previous existence as larvae, he said that almost all caterpillars ate only one kind of food . . . and they stuffed themselves with that chosen food, said Alphonso, until they became well-nigh senseless, whereas the moths ate nothing more at all for the rest of their lives, and were bent solely on the business of reproduction" (91–92). In a Nabokovian echo, apart from chess the amateur study of moths is one of Austerlitz's few diversions. In later life Austerlitz even collects them, but only after they have already died of natural causes. Another passage Sebald notes in his copy of *Speak, Memory* is exemplary of this aspect of Nabokov's influence upon *Austerlitz* (the underlining is Sebald's):

> That summer I had been collecting assiduously on moonless nights, in a glade of the park, by spreading a bedsheet over the grass and its annoyed glowworms, and casting upon it the light of an <u>acetylene lamp</u> . . . Into that arena of radiance, moths would come drifting out of the solid blackness around me, and it was in that manner, upon that magic sheet, that I took a beautiful *Plusia*. (1989, 133–34 [*Speak, Memory* 1987, 105])

In the remediated passage in *Austerlitz* the action is transposed in space and time from the prerevolutionary Russian countryside to rural postwar Wales, where the adolescent protagonist—in his account to the narrator—is enjoying one of the only idylls of comparative happiness in his post-Prague life:

> On another occasion, said Austerlitz, Great-Uncle Alphonso took us up the hill behind the house on a still, moonless night to spend a few hours looking into the mysterious world of moths . . . Soon after darkness fell we were sitting on a promontory far above Andromeda

Lodge . . . and no sooner had Alphonso placed his incandescent lamp in a shallow hollow surrounded by heather than the moths, not one of which we had seen during our climb, came flying in as if from nowhere, describing thousands of different arcs and spirals and loops . . . while others, wings whirring, crawled over the sheet spread under the lamp. (Sebald 2001, 90)

Each of these passages evinces a sympathetic and observant eye for the insects in question, but where the artist in Nabokov is always negotiating with the scientist, Sebald's authorial concern for these nocturnal creatures is an extension of his more general concern for the natural world, which for him also includes human beings, connected with other living—and nonliving—things through the vast "networks of a complexity that goes far beyond the power of any one individual to imagine" (Sebald 1998, 91). The most significant change introduced by Sebald therefore is to shift Nabokov's thematic emphasis away from the insects and onto the human subjects in the narrative. One can say of Nabokov that, as a practicing entomologist, his frequent and knowledgeable invocation of insects only rarely functions metaphorically (one such exception is explored above). When insects show up in Sebald's books, by contrast, their typical function is to augment the thematic significance of the human characters, but in an obliquely ironic fashion. Moths, for instance, proliferate throughout *Austerlitz*, but their relative significance resists conventional symbolic interpretation.[30]

As I argued at the outset of this chapter, Nabokov can be described as the "tutelary deity" of *The Emigrants*. But in *The Rings of Saturn* and *Austerlitz* the emphasis is somewhat different: not only is the moth or butterfly patently *not* a clichéd allegory for the psyche or "soul," in fact the moths and other insects in these books do not really seem to have any conventional metaphorical function. Swinburne is figured as the "ashy grey silkworm," genus *Bombyx*, metaphorically entombed in a "Leiden jar."[31] As is noted in part 10, "the silkworm moth, *Bombyx mori* . . . is a member of the *Bombycidae* or spinners, a subspecies of the *Lepidoptera* which, together with the *Saturnidae*, includes some of the most beautiful of all moths" (Sebald 1998, 274). In the analogy the silkworm produces silk and the moth eats the resulting fabric; the man consumes prodigious quantities of meat ("munch[ing] his way through his food bit by bit"), and the poet produces his famously decadent poems. Sebald, far more overtly than Nabokov, exploits and subverts the metaphorical potential of entomology, crossing it with an ironic autoerotic-salvific economy, collapsing pupa and transfigured moth into one figure. In the suggested positive Neoplatonic model silk production is to artistic-poetic creation as physical transformation or metamorphosis is to redemption or "rebirth." Sebald goes even further than Nabokov's ironic inversion of this too easy, too affirmative sense, however; his deeper interest throughout *The Rings*

of Saturn is *death and destruction generally: its* productivity out of negation,
its crucial role in determining meaning in human life within what Theisen
(2006, 578) calls the "saturnine principle of opposites . . . an allegory for
Sebald's attempt to reconstitute the scattered 'ruins of history' by drawing out
connections across time." After all, Swinburne is in a sense both subject and
agent of dissolution; the passive-masculine and active-feminine principles of
the received literary model are conflated in one figure in which metaphorical
change stands for physical and not metaphysical transformation: inevitable
and impending death, not transfiguration.[32] According to Theisen (2006, 580),
Swinburne functions here in Sebald's comparison to show his awareness of
"the radically self-destructive trait" perceptible in the writer's poems. This
trait is another example, in the book's intra- and intertextual network of
meanings, of an alternative to the redemptive economy of productive destruction characteristic of capitalism. Theisen (2006, 576) refers to these moments
as instances of "non-exploitative behavior," of which the silk moth is "the
most prominent emblem" in *The Rings of Saturn*.[33] The complexity and ironic
ambiguities of the redemption theme in *The Rings of Saturn*—emblematized
in the moths and silkworms, as argued above—require more space than is
possible in the present study. The obliquity of the allusion to Nabokov here
acquires enhanced meaning, however, in the context of Sebald's invocation of
the "butterfly man" in *The Emigrants* and his continued intertextualization of
aspects of *Speak, Memory* in *Austerlitz*. In this latter book moths, for all their
suggestive metaphorical value, again clearly lack any redemptive meaning in
the narrative. At one point Austerlitz recounts to the narrator how

> in the warmer months . . . one . . . of these nocturnal insects quite
> often strays indoors . . . I find them clinging to the wall, motionless.
> I believe, said Austerlitz, they know they have lost their way, since if
> you do not put them out again carefully they will stay where they are,
> never moving, until the last breath is out of their bodies, and indeed
> they will remain in the place they came to grief even after death . . .
> until a draft of air detaches them and blows them into a dusty corner.
> (Sebald 2001, 93–94)

With this echo of Samsa-turned-insect's fate in Kafka's "Metamorphosis,"[34]
it becomes gradually clear that the dead moth is one instance of a kind of
oblique allegory for Austerlitz's complex and only semiconscious identification with a group of people and a time and place, which for most of his life
had no tangible geographical or historical existence. In this light the dead
moth does not "represent" or allegorize Austerlitz as he is but rather as he
might, or perhaps in a certain sense, should, have been.

As Theisen (2006, 576) argues, the anticapitalist and anticolonialist themes
in *The Rings of Saturn* are linked in Sebald's fascination with the self-destructive
behaviors of eccentric, generally creative individuals: "Such refusals to take

part in any economy of use and abuse are paired by the empathy that [Edward] FitzGerald, [Roger] Casement, or [Joseph] Conrad have for the cause of the enslaved and oppressed." In a strong but persuasive reading, Theisen suggests that "the silkworm [in *The Rings of Saturn*] signifies serfdom and bondage without recompense, a fatal self-entanglement in the service of commercial greed, and is thus a prominent emblem for the enslaved, victimized, perse- cuted, marginalized, and perishing. In short, it is an emblem for the identi- fication with all those forced to live in the shadows, an identification that constitutes one of Sebald's dominant concerns" (572). I return, in the chapters that follow, to the significance of this identification with the disenfranchised and subaltern subjects of history for Sebald in relation to three other authors: Magris, Nabokov, and Canadian Alice Munro.

Chapter 5

"A Vision Intended for My Liberation"

Ironic Eschatology and Masculine Identity in Kafka, Sebald, and Magris

It is only our conception of time that makes us call the Last Judgment by that name; in fact it is a kind of martial law.
—Franz Kafka, *Collected Aphorisms*

Telling stories was as much a torment to him as an attempt at self-liberation. He was at once saving himself, in some way, and mercilessly destroying himself.
—W. G. Sebald, *The Emigrants*

Like Heine, he has been searching for his homecoming, but is distracted by the sirens of memory.
—Ben Hutchinson, "Egg Boxes Stacked in a Crate"

As noted in the introduction, Claudio Magris offers an instance of a contemporary novelist who takes Sebald's arguments on history and eschatology a step further from his liminal position between modernism and postmodernism. Relatively little scholarly attention has been paid so far to the very meaningful relation between Sebald and the Triestine writer.[1] In this chapter I use an analysis of the concluding section of Magris's 2008 novel, *Blindly*,[2] as the basis for a critical comparison with *Vertigo* (1999), in the process exploring each text's intertextual and intermedial relation to a constellation of works by Franz Kafka, Walter Benjamin, Max Ernst, Giuseppe Verdi, and East German playwright Heiner Müller, as well as an array of premodern katabasis narratives—Dante's *Inferno*, Homer's *Odyssey*, book 12, the myths of Orpheus[3] and, of special significance for Magris, of Jason and the Argonauts. In casting an introductory light on Sebald's relation to Magris, his fellow geopolitical, linguistic, and imaginative border crosser, I show how *Vertigo*'s fictional world intersects with that of *Blindly*, in a scene set by Sebald in the northern Italian city of Trieste when it still belonged to the Austro-Hungarian Empire, involving an angelic visitation whose original is in a dreamlike passage in Kafka's *Diaries*. The most striking element in this passage's mise-en-scène, the messenger-angel-cum-ceiling-light-fixture, war-rants close comparison with the ship's figurehead that is the guiding motif in Magris's novel. Each of these figures stands moreover in meaningful relation to Benjamin's angel of catastrophic history, famously inspired by Paul Klee's 1920 painting *Angelus Novus*, his "new angel." As models for Magris's and Sebald's textual constructs, Kafka's and Benjamin's angels convey in their different ways a peculiarly ironic sense of eschatological hope: in Benjamin for potential salvation indefinitely deferred while the catastrophe of histor-ical Progress accumulates; in Kafka for the more immediate "salvation" of writing—both, ironically, forms of "hopeless hope."[4] As seen in chapter 3, Sebald's reimagining of Kafka's time in Italy and what was then the Habsburg Empire presents a highly idiosyncratic figure as an emissary of a comparably ironic and even more contemporary allegory of destruction both general and imminent. For Magris, by contrast, the ship's female figurehead becomes an Ovidian figure of mythic transformation, at once the focus of the novel's pro-tagonist's love and hope for redemption and the nonsubjective agent of his ultimate destruction, which is tantamount, in the novel's post-postmodernist antirealism, not to the final silencing of the narrative's various voices but to a final "vision" of their perpetual drifting in a sea of ironic self-contradiction, of death-within-life and life-as-death.

Kafka in Italy

Much work has already been done on Sebald's complex intertextualization of Franz Kafka's diary of his travels through northern Italy in 1913, as well as regular diary entries and letters of 1914, the year he began writing *The Trial* and "In the Penal Colony" and became engaged to Felice Bauer.[5] In Elias Canetti's (1974, 63) estimation these things are intimately connected: what he calls Kafka's other trial was his engagement, the prospect of marriage proving too horrifying to contemplate.[6] The mutual exclusivity of bourgeois marriage and a life of writing is a complex motif at the center of Kafka's life and writing, contributing to the unavoidable conflation of his autobiograph-ical and his fictional output. This motif resonates across his oeuvre, proving a major aspect of Kafka's influence upon contemporary writers as diverse as Magris and Sebald.

For the present discussion it is instructive to quote at length from Kafka's diary entry of June 25, 1914:

> Towards evening I walked over to the window and sat down on the low sill . . . I happened calmly to glance into the interior of the room and at the ceiling. And finally . . . unless I were mistaken, this room . . . began to stir. The tremor began at the edges of the thinly plastered white ceiling. Little pieces of plaster broke off and with a

distinct thud fell here and there, as if at random to the floor . . . a bluish violet began to mix with the white; it spread straight out from the centre of the ceiling, which itself remained white . . . where the shabby electric lamp was stuck.[7] Wave after wave of the colour—or was it a light?—spread out towards the now darkening edges . . . But the ceiling did not really take on these different hues; the colours merely made it somewhat transparent; things trying to break through seemed to be hovering above it, already one could almost see the outlines of a movement there, an arm thrust out, a silver sword swung to and fro. It was meant for me, there was no doubt of that; *a vision intended for my liberation was being prepared.*[8]

I sprang up on the table to make everything ready, tore out the electric light together with its brass fixture and hurled it to the floor, then jumped down and pushed the table from the middle of the room to the wall. That which was striving to appear could drop down unhindered on the carpet and announce to me whatever it had to announce. I had barely finished when the ceiling did in fact break open. In the dim light, still at a great height, I had judged it badly, an angel in bluish-violet robes girt with gold cords sank slowly down on great white silken-shining wings, the sword in its raised arm thrust out horizontally. "An angel, then!" I thought; "it [*er*] has been flying towards me all the day and in my disbelief I did not know it [*ich in meinem Unglauben wußte es nicht*]. Now it will speak to me." I lowered my eyes. When I raised them again the angel was still there, it is true, hanging rather far off under the ceiling (which had closed again), but it was no living angel, only a painted wooden figurehead off the prow of some ship, one of the kind that hangs from the ceiling of sailors' taverns, nothing more [*eine bemalte Holzfigur von einem Schiffsschnabel, wie sie in Matrosenkneipen an der Decke hängen*].

The hilt of the sword was made in such a way as to hold candles and catch the dripping tallow. I had pulled the electric light down; I didn't want to remain in the dark, there was still one candle left, so I got up on a chair, stuck the candle into the hilt of the sword, lit it, and then sat late into the night under the angel's faint flame.[9]

The ultimate intertext for this passage is the Book of Revelations 18:1, where, in a kind of apocalyptic complement to the Annunciation as harbinger of Christ's initial appearance at the beginning of sacred history, and the promise of grace embodied therein, an angel of the lord appears to the speaker at the end of time: "After this I saw another angel coming down from heaven, having great authority; and the earth was made bright with his splendour."[10] The angel goes on to announce the fall of Babylon, allegorically aligned with the figure of the Whore of Babylon, traditionally interpreted as the feminine embodiment of sin. As a city, Babylon is condemned to redemption through apocalyptic destruction rather than by grace: "So shall her plagues come in a single day, / pestilence and mourning and famine, / and she shall be burned with fire; / for mighty is the Lord God who judges her" (Revelations 18:8).

In aphorism 40 Kafka (1994, 11) writes, "It is only our conception of time that makes us call the Last Judgment by that name; in fact it is a kind of martial law." Two alternative eschatological paradigms are contrasted here: on the one hand, Judgment and Retribution, the old dispensation of Jewish Scripture; on the other, Forgiveness and Redemption, the new dispensation of the Christian New Testament. Kafka's reading of the Last Judgment as "a kind of martial law," in conflict with a notion of time as linear narrative with beginning, middle, and end—as "history"—can be interpreted as Kafka's representation of the dissemination of judgment *across* time, the temporal axis of human life, as "the Law," as something omnipresent, infinite, and, in this sense, absolute. This results in a hybrid figure combining, but not synthesizing, the two paradigms, Jewish and Christian. Walter Benjamin, in a letter to Gershom Scholem (Benjamin and Scholem 1992, 128), addresses the question of how to think this unthinkable introduction of something properly transcendent, outside time, into the human experience of time: "[You raise] the question of how one has to imagine, in Kafka's sense, the Last Judgment's projection into world history. Does this projection turn the judge into the accused? And the proceedings into the punishment? Is it devoted to raising up the Law on high, or to burying it?"[11] "The Last Judgment's projection into world history" is a classic Kafkan move, in its impossible conflation of complementary but incommensurable orders. Benjamin is responding here to a "theological didactic" poem by Scholem that accompanied a copy of Kafka's *The Trial* (123). Benjamin's "Ninth Thesis on the Concept of History" is also written in dialogue with another Scholem poem, "Gruss vom Angelus," like Benjamin's text also a response to the Klee painting *Angelus Novus*, which

> shows an angel looking as though he is about to move away from something he is fixedly contemplating. His eyes are staring, his mouth is open, his wings are spread. This is how one pictures the angel of history. His face is turned toward the past. While we perceive a chain of events, he sees one single catastrophe which keeps piling wreckage upon wreckage and hurls it in front of his feet. The angel would like to stay, awaken the dead, and make whole what has been smashed. But a storm is blowing from Paradise; it has got caught in his wings with such violence that the angel can no longer close them. The storm irresistibly propels him into the future to which his back is turned, while the pile of debris before him grows skyward. This storm is what we call progress. (Benjamin 1969, 257–58)

Far from a culmination of Kafka's dreamlike diary entry of 1914 and Benjamin's iconic "angel of history," Sebald's synthesis in *Vertigo* of these two texts, along with several others, is symptomatic of the proliferation of angelic figures, an angel topos or constellation, in modern and contemporary European literature. This can manifest as messianic angel, promising collective or singular salvation; or as angel of history looking on as transcendent witness; or as angel of death heralding apocalyptic destruction; or as some other angelic avatar of modernity. Rilke's angel in the first *Duino Elegy*, set to guard the Garden after humankind's expulsion, comes to mind—one inspiration for Paul Klee's painting (Hell 2004, 376)—as does Heiner Müller's "luckless angel" in his 1958 work *Germania*, a direct response to Benjamin's angel of history.[12] This inventory must also include the other angels in Kafka, most notably in *Amerika*, originally titled *The Man Who Disappeared* (*Der Verschollene*), and *The Trial*. In the first unfinished novel, for example, Kafka's reconceived Statue of Liberty in New York harbor, with its upraised sword, "seems full of promise" but is entirely ambiguous as a symbol (Hayman 1982, 142). The statue in *Amerika* is like an angel of vengeance or retribution as much as liberty or salvation. It recalls the cherubim posted by the Lord at the gates of paradise in Genesis 22, brandishing flaming swords as a sign that Eden, from the front at least, is irrevocably closed. This type of ambiguously gendered allegorical figure recurs throughout Kafka's work.

In *The Trial*, by contrast, Josef K. is informed by Leni, Lawyer Huld's maid, that the court painter Titorelli's "judge" paintings are all about pseudoallegorical misrepresentation. K. and Titorelli speak in allegories as they discuss this hybrid figure: *Gerechtigkeit* (Justice) as *die Siegesgöttin* (the Goddess of Victory), a personification of the triumph of Justice, far removed from any properly modern notion of Justice, more like a Fury or avenging angel, a transgendered Old Testament "angel of the Lord." In this chapter the tradesman Block quotes for K.'s benefit an "old maxim," which stands as a kind of gloss on Titorelli's portrayal of a martial Justice: "People under suspicion are better moving than at rest, since at rest they may be sitting in the balance without knowing it, being weighed together with their sins (1992b, 191). In other words, it appears to be not a question of whether but *when* Justice, figured as a woman, ever in hot pursuit, will catch up; a question of how long you can postpone if not avoid the Day of Atonement, Yom Kippur. Kafka's "hybrid figure" in *The Trial* of Justice as an angel is cousin to the Angelus Novus of Klee's painting.[13] It is positioned, however, not in an attitude of frozen rearward flight, as in Benjamin's Ninth Thesis, but in a dynamic posture of *pursuit*, at the other end of history—which, from the angel's vantage is the *same* end, merely seen from the opposite direction, hence the attitude of simultaneous waiting and pursuit. (This also goes some way toward justifying the parallel biblical intertexts from Genesis and Revelations: the end meets the beginning in the circular logic of sacred history.) In *The Trial* Titorelli's allegorical painting of Justice as Niké, the Goddess of Victory, is such a hybrid martial image, an allegory of the triumph of Justice (176). Titorelli even draws in a sort of aureole or halo, such as in medieval representations of saints (177).

The figure of Justice mutates into "the goddess of the Hunt in full cry," Diana or Artemis, who is radically distinct, allegorically speaking, from any modern notion of Justice. As noted, she is more like a Fury or avenging angel, whose ambivalent meaning is implicitly echoed in Titorelli's rendering of the attitude of the judges: at once menacing, ready to pounce, and yet maddeningly passive, sitting in judgment as if "the Day of Judgment [were] a summary court in perpetual session."[14]

The recurrent ship's figurehead in *Blindly* is Magris's unique contribution to this filiation of female or ambiguously gendered personifications at the intersection of history viewed as it were horizontally, as a serial catastrophe, over against the transcendent verticality of a vision of a singular apocalyptic or redemptive event.[15] Privileging Benjamin, Julia Hell (2004) views the angel topos in a specific historical context. In her estimation, "after 1945, Benjamin's angel appears in an even more apocalyptic, more pessimistic guise . . . While there is continuity in German culture between the apocalyptic thinking after World War II and the catastrophic visions so prominent after World War I, there is also a significant difference: after World War II, the belief in redemption, or in the redemptive potential of violence and revolution, no longer exists"(363). This difference is further complicated by the question of subjectivity either explicitly or implicitly indexed in the various manifestations of angelic visitation—the question, in other words, of agency, and of represented point of view: that of the human participant in or victim of "History," or that of the angelic, as it were transcendent, witness. Such a clear distinction between radically subjective and radically objective is already impossible after Kafka, however, who in a characteristic move translates a single, ever-imminent apocalypse into a *singular* event of significance only to himself—or rather to his writerly protagonist. In Kafka's dreamlike diary entry, one of the other key intertexts, subjectivity is radically alienated, and the angel's visitation somehow deallegorized into a scene of ironic autosalvation—not through love or violence but what Kafka calls the impossible labor of writing.[16]

Sebald's Angel

Part 2 of Sebald's *Vertigo* is titled "*All'estero*" (away, abroad) and is recounted in the first person; part 3, "Dr. K. Takes the Waters at Riva," is recounted in the third person. In the former Sebald already anticipates intertextually the events he represents in the latter, in a shift in voice and perspective clearly derived from Kafka's later novels. In a scene in part 2 the narrator meets an old friend in present-day Verona, outside the open-air opera house during a production of Verdi's *Aida* (his name, Salvatore—the one who saves, also invoked in *Blindly* as one of the narrator's names or personae [Magris 2008a, 21]—is an allusion to Kafka's "Hunter Gracchus" story, another major intertext): "The opera, said Salvatore, is not what it used to be. The audience no longer understands that they are a part of the occasion" (Sebald 1999, 132).[17] "Verdi's earlier operas . . . stimulated his audiences to frenzies of participation, so immediate was their impact, the clarity of their contemporary reference, and the sheer skill of his efficiency at whipping everyone into urgent, big theatrical climaxes" (Said 1994, 113–14). Edward Said also notes, however, that despite the fact that *Aida*'s so-called "Triumphal scene" is "the biggest thing Verdi wrote for the stage," as a later work with a potentially alienating orientalist setting, the opera is "self-limiting . . . and there is no record of any participatory enthusiasm connected with it" (114). Nevertheless, Salvatore's account of the history of the Verona arena, where he dwells on the inauguration of the opera festival in 1913, connecting as well the narrator's present (1987) with the premiere of Verdi's *Aida* in Cairo on December 24, 1871 (Said 1994, 133), seems to draw upon the reputed reception of the earlier Verdi operas. Salvatore ends with an imagined scene of operatic apocalypse, in which *Aida*'s first audience literally becomes part of the spectacle:

> And now, fire breaks out in the opera house. A crackling conflagration. With a crash the seats in the stalls, together with all their occupants, vanish into the orchestra pit. Through the swathes of smoke beneath the ceiling an unfamiliar figure comes floating down. *Di morte l'angelo a noi s'appressa. Gia' veggo il ciel discindersi* [The angel of death is approaching us. I already see the heavens coming down]. But I digress. With these words, Salvatore stood up. You know how I am, he said as he took his leave, when it is getting late. I for my part, however, remained on the piazza for a long time with that image of the descending angel before my eyes. (Sebald 1999, 133–34)

Here we see the angel completing its ironic transformation from witness of to participant in the apocalyptic spectacle. The quoted lines in this passage intertextualize Verdi's *Aida*: a tragic love story set against the spectacular backdrop of the warring Egyptian and Ethiopian dynasties in the time of the Pharaohs. Aida, an Ethiopian princess, is being held captive by the Pharaoh. Her father's attempt to free her precipitates the conflict and underscores the theme of delivery from slavery. She is in love with Radames, the captain of the Imperial Guard and a great warrior, who returns her love but is also beloved of the Pharaoh's daughter, Amneris, whose affection he does not reciprocate. There are two key scenes, both in the final act, that inform Sebald's appropriation of Kafka's angelic vision:[18] Act 4, scene 1 of the opera is set in "the Temple of Justice." Radames, caught between his loyalty to the Pharaoh and his love for the enslaved Aida, has been unjustly condemned to death by a tribunal of priests; the sentence is that he shall be buried alive. Set in the hallway outside Radames's prison cell, the "Judgment scene" features the high priest Ramfis and the chorus, who together sing, "Heavenly spirit descend upon us! / Strengthen us in the beams of the light eternal; / through our lips make known thy justice" (*Spirito del Nume, sovra noi discendi! / Ne avviva al raggio dell'eterna luce; / Pel labbro nostro tua giustizia apprendi*).

In act 4, scene 2, Aida, out of love for Radames, hides in the underground tomb in which he is to be buried alive so that she can accompany him in death. In a delirium (*vaneggiando*), she sings, "Do you see? . . . / Death's radiant angel / Hastens toward us, / And carries us to eternal joy / Upon his golden wings. / Already I see heaven opening, / There all torment ceases, / There begins the ecstasy / Of an immortal love" (*Vedi? . . . di morte l'angelo / Radiante a noi s'appressa, / Ne adduce eterni gaudii / Sovra i suoi vanni d'or. / Già veggo il ciel dischiudersi, / Ivi ogni affanno cessa, / Ivi comincia l'estasi / D'un immortale amor*).

Vertigo's ironic remediation of Verdi's famous opera links the book with a thematic web stretching across all four of Sebald's prose works, taking a different form in each.[19] In *Vertigo* this master theme functions to complicate even as it reinforces Sebald's adaptation of a Kafkan typology: a model of incommensurable eschatological paradigms—one promising imminent redemption marking the end of history, the other an open-ended messianicity, what Derrida (1996, 72), after Benjamin, calls "messianicity without messianism": the promise of meaning or "truth" indefinitely deferred. In this light, Brad Prager (2006, 115–16) reads the "messianic overtones" of Kafka's Hunter Gracchus in Sebald:

> Taking a different direction from that of Benjamin, Adorno links Gracchus to the historical category of the bourgeoisie, which refuses to die despite its utter uselessness. He links this understanding of Gracchus to the horrors of Auschwitz . . . "History becomes Hell in Kafka because the opportunity for salvation was missed. The late bourgeoisie itself brought this about. In the concentration camps, the boundary between life and death was eradicated. A middle ground was created, inhabited by living skeletons and putrefying bodies, victims unable to take their own lives."

Politics and eschatology intersect in the Adorno text: "Satan's laughter at the hope of abolishing death. As in Kafka's twisted epics, what perished [in the camp] was that which had provided the criterion of experience—life lived out to its end. Gracchus is the consummate refutation of the possibility banished from the world: to die after a long and full life" (Adorno 1981b, 260). We can connect this to the motif of the angel, delivering either death or a vision intended for a singular liberation, where bourgeois domesticity equals either the one or the other, depending on one's point of view and on the attendant valuation of long since revalued terms such as "redemption," "freedom," "the transcendence of death."

These Kafkan and Benjaminian (and Adornian) threads are interwoven in *Vertigo*'s four-part narrative, whose formal closure offers no resolution and whose logical and chronological position in relation to "History" is at best ironic. More broadly, as exemplified in *Austerlitz* and *The Rings of Saturn*,[20] this irony issues in Sebald's idiosyncratic appropriation of the Old Testament topoi of the "Promised Land" and "Chosen People." As Hitler once ominously put it, there can be only one chosen people (Sebald 2005, 164). Following Kafka, for whom any general Law always also signifies as individual prohibition, Sebald in much of his fiction is more interested in negotiating the liminal space between these extremes rather than adopting one position or another, as he does so starkly in the "Air War" lectures, where he speaks as literary critic.

Salvatore's "quotation" from *Aida* in the passage from *Vertigo* appropriates elements from both the scenes described above, in particular the verb *discendere* and the phrase *di morte l'angelo*: the vivid "image of the descending angel" that remains before the narrator's eyes after Salvatore's departure, an image, to paraphrase Kafka, of a highly ambiguous liberation, only here, in Verdi's operatic source text, the vision is *not* one of a personal liberation, prepared especially for the singular viewing subject within the scene. By the same token, Salvatore's redaction inverts the sense of the original by cutting certain phrases while adding specific qualifiers: the lines "Death's radiant angel / hastens toward us, / and carries us to eternal joy / upon his golden wings. / Already I see heaven opening, / there all torment ceases, / there begins the ecstasy / of an immortal love" become "The angel of death is approaching us. I already see the heavens coming down." In this recontextualized passage Sebald stages the violent collision of the lateral, open-ended narrative and eschatological paradigm of exile from the Promised Land, of exclusion and wandering as a state of being—a recurrent motif in *The Emigrants*, *The Rings of Saturn*, and especially *Austerlitz*—with the radical, vertical, irruptive intrusion of the angel of death, crashing down from on high, announcing some kind of apocalyptic closure.

Here is the relevant passage from *Vertigo*, part 3, "Dr. K. Takes the Waters at Riva" wherein Kafka's 1914 diary entry is transposed in both time and space:

> On the 14 of September [1913] Dr. K. travels to Trieste . . . In the hotel he reclines on the bed, hands clasped behind his head, and looks up at the ceiling . . . Dr. K. is aware that in this city there is an iron angel [*einen erzenen Engel*] who kills travelers from the north, and he longs to go out . . . The circling reflections of the streetlights on the ceiling above him are signs that any moment now it will break open and something will be revealed. Already cracks are appearing in the smooth surface, and then, in a cloud of plaster dust, gradually showing itself against the half-light, a figure descends on great silk-white wings, swathed in bluish-violet vestments and bound with golden cords, the upraised arm with the sword pointing forwards. A veritable angel, thought Dr. K. when he could breathe again, all day long

it has flown towards me and I of little faith knew nothing of it [*ich in meinem Unglauben weiß es nicht*]. Now he [*er*] will speak to me, he thought, and lowered his gaze. But when he looked up again, the angel, though it was still there, suspended quite low under the ceiling, was no longer a living angel but a garishly painted ship's figurehead, such as hang from the ceilings of sailors' taverns [*eine bemalte Holz-figur von einem Schiffschnabel, wie sie in Matrosenkneipen an der Decke hängen*]. The sword guard was fashioned to hold candles and catch the dripping tallow. (145–46)[21]

The enigma of Sebald's interpolation, "an iron angel who kills travelers from the north," may be because of a mistranslation. The German *einen erzenen Engel*, "bronze angel," is somewhat misleadingly translated as "iron angel," which would be *eisernen Engel*. However, on one level Sebald seems to have appropriated Kafka's highly ambiguous image for a historically specific purpose: the angel becomes the active masculine harbinger of destruction, a literal angel of death, a veritable threat to those "travelers from the north" who may include the soldiers of the German army, as a nationalistic, irredentist Trieste girded itself for self-defense in the war that would begin the following year (1914). There does indeed stand overlooking the harbor in Trieste a bronze angel, a statue of a winged Victory atop a lighthouse—the *Faro della Vittoria*—first conceived in 1918 as a symbol of Trieste's return to Italy following World War I but not raised until 1927. One crucial element is missing from the appropriated scene, however, which here ends with the "garishly painted ship's figurehead": Sebald eliminates the ironic "salvation" of writing with which Kafka's entry concludes—that is, the angel's reduction to ceiling fixture, providing light, however weak, by which to work. In denying Dr. K. this solace, however mundane or illusory, Sebald emphasizes the objective significance of the angelic visitor, its portentous value as harbinger of a general catastrophe whose specific historical locus is World War I but which manifests at the end of the book in the narrator's apocalyptic dream vision of the Great Fire of London in 1666.

In his reimagining of this episode from Kafka's *Diaries*, Sebald presents "Dr. K." "in a condition in keeping with his nature and ordained for him by a justice not of this world, a condition that he could not transcend and which he would have to endure till the very last of his days" (Sebald 1999, 148). There is an echo here of Max Brod's biography of Kafka, where the writer is alleged to have denied any conventional nihilism on his part, asserting that there is "plenty of hope, an infinite amount of hope—but not for us."[22] The two strands in Kafka are inseparable: the self-denying writing and the possibility or impossibility of redemption; in the novels, at least, the ironic denial of any positive transcendence manifests itself in a narrative structure of paradoxically finite interminability, in quasi-unrepresentable, fictional forms and in the apotropaic avoidance of metaphorical figures. Out of these formal strategies emerges not a new ground for hope as such but an alternative to the empty promise of redemption embodied in metaphor, for example, whose meaning stems from a verticality predicated on the collapsing of difference into identity and simultaneity. This alternative emerges in the nonmetaphysical space that opens up in the text on the horizontal level of differentially produced meaning. It is along this axis that Kafka negotiates a new relation to fiction's value. The alternative, it seems, is to read Kafka as not just thematically but also formally nihilistic—an interpretive dead end, and one I therefore reject.

In part 2 of *Vertigo* the narrator comes upon his friend, Salvatore, reading the Leonardo Sciascia novel *1912 + 1* (Sebald 1999, 127). The year 1913 signifies throughout *Vertigo* in a variety of contexts: "1913 was a peculiar year," the narrator remarks. "The times were changing, and the spark was racing along the fuse like an adder through the grass" (121); "It is curious to observe . . . how in that year [1913] everything was moving towards a single point, at which something would have to happen, whatever the cost" (129). In this context Sebald's appropriated angel reveals itself as an allegory open to multiple simultaneous readings, from the intensely singular and personal to the generally catastrophic. On one level the masculine *angelo di morte* is equivalent to what 1913 represents as harbinger of World War I (e.g., 128–34). The ambiguously gendered ship's figurehead, on the other hand, can be read as an avatar of either "Woman" in general or a *specific* woman— particularly the nameless Swiss girl Dr. K. meets at Riva, who is both ironic saving angel and "mermaid" (*die Seejungfer*; 158–61)[23]—as well as a handful of other women, not including Felice Bauer, his fiancée. Finally, in Sebald's intertextualization of Kafka's 1914 diary entry, the angel may also herald his sexual liberation by a man—something Kafka actually does hint at in his diaries and letters, but only negatively, as yet another impossibility (see Sebald 1999, 167).

Magris's (Voiceless) Women

The image of the ship's figurehead with which Sebald's remediation of Kafka's diary entry concludes connects these intertexts to Magris's novel, albeit in a more clearly gendered form. In contrast to the Sebald and Kafka texts, the sexual politics—and aesthetic—of *Blindly* are markedly (if complexly) heteronormative, and the figurehead motif so crucial to the novel's symbolic economy is explicitly the focus of the book's thematized critique of Western culture's hallowed fetishization of woman as savior of undeserving man. "In general," explains Magris (2009, 27) in "The Self That Writes,"

> in my recent books, there is this strong sense of a woman passionately loved but also shamefully used by a man to protect himself, interposed like a shield between the man and the storms of life, so

that it is she who is first to bear their brunt, and it is her breast, like a buckler, that the poisoned arrows will penetrate, thereby protecting the man. She resembles the figurehead set in the prow of the ship, the first to receive, as in *Blindly*, the tempestuous blows of history and life. It is the subject in *The Exhibition*, in *Blindly*, in *To have been*, based, in some way, on the archetype of Jason and Medea, used and abused by Jason, victim even when she commits the terrible crime of killing her own children.

Blindly also offers an amplification of Kafka's revaluation of the Last Judgment as the dissemination of judgment *across* time (the temporal axis of human life), its projection into world history as "the Law." In Magris, death becomes the eternal living hell, the Day of Judgment conflated with the impossibility of salvation in a historically specific sense whose locus, ultimately, is the concentration camp: "Why awaken those who are sleeping? I would have been so happy if they had let me rest in peace; it's horrible, that idea of having to wake up all together, on the last day, a joyful last day that instead becomes a wretched first day, the beginning of eternity, of that Lager that will never end" (2008a, 45).

Important here is the historical context of travel and travel literature: insofar as all the primary texts—Kafka's, Sebald's, Magris's—relate a journey of some kind, the first two fall (however loosely) under the modern category of "tourism,"[24] while *Blindly*'s mixture of journeys of exploration, discovery, conquest, and nation-building, on the one hand, over against exile, diaspora, incarceration, and penal life, on the other, falls under a wholly other category of travel literature. Furthermore, while in Kafka the ethical or political dimensions of travel are subordinated to the subjective and epistemological, in Sebald and Magris, in their different ways, travel is treated in a manner clearly conversant with contemporary postcolonial critiques of late nineteenth- and early twentieth-century modernity. In other words, where Kafka's travel writing is never free of the specter of orientalism,[25] the more contemporary authors inevitably engage on some level with the postcolonialist theories of Edward Said, Foucault, and others.[26] This is clear from the example of Sebald's complex intertextualization of Verdi's *Aida*, and in what follows will be seen to hold true as well for Magris, who in *Blindly* for the first time ranges far beyond a specific middle European psychogeography.

Julia Hell (2004, 363) notes the emphasis in Benjamin's Ninth Thesis on the angel's eyes and their witnessing gaze: "'This is how one pictures the angel of history', Benjamin writes . . . 'looking as though he is about to move away from something he is fixedly contemplating. His eyes are staring, his mouth is open, his wings are spread.'" In *Blindly* the figurehead as extension or avatar of woman-as-saving-angel also intertextualizes Benjamin's angel of history while changing its gender. This is most apparent in the narrative's repeated attention to her "astonished, dilated gaze focused on the sea" (Magris 2008a,

157), as if perceiving "the inevitable catastrophe" (101). In certain moments in the story this catastrophe is the sight of Orpheus turning and abandoning Eurydice "forever to the void" (Eurydice is also identified with Maria, and with the figurehead [327–28]);[27] at others it is shipwreck; at still others the all-encompassing catastrophe that is the twentieth century. Eventually the contrast is made explicit between this female figurehead, gazing fixedly, stereoscopically, at "imminent disasters" and the telescopic or monocular eye of history, which is blind. This difference is gendered—"those eyes wide open on the beyond, on imminent, unavoidable catastrophes. Maria's eyes . . . not at all like mine, blind . . ." (181)—as well as generalized: "The astonished, dilated gaze of figureheads is focused on the sea and its unvarying horizon, on the disasters that are about to come from that horizon and which men cannot see" (353–54).

The speaker is rendered "blind" by the loss of his beloved, at times called Maria, a discrete personage in the narrative who also at times merges with the ship's figurehead, which is at times that of the *Rebecca*, Jørgen Jørgenson's ship, at others that of Jason's *Argo*. This blindness is tantamount to historical and autobiographical oblivion, the speaker merging even with Odysseus, in Magris's elegiac rewriting of the Polyphemus episode: "I left her on land, I lost sight of her face. It vanishes in the sea of years and events, and along with that face, swallowed up by the waves, I too sink and am lost; I am no longer anybody, yet this doesn't help me avoid the Cyclops, the dark, blind eye aimed at me. I don't see a thing" (106). Myth, history, and autobiography merge in a characteristically polyvalent, multivocal passage: "Maria disappears and the world is dark. After the shipwreck the sea returns the figurehead, corroded and eaten away by the water, the worn features almost mere wood again, the folds of her garment the grooves of a tree trunk, mouth nose and eyes chinks or nodes of a tree" (106). In this complex image of "Maria" as Eurydice-cum-figurehead, Magris goes beyond Kafka's hotel-room vision of the angel-become-figurehead-cum-ceiling-light-fixture, furthering the novel's critique of a banalized redemption. In *Blindly* Magris extends his ongoing project of rewriting both history and autobiography as myth, to the extent that, as these dual projects converge in the rewritten myth, he is also in the end rewriting and revaluing not merely individual myths but also the cultural category of myth itself.

Eventually the salient difference emerges between the ship's figurehead and the Benjaminian "new angel" of history, gazing fixedly at the ever-growing pile of detritus from the catastrophe that is progress: "Real figureheads are those in the form of a woman, a hand at her breast securing her dress which flutters and ripples like a wave, her astonished, dilated gaze focused on the sea and imminent disasters" (157, 353). In this image the disasters upon which she gazes are "imminent," still coming up, in the near future. Unlike Benjamin's angel, she is at the ship's prow, looking forward, toward the future as horizon, toward "the disasters that are about to come from that horizon" (354). This difference in orientation, in direction of the gaze, is crucial: where Benjamin's angel offers a radically other viewpoint upon history, countering dominant linear or teleological historioscopic models, Magris's figurehead represents a point of view not upon history or the past but upon the future, or futurity; she is a Cassandra-like figure of foreboding, of prophetic knowledge, neither actor, agent, nor subject but a passive spectator upon the shipwreck to come.

In all three texts—Magris's, Sebald's, Kafka's—the two figures, angel and figurehead, come together, however, around the ironic transformation of the "real" woman or angel—harbinger of either salvation or destruction—into the mundane and immanent, as in Magris's appropriation of another mythical female: "This is Galatea. She was found on an African beach following a shipwreck, and was worshipped like a goddess by the aborigines; other figures ended up adorning inns and taverns, so that the sailors might feel a little more at home even when they were on land" (326). This passage recalls Kafka's (1976, 292) ironic banalization of revelation: "only a painted wooden figurehead off the prow of some ship, one of the kind that hangs from the ceiling of sailors' taverns, nothing more." The marked difference also emerges between Kafka's and Sebald's angelic light fixtures: the first a light for the autosalvific act of writing, the second merely a light by which to drown one's sorrows— but looking ahead, obliquely, to its literalization in Magris's novel.

The protagonist's relation to women, to Woman, is also inverted in *Blindly*, in relation to Kafka's "allergy"—reproduced in *Vertigo*—to "intercourse" or *traffic* (*Verkehr*) in every form: economic, conjugal, sexual—what Kafka (1976, 228) in the *Diaries* refers to as "coitus as punishment for the happiness of being together." In Magris the speaker's relationship to the woman called variously Maria, Medea, or Eurydice is one of tempestuous sexual attraction (and consummation)—in short, of love—culminating in her betrayal by him: Jason, Jørgen, Salvatore.[28] In this Magris remediates elements of all these myths and stories: Eurydice's second, irreversible, death; Medea's betrayal by and revenge upon Jason; and so on. But here the betrayal has a far more cynical, self-centered motivation and is therefore thoroughly modern: the male protagonist's own survival at all costs. As the speaker succinctly puts it late in the story, "It was I who pushed Maria, on the open sea and under the sea; I threw her to the sharks as food and so I was spared by them" (Magris 2008a, 327).[29]

The recurrent scene of the burning in 1794 of the palace at Christiansborg in Denmark underlines the novel's preoccupation with specific historical disasters metonymizing more general apocalyptic destruction: "Christiansborg burns, for three days and three nights the Royal Palace burns . . . Fire is righteous, it destroyed Sodom and Gomorrah and one day it will destroy the new infernal cities" (360–61). As at the conclusion of *Vertigo*, with its dream vision of the Great Fire of London brought on by the narrator's reading of Samuel Pepys's *Diary*, fire returns as an actual and symbolic antidote to either narrative's thematization of water, the pitfalls of ocean voyages, and the ever-present threat of drowning. The novel's enigmatic conclusion merges the singular, as it were appointed fate of Kafka's Hunter Gracchus—the initial fall from the cliff while out hunting—ironically avoided, as in his dream the narrator traverses a nocturnal Alpine road bordering upon "a drop into truly vertiginous depths" (Sebald 1999, 262), with a more general apocalypse: "Is this the end of time?" (262).

As well, a comparable (ironic) binary logic applies to the visual dialectic of light and dark, blindness and insight announced in Magris's title, the clear light of noon in which (since Plato) the "truth" shines forth, itself revealed to be as much of a barrier to understanding as is the black hole of historical blindness:

> The light was blinding me . . . I lay down under the prow of the ship, in the patch of shade that the prow and the figurehead cast on the beach . . . This is how catastrophes occur, a defect of vision, a misunderstanding, the helmsman who doesn't see the rocks because he's looking someplace else . . . No, I don't think I heard the creaking of the figurehead breaking away from the ship and I think it fell on top of me. Undoubtedly I didn't ward it off; maybe I was asleep . . . I don't remember. (Magris 2008a, 359–62)

Magris goes beyond Sebald in his invocation of the "Hunter Gracchus" intertext, linking the significance of the story for a specific individual subject to the ongoing problem of historical blindness, a problem of vision, of a way of seeing, which is also connected to identity. As Magris (2008b, 1) writes elsewhere, "Our identity is our way of looking at things."[30] Rather than a fall from a precipice while out hunting, here the protagonist is crushed beneath the fallen weight of the figurehead's feminine form.

"Nothing Is Left but Looking"

The links emerge among Magris, Sebald, and Heiner Müller. Where in *Vertigo*'s postcolonialist remediation of Kafka Sebald incorporates elements of an "Old World" form like opera, Magris's text can as readily be compared with more typically twentieth-century cultural forms, such as the avant-garde theater work of the East German playwright. After all, *Blindly* is stylistically and structurally distinct from Magris's earlier novels and has in common with his works for the theater the quality of a highly dialogic monologue for spoken voice, in the manner of Beckett's later prose and theater pieces. What sets both contemporary writers apart from their modernist (and even some postmodernist) forebears, however, is a mutual interest in negotiating, even in a negative fashion, a relationship with a world increasingly determined by the forces of globalized capital.

As I argue in chapter 2, while Sebald's project *cannot* be reduced to a nostalgic reclamation of territory lost to modernity's ineluctable eroding of a former, "better" world, there is in it a recurring critique of the relentless expansion of capital—a process directly proportionate to the destruction of any stable position from which the subject can survey in relative objectivity the scene of its own striving: "the dissolution, in line with the inexorable spread of processed data, of our capacity to remember" (Sebald 2001, 286). The collapsing of subject and object within what I call the visual and spatial coordinates of modern catastrophe is succinctly announced in the conclusion to Benjamin's "Work of Art in the Age of Its Technological Reproducibility" (2002b, 147). In his review of Hanns Zischler's *Kafka Goes to the Movies* (which addresses the same period of Kafka's travels through Italy) Sebald combines Benjamin with Barthes in his approach to visual cultural history. He notes the recurrent passages in Kafka's *Diaries* that feature an "observer . . . who stands a great distance away yet is consumed by longing"—the observer who is absorbed in the individual, isolated aspects of a physicality beyond his reach because it is up on the screen (Sebald 2005, 156).[31] In the cinema, as Sebald claims, "nothing is left but looking, an obsession in which real time is suspended while, as we sometimes feel in dreams, the dead, the living, and the still unborn come together on the same plane" (156). Here, cinema is figured as a peculiarly modern land of the dead, to which the spectator is granted temporary access, a journey with certain paradoxical consequences for an image-based culture. Sebald underscores the blindness inherent to the dominant visuality: "The innermost mystery of secular metaphysics is this strange sensation of physical absence, something evoked by what might be called an overdeveloped gaze" (156). The film viewer, like Kafka, according to Sebald, becomes pure gaze, an eye without a body, in the peculiar phenomenology of cinematic perception—the early twentieth-century incarnation of the single unblinking mobile eye demanded by the sovereign gaze of artificial perspective and of the rational, Cartesian ego.[32] But this spectator is not gazing at a static painterly or even photographic image, aligned in its referential indexicality to both death and memory and therefore the possibility of historical consciousness. This is not the sublime visual sovereignty of the infamous opening shots of Leni Riefenstahl's *Triumph of the Will* (1935); it is the complementary "human" point of view of *another* modernity, constantly threatened with negation.

Sebald had already considered these themes in his scholarship on other contemporary literary and dramatic modes. As he wrote in an introduction to a collection of essays on 1970s and 1980s German theater, "[t]his prospect in which the subject and object of destruction are one is a central theme of playwriting in Germany today" (1988, 8). He cites as an example Müller's *Despoiled Shore Medeamaterial Landscape with Argonauts* of 1982: "That there is an audience watching the calamitous scene of destruction brings the whole arrangement in line with one of the most pervasive *topoi* of Western literature and art identified by Hans Blumenberg as *Schiffbruch mit Zuschauer* ('Shipwreck with Spectator')" (8).

Taking this in a different direction from that in chapter 2, I emphasize here Carl Weber's description of the final image of Müller's play: "the extermination of the voyager who turns into a landscape, the landscape of his death" (Müller 1984, 125)." Here we can contrast a potentially even more affecting final scene, that of Müller's (in the West) more famous play, *Hamletmachine* (1977), which concludes with a concatenation of mythical, literary, and contemporary popular cultural intertexts:

> *The deep sea. Ophelia in a wheelchair. Fish, debris, dead bodies and limbs drift by.*
> OPHELIA:
> *While two men in white smocks wrap gauze around her and the wheelchair, from bottom to top.*
> This is Electra speaking. In the heart of darkness. Under the sun of torture. To the capitals of the world. In the name of the victims. I eject all the sperm I have received. I turn the milk of my breasts into a lethal poison. I take back the world I gave birth to. I choke between my thighs the world I gave birth to. I bury it in my womb. Down with the happiness of submission. Long live hate and contempt, rebellion and death. When she walks through your bedrooms carrying butcher knives you'll know the truth.[33]
> *The men exit. Ophelia remains on stage, motionless in her white wrappings.* (1984, 58)

Specific aspects of this scene are echoed in Magris's 2006 monologue (Magris 2011), *You Will Therefore Understand* (*Lei dunque capirà*), a rewriting of the Orpheus myth from Eurydice's perspective: "I like this veiled, opaque light; it makes me feel like I'm at the bottom of the sea, where everything is fixed, motionless, even time" (2006, 11). More generally the intertextual and associational density of Müller's text is echoed at points in *Blindly*: "Maria, Marie, Márja, Marica, Norah, down there in the putrid waste of the heart, to die, to rot. Black divinities of the abyss, shadowy rites of Hecate in which Medea, sorceress of the night, indulges" (2008a, 358). As Sandra Parmegiani points out, in *Blindly* as well as in Magris's recent play, *The Exhibition*,

> the female protagonists in their endless protean reincarnations—Maria, Mariza, Norah, Medea, Alcestis—although subject to the deceptions of history and of the men they love, emerge somehow intact from the wreckage of that world, yet they do not have a voice though which to express their agency. Magris' female characters are always first and foremost victims, even when—like Medea—they perpetrate an atrocious crime. They are the target of man's blind and

egotistical self and always end up towering above their male counterparts. (2011, 117)

In *Blindly* Magris thus gives form to the paradox of a voiceless woman, not
a subject properly speaking, who nevertheless becomes the undoing of her
male counterpart but only by means of an objectification so outrageous that
she literally crushes the man who is guilty of denying her subjectivity in the
first place.

These diverse examples of postmodern literature, self-consciously informed
by postcolonial theory, also reveal the distance traveled from a work like
Verdi's *Aida*, emblematic as it is of grand opera's spectacularly melodramatic
staging of Romantic love's apotheosis, in tacit dialectic with the bourgeois values of its original, ideal audiences, for whom gendered stereotypes, for all their
artistic complexity, are all too readily naturalized. In *Blindly*'s concluding
chapter, as in the above-quoted final scene of *Hamletmachine*, the apocalypse
is personal and specifically gendered, Müller's postmodern, post-Communist
"feminist" politics receiving an extra twist in what we might now have to
call Magris's *post*-postmodern gender critique. Furthermore, the play's final,
surreal setting at the bottom of the sea finds in Magris's novel its postrealist
counterpart: the bottom of the world as figure for an ironic Dantean eschatological other-world or afterlife, the goal of the novel's "psychokatabasis."[34]

Every Day Is Judgment Day

In *Blindly*'s final chapter the resolutely masculine speaker—Jason? Jørgen?
Salvatore?—finds himself on what is primarily a beach in Australia, at the
bottom of the world ("Down the Bay, in Terra Australis Incognita, upside-
down again" [Magris 2008a, 359]), in antipodal relation to his origins in
Northern or Central Europe. Like Dante-pilgrim in the *Inferno*'s final canto,
at the bottom of Hell, the speaker has reached the point where the subject of
the narrative and the narrating subject are as far apart as they could possibly
be; from here they can only begin to converge once more, or so this premodern narrative and eschatological model dictates. Here, in Magris's post-
postmodern view, there is no possibility of the redemption represented by such
convergence, such self-transcendence, at the end, at the gates of paradise (if
not within). This is the end, and the speaker is no closer to understanding who
he is or where he is going. That the speaker is in some kind of hell, both here
and throughout, is evident in the repeated and specific references to actual
historical hells: from Port Arthur to Goli Otok, where he invokes the Croatian
slang for "through the machine": "*kroz stroj kroz stroj*. Flesh, racked and
harrowed in the great meat grinder" (356). And, although he does not literally
climb over Satan's buttocks to get out, the speaker does indulge in this final
section in a peculiarly excremental vision of the world as a living hell: "I look

down into that black well, that slime is the reflection of my face. I am down there, I thrive in that sludge; man is an autophagic and stercoraceous insect, he enjoys devouring himself . . . In the back hole of that shithole, head down in the *kroz stroj*, I vomited but at least I could see the rising sun, hidden at the bottom of that muck" (358–59).

Even more than the Dantean katabasis narrative, it is the all-important Orpheus intertext that provides a key to understanding the form and structure of *Blindly*, in particular the ending: the constitutive fragmentation of voice, or narrative personae (à la Beckett's novel trilogy, e.g.), on the formal level is directly analogous to Orpheus's dismemberment at the hands of the maenads, after his return from his failed mission to the Underworld, in the myth's diegesis. In this sense, then, the narrator or speaker—a concatenation of voices—is speaking, from the start, from beyond the grave; he is/they are already dead, even though the event of his/their death beneath the ship's figurehead comes at the very end. As in Beckett's novel *The Unnamable* (1953), the voice continues to speak, just as it is already speaking at the beginning, when the narrative of this death, as one event in his life, begins, even as the enveloping narrative of his life is recounted from a postdeath perspective. Again, it is Kafka who shows us the way out of this paradox, this labyrinth. After all, it is from Kafka that Benjamin gets the notion of the "Last Judgment projected across history," the modern(ist) conflation of the "Last Day" with the day of one's individual death; thus (for Kafka at least) every day is Judgment Day. In *Blindly*'s concluding scene of the protagonist's death on the beach is manifest the contradictory conflation of the angel's two principal faces: on the one hand, "the angel of death is approaching us"; on the other, "a vision intended for my liberation was being prepared." The Dantean slippage from third-person plural to first-person singular is the reverse of the *Inferno*'s opening lines, a fortuitous but meaningful coincidence.

In the eschatological cosmos of Magris's novel, "the Last Judgment will take place under water" (244), for it is "on land that hells are found. Those who die at sea are fortunate" (354). Here, Jason/Jørgen/Tore dies (or appears to die) on the shore, ignominiously, when the figurehead beneath which he reclines to escape the blinding noonday sunlight breaks off from the ship's prow and crushes him (363). This detail, too, is grounded in the mythic cycle, as an extension of Medea's revenge for his betrayal. In the myth as received, however, Jason is not killed under the ship's prow but its stern: "Reports of the death of Jason differ greatly." In one version he is "killed by a falling beam as he rests under the stern of the *Argo*" (Moog-Grünewald 2010, 366). It is highly significant of course that in Magris's version not the stern but the ship's prow, specifically the figurehead, kills Jason, as if Medea's revenge upon the traitorous Jason had been transferred to the wooden figure of idealized womanhood.

From this point to the narrative's end, the speaker is both dead and not dead, speaking his own death, from a position posterior to death, even as he continues to recount his various interfolded lives—a twenty-first-century updating of Beckett's ceaselessly babbling narrative voice. This is self-reflexively thematized in the recurrent mention of tape recordings being played back and finally erased, of documents deleted by a computer virus, and so forth (e.g., Magris 2008a, 363–64). These (ironic) negations represent at the same time the (ironic) possibility of immortality, of triumphing over death either by returning to life or by being "assumed" directly into some transcendent zone after passing through the purifying fire: "Fire . . . of course, I've got it! Better to be assumed among the gods like the greatest of the Argonauts, Heracles, burned on the pyre on Mount Oeta, transported to Olympus by the flames." (365). This allusion to the myth of Heracles invokes one of the original meanings of *translation*: to be taken up directly into heaven without passing through physical death, or in this case through the underworld or land of the dead. Such an apotheosis may be a possibility, however ironic, for the privileged masculine hero, but for the woman, here in the form of the figurehead, it is not possible: "Indeed [the *Argo*] was assumed into heaven, among the eternal constellations . . . But it's empty, without a crew . . . even without the figurehead" (363). At the same time, as Jørgen now, the speaker speaks of his death in "the Antarctic ice fields" by ice and by fire: "despite the permafrost—fire destroys everything . . . my memory, that of others, of everyone, who knows." (366).

In late May 1914—the year he turned thirty and the year before he first coughed blood—Kafka became engaged for the first time to Felice Bauer, whom he had known for two years. On June 6 he famously wrote, "Back from Berlin. Was tied hand and foot like a criminal. Had they sat me down in a corner bound in real chains, placed policemen in front of me, and let me look on simply like that, it could not have been worse. And that was my engagement" (1976, 275–76). Around the same time he began writing *The Trial*, one of three unfinished novels, and the first draft of the story "In the Penal Colony." In July 1914 the engagement was broken off, following what Kafka called the "tribunal" (*Gerichtshof*) to which he had been subjected by Felice's family (293).[35] By 1917 their relationship was over for good. And, while he would be involved with other women before his death from tuberculosis in 1924, he would never marry.

It would be overly reductive and even fallacious to read the whole of *The Trial* with Elias Canetti as an oblique response to Kafka's relationship with Felice. More significant is what this perspective reveals regarding Kafka's attitude toward women in general (his "failure" to live up to expectations, what he calls at one point in the *Diaries* "the broadening and heightening of existence through marriage," family, etc. [223][36]) vis-a-vis his relation to authority: together these constitute what might be characterized as his relation to the "law of the Father," addressed explicitly in his *Letter to My Father* (1919). In a reconstituted letter to Felice's friend Grete Bloch (present at the *Gerichtshof* in Berlin), Kafka writes, "You sat as a judge over me in the Askanischer Hof [hotel]—it was awful for you, for me, for everyone—but it only *seemed* so; in reality all the time I was sitting in your place and sit there to this day" (315). The "accused" in *The Trial*, it should be noted, are all men. More significant than this, though, is the strange element of self-judgment he evinces, as if in oblique reference to the Officer's assumption in his story "The Penal Colony," of all the roles: executioner and victim alike. This story ends, famously, with the Officer successfully putting himself to death (an action for which he still requires the Explorer as witness, however).

Kafka's writing of "The Judgment" was in part a response to what he saw as his family's, especially his father's, hypocritical attitude regarding the observance of Jewish high holidays, notably Yom Kippur, the Day of Atonement (*Versöhnung*), the time when judgment sits heavily, and one prays for forgiveness. One puts oneself before the divine Seat of Judgment in anticipation not only of the year ahead but also of life after death: *the* Day of Judgment. Much ink has been spilled on the question as to the connections between the father's "judgment" of the son and this sort of Judaic theologico-legalistic judgment. Cabalistic tradition describes a perpetually sitting "celestial court of justice," determining an omnipresent judicial world of accusation and punishment. Such a court is spoken of in detail and at length in Hasidic literature, which Kafka knew secondhand.[37] "The Judgment" and the work that follows, culminating in *The Trial*, constitute Kafka's "legalistic" writings: a multivalent and enigmatic response to the question of the individual's relation to "the Law." At the risk of too violent an analogy, we might see in this the modernist literary expression of what Jan Assmann (2006, 38) calls a *normative* sacred text, whose purpose is to answer the question for a specific people: "What do I do?" The counterpart to this is the *formative* text, which answers the question, "Who am I?" This question, the double question of identity and agency, is in a sense the central question of modernist cultural exploration, if not modernity more broadly. Kafka's evident failure to write such a text is more than compensated for by his many attempts to do so. And, since his death, the task has been taken up by numerous others, of whom Sebald's and Magris's recent contributions to the long prose narrative form are among the more significant.

As I note in chapter 2, the metaphysical category of redemption has been long since revalued in the gradual shift to a so-called secular late modernity: the Western world's semiconscious disavowal of its abiding allegiance to categories like God or an afterlife. Sebald's prose narratives in their different ways extend Kafka's (and other modernists') critique of the persistence of a positive metaphysical worldview that is nevertheless often affirmed in the work of Kafka scholars. I have focused in this chapter on *Vertigo*'s initially metonymic "identification" of the narrator with Kafka, leaving to one side several other figures, all men, all writers, such as Stendhal, Casanova, and Dante (since these are discussed in other chapters in this book). My partial aim was to shed light on Sebald's unique contribution to the transformation of a salvific model predicated on a specific relation between a narrative subject and an *other* as embodiment of the promise—or hope—of redemption. What is of interest here is the manner in which Sebald responds to the interminably open-ended nonsolution adumbrated in Kafka—a space in which Maurice Blanchot (1982, 79) sees the very possibility for the production of verbal images in the state of interminable exclusion, the condition of "exile" within the "space of literature," the "bad" or artificial infinite that gives rise to the "principle of figuration" that makes possible the image, the work, images that then interpose themselves between subject and "inaccessible unity" (the absolute, the infinite, etc.). Sebald's response takes place in the larger context of his abiding concern with the manner in which we—as subjects of late modernity, of yet another dispensation—have yet to come to terms with what we have already left behind. And, as in Kafka's last novels, the thematized failure or impossibility of salvation on the eschatological level in Magris's *Blindly* translates on the narrative level into the failure of *closure*, of narrative redemption. Whereas in Kafka this lack of closure is in part the result of the texts' unfinished status, however, in *Blindly* it is entirely intentional. Therefore, for Magris (in this novel), there is no salvation, not even in writing—no salvation, that is, except for salvation from salvation.[38]

Blindly's final chapter builds upon and goes beyond the achievement of Heiner Müller, whose work, although formally very different, nevertheless shares many thematic preoccupations. For his part Magris offers a differently—and perhaps more productively—negative outlook on such long-standing eschatological concerns by framing them in the highly gendered, postcolonial terms of a post-postmodern psychokatabasis narrative. In a line extending circuitously back through Beckett to Dante and the Orpheus myth, Magris (2008a, 118) presents a radical critique of a specific masculine subject speaking from beyond the grave, like the hybrid Flying Dutchman–Wandering Jew protagonists of *Vertigo*: "doomed to live in permanent exile," even (as in Beckett) this voice remains at the end the only certainty in a sea of oblivion. In *Blindly*'s post-postmodern cosmos, even more markedly than in Sebald, all Christological trappings have been thrown over for mythological ones, and the masculine or transgendered "descending angel" who announces the day of judgment is always already transformed into a wooden ship's figurehead of decidedly feminine shape. Here, at this highly inconclusive ending, Magris gives concrete form to Kafka's (1976, 225) contradictory desire to both be with an other and yet to be always alone, "the feat of the connection, of passing into the other." Thus the most positive reading of this ending, in which the woman's otherness remains so radically unknowable, emerges as it gives voice to the only possible form of salvation: to be saved from the need or desire for even a metaphorical salvation. To recognize and to embrace the richness of this failure, to pass through the heteronormative inferno of love, marriage, and betrayal (what Zilcosky [2003, 108] calls "eternal heterosexual return"), emerging on the other side, no longer alive exactly but having lived, and able to speak, which is to say to write.

Chapter 6

"The Gift of Being Remembered"

Speak, Memory and Austerlitz

Everything is as it should be, nothing will ever change, nobody will ever die.

—Vladimir Nabokov, *Speak, Memory*

Every entry into the sphere of meanings is accomplished only through the gates of the chronotope.

—Mikhail Bakhtin, "Forms of Time and of the Chronotope in the Novel"

Introduction: Chronotopes of Memory

This chapter and the one following seek to expand the exploration of Sebald's (and others') engagement with literary realism through the lens of Bakhtin's chronotope, which provides the ground for a meaningful connection between realism and the trope or theme of redemption via the category of memory. For Immanuel Kant, time and space are distinct forms of intuition informing categories of knowledge (epistemology) and of representation (aesthetics). In contrast, Russian literary theorist Mikhail Bakhtin gives "the name *chronotope* (literally, 'time-space') to the intrinsic connectedness of temporal and spatial relationships that are artistically expressed in literature."[1] The literary instantiation of the chronotope can be seen as one of the pillars of modern literary realism, insofar as it is effectively a constitutive component of any project that seeks to realize the miracle of a substantive and verisimilitudinous fictional world via the medium of verbal discourse: words printed on the page. "In the literary-artistic *chronotope*, spatial and temporal indicators are fused into one carefully thought-out, concrete whole. Time, as it were, thickens, takes on flesh, becomes artistically visible; likewise, space becomes charged and responsive to the movements of time, plot and history. This intersection of axes and fusion of indicators characterizes the artistic chronotope" (84). Bakhtin's chronotope, a concept adapted from Einstein's theory of relativity, is an ideal tool by which to gain a deeper understanding of the nature of contemporary literary discourse in Europe, North America, and beyond. "In literature, the primary category in the chronotope is *time*. The chronotope as a formally constitutive category determines to a significant degree the image of man [*sic*] in literature as well. The image of man is always intrinsically chronotopic" (85). The chronotope is representative of Bakhtin's crucial contribution to the history of ideas, whose most salutary achievement is the ongoing displacement of "man" from any kind of "center," real or imagined, literal or figurative, the thoroughgoing deconstruction and replacement of "man" by other concepts. Bakhtin analogizes this process repeatedly in relation to the rise of the novel—discourse, the *word* in all its heteroglossic and dialogically emancipatory potential—and its Copernican displacement of the Ptolemaic forces of monologistic textual authority. In an ideal sense, historically, the chronotope partakes of revolutionary centrifugal cultural forces, in perpetual struggle with the centripetal forces of official or mainstream culture.

As the term "chronotope" suggests, the temporal and spatial dimensions or axes are inseparable in most literary representations of the subjective, human experience of being-in-the-world. It is part of Bakhtin's anti-Kantianism, after all, that leads him to the dialogization of the relation between time and space in the chronotope. Nevertheless, Sebald, in *Austerlitz* at least, privileges space in his narrative account of time. For Austerlitz, time is a "higher form of stereometry," a kind of visual-spatial plane, like a giant chessboard upon which the pieces move according to laws knowable only to those outside the game (see Sebald 2001, 136):[2]

> It does not seem to me, Austerlitz added, that we understand the laws governing the return of the past, but I feel more and more as if time did not exist at all, only various spaces interlocking according to the rules of a higher form of stereometry, between which the living and the dead can move back and forth as they like, and the longer I think about it the more it seems to me that we who are still alive are unreal in the eyes of the dead, that only occasionally, in certain lights and atmospheric conditions, do we appear in their field of vision. (185)

In *The Rings of Saturn*, similarly, time does not flow so much as weigh upon the narrator's being, in an almost physical way, increasing as he turns in full consciousness toward the past, decreasing as he focuses on the present at the exclusion of the past—the all-too-bearable heaviness of being in time. Across Sebald's oeuvre, time is a force, like gravity, a law of physics whose metaphysical expression is memory: "I feel, almost physically, the current of time slowing down in the gravitational field of oblivion. It seems to me then as if all the moments of our life occupy the same space, as if future events already existed and were only waiting for us to find our way to them at last, just as when we have accepted an invitation we duly arrive in a certain house at a given time" (Sebald 2001, 257–58).

Austerlitz's presiding spirit is quite literally Time, the reigning deity of narrative and of the capitalist age alike, emblematized by Europe's great train stations (12).[3] The first colloquy between Austerlitz and the narrator takes place under the bored gaze of the "goddess of time past," in the person of a peroxided barmaid ensconced beneath an enormous clock, whose six-foot-long hand jerks forward like a "sword of justice . . . slicing off the next one-sixtieth of an hour from the future and coming to a halt with such a menacing quiver that one's heart almost stopped" (8–9). Austerlitz describes clock time as one of modernity's greatest inventions. After all, it was only by standardizing time in the mid-nineteenth century—by synchronizing clocks and dividing the world up into time zones and thus imposing a new kind of order, says Austerlitz—that we could then "hasten through the gigantic spaces separating us from each other" (12). But Austerlitz is critical of prevailing conceptions of time. Time, for him, is inherently artificial, and the view of time he advocates is one that recognizes the conceptual interpenetration of time and space. Far from the objectivity of time zones, time in this view is also subjectively determined, predicated on the individual's experience of duration and change. In effect, Austerlitz represents a kind of phenomenology of time that, in its complex function, owes as much to theories of visual perspective (and other technologies of seeing) as it does to Nabokov, Proust, Bergson, Saint Augustine, or classical thought (see, e.g., Panofsky 1997). Time for Austerlitz is a kind of prosthetic organ of human sense perception, extending our apprehension of the external world understood as the material manifestation of past, present, and future. In fact, it gradually becomes clear that what Austerlitz is interested in is not time per se—however one defines it—but *memory*, which, instantiated through specific spatial-visual metaphors, can be seen to determine a particular phenomenology of time. It is in this respect that cinema enters in a fundamental way into the book's fictional world—even as it is foregrounded in the narrative—to provide Sebald with yet another frame of reference that is at once necessarily time bound (as a narrative medium) and yet inescapably spatial in its hegemonic visual realism. It is also this concrete, spatial exteriority characteristic of cinema as a predominantly visual medium that will be revealed, much later in the narrative, as a paradoxical obstacle in Austerlitz's quest to uncover the "truth" of his past via the technologies of a century biased toward visual modes of representation, within a culture increasingly determined by the logic of mass production.

In one example, when Austerlitz takes his leave of the elderly Vera, his guide to his Prague childhood, she suddenly recalls how, on the day in 1939 that they put him on the train for England from that same station platform, Austerlitz's mother had turned to her, Vera, and remarked how it had been only last summer that they had all left together for a vacation at Marienbad—last year at Marienbad (Sebald 2001, 205–6). Originating in Alain Resnais's 1961 film about the endless, circular quest for the truth of the past within a planar model of time, "Marienbad" becomes in *Austerlitz* a signifier for an irretrievably idyllic interlude of happiness (206). At the mention of the "three wonderful, almost blissful weeks" he and his family spent at the resort—a trip of which he retained no conscious memory—Austerlitz is suddenly reminded of a subsequent trip to Marienbad he made in the early 1970s with the one woman in the narrative with whom he has what might be called a romantic relationship (206).[4] This second trip, intended by his friend Marie de Verneuil as a means of liberating Austerlitz "from his self-inflicted isolation," turns out to be a quiet disaster, like a trip to a decadent looking-glass underworld in which the ironically Orphic hero loses his beloved to life while he is drawn uncomprehendingly toward death (216).[5] He is constitutively incapable of accepting Marie's offer of love and the salvation it represents.

In contrast to the discursively constituted psychokatabasis at the heart of Magris's *Blindly*, and as a testament of Sebald's greater investment in the realist tradition, Austerlitz's second trip to Marienbad thus stands as one of the book's several ironically literal katabases. As with the Liverpool Street Station disused ladies' waiting room scene, Marienbad as a physical place is really a metaphorical city of the dead or underworld in *temporal* terms: Austerlitz is incapable of seeing that the profound unease he experiences while there is caused by the fact that he was there before in a time of happiness, access to which he has lost by virtue of his willful "unremembering" of all his memories of his childhood in Prague (216). That the act of will involved effaces itself in the process is emblematic of the irony of his entire situation. Austerlitz tries to explain himself: "I had always believed I must be alone, and in spite of my longing for [Marie] I now felt it more than ever before" (216). Austerlitz then retraces his own journey by train, made in 1939 when he was just five years old, across Germany to the English Channel and, by boat, to Great Britain, where he has resided ever since. At this point the adult Austerlitz realizes that his having discovered the "sources of [his] distress" had done him little good; his "reason was powerless against the sense of rejection and annihilation which [he] had always suppressed, and which was now breaking through the walls of its confinement" (228).

As observed in chapter 4, the erotic-salvific paradigm Sebald traces in Nabokov links the presence of specific female characters, such as Marie de Verneuil, with other "agents" of potential metaphorical redemption or salvation, some of whom also act as mediators of mnemic retrieval.[6] Sebald's general attitude toward any potentially erotic dimension, however, seems more influenced by Kafka than by Nabokov. In Sebald's reading, Nabokov is exemplary among visionary memoirists in his preoccupation with "the study of spirits, of which his famous passion for moths and butterflies was only an offshoot" (Sebald 2005, 142). This rather strong opinion it must be said only *seems* to shore up a conventional metaphysical reading of Nabokov's fictional texts. As evidence Sebald cites the well-known conclusion of *Speak, Memory*'s second chapter:

> Whenever in my dreams I see the dead, they always appear silent, bothered, strangely depressed, quite unlike their dear, bright selves. I am aware of them, without any astonishment, in surroundings they never visited during their earthly existence, in the house of some friend of mine they never knew. They sit apart, frowning at the floor, as if death were a dark taint, a shameful family secret. It is certainly not then—not in dreams—but when one is wide awake, at moments of robust joy and achievement, on the highest terrace of consciousness, that morality has a chance to peer beyond its own limits, from the mast, from the past and its castle tower. And although nothing much can be seen through the mist, there is somehow the blissful feeling that one is looking in the right direction. (Nabokov 1989, 50)[7]

His essay on Nabokov is a likely pretext for Sebald's annotations in this chapter of his Vintage paperback copy of *Speak, Memory*, in which he privileges the first half of this passage over the often-quoted second half. (In his copy he underscored the first four lines of this paragraph.[8]) This preoccupation with the dreamlike afterlife of the dead in *Speak, Memory* is a function of Nabokov's principal theme, memory—but not in the way this is typically formulated by scholars swayed by the rhetoric of his conclusion: "It is certainly *not* then—*not* in dreams—but when one is wide awake . . . from the highest terrace of consciousness" that one is able to transcend the limitations of individuated being. Sebald's reading is a highly idiosyncratic one that says as much about his *own* literary preoccupations as it does about Nabokov's— especially regarding not "spirits" in any literal sense but rather *memory*.

The above-quoted passage from *Speak, Memory*'s second chapter introduces a crucial contrast between the vividly *visual* quality of dreams in which one *sees* the dead (inevitably invoking Nabokov's elderly mother in Prague, about whom he has just been reminiscing) over against the "nothing much" to be seen of the generally privileged, ironically *anti*visual transcendent position. Neither of these spectacles—the indexicality of dream versus an unrepresentable transcendence—is equivalent to that of the visual iconicity of memory, in which, presumably, Nabokov can clearly see the dead as "their dear, bright selves," *vividly* alive (50; see Wood 1994, 87). In this regard, Brian Boyd (1991, 151) points out that Nabokov writes at length about only *certain* people in his past, and of those, "only when they are dead, like his parents . . . will he let real people play a large part under their own names."

Nabokov "the hunter of elusive memory" is emblematized in the imaginative world of his memoir by *Parnassius mnemosyne*, the butterfly species that Brian Boyd calls "a sort of tutelary deity in *Speak, Memory*—which Nabokov would have liked to call *Speak, Mnemosyne*" (1991, 563–64). As argued in chapter 4, Nabokov is himself the "tutelary deity" of *The Emigrants*. In this light the butterfly is not simply a clichéd allegory for the psyche or "soul"[9] but more specifically and idiosyncratically for *memory*: memory as primary mode of self-reflective consciousness, confined bodily in space, capable of transcending the present through active reimagining of the past; hence in his remark about Nabokov's preoccupation with spirits or ghosts Sebald is referring to memory. In Sebald, memory either thwarts time's passage à la Proustian recuperation, a making present through memory as quasi-involuntary re-presentation, or torments the subject via the knowledge of precisely the opposite: the past's irrecoverability and the other's now-absolute absence. Memory in this Sebaldian context is therefore posed as *either* the key to the suffering subject's salvation *or* as the very source of its suffering and thus the thing whose negation through death is to be desired as an escape from an ever-present knowledge of an unbearable past. Nabokov is thus literally introduced into the narrative of *The Emigrants* as a kind of personification of memory's ambivalently redemptive potential in terms of its centrality to his peculiar poetics of mnemonic divestment—Nabokov's art of memory, to use Foster's term, but also in the proper sense of a conscious ensemble of techniques.[10] (My use of the term "art of memory," in contrast to Foster's, in application to either Nabokov or Sebald *does* allude to Frances Yates's title and to those premodern memory systems, whose transmedial impact on modern memory texts runs much deeper than the kind of conscious influence to which Foster refers.) The butterfly hunter embodies for Sebald the salvific potential of the Nabokovian art of memory, in a bitterly ironic symbolism whose radically negative significance at key points in the narrative underscores the peculiar situation of Sebald's four (five, with Luisa Lanzberg) protagonists as not so much subjects *of* as subjected *by* memory. All five, not incidentally, are directly or indirectly victims of the Holocaust.

In subsequent works—*The Rings of Saturn* and especially his last book, *Austerlitz*—Sebald extends and complicates his intertextual relation to Nabokov. In this chapter I elaborate on Sebald's deliberate incorporation of specific passages and images from Nabokov's 1967 memoir in the narrative of *Austerlitz*, the only one of his long prose works he called a novel.[11] I focus primarily on the eponymous protagonist's attempts to recuperate some kind of memory, or rather a mnemic *image*, of the mother he cannot remember having known. I say Sebald's "*deliberate* incorporation" insofar as I draw here on research conducted at the Sebald archive in Marbach, Germany, where in Sebald's copy of *Speak, Memory* one can see marginal notations and other indications of the manner in which he adapted or remediated certain scenes or elements into his version of a fictional biography.[12]

Mnemic Divestment: *Apomnesis* ("Unremembering")

What is the difference between the mnemonic poetics of *Speak, Memory* and the "art of memory" Nabokov employs in his fictions? This might be articulated in the well-known opening to chapter 5, which Sebald notes in his copy of the book. Here Nabokov proposes to "save what is left of poor Mademoiselle," his "old French governess" (1989, 95 [1987, 75]),[13] from what I outline in chapter 4 as the compositional process employed in his novels of the conscious mnemic divestment, an *apomnesis* or "unremembering," framed as a kind of "gift giving," a gratuitous act of authorial grace. "Have I really salvaged [Mademoiselle] from fiction?" (1989, 117), Nabokov asks, rhetorically. It is worth noting the eschatological connotations of "salvage," suggesting a contrast between salvation as a rescuing *from* fiction and its distortion of an authentic image of things versus salvation *by* fiction: the redeeming and, as Nietzsche would say, justification of life through art.

This tension has its complement in Sebald, alongside other comparably intermedial authors whose poetics involve the conscious appropriation of specific elements from their predecessors, incorporating and resignifying them in new contexts. In each case this is a repertoire of techniques learned from, attributed to, or associated with the author's mother. Michael Wood (1994, 93) makes a related point: "Writing, the disappearance of ordinary identity into writing, is a dissolution of the self, and this too, or the awareness of this, may be part of Nabokov's legacy from his mother . . . she allows him to see that writing too is loss, a form of dishevelment"—a dissolution for which *Speak, Memory*'s text stands as a form of redemption. As will be seen in the next chapter, this poetics of mnemic divestment complements the comparable technique employed by Canadian writer Alice Munro. Munro's novelistic short-story cycle *The View from Castle Rock* (2006) makes a mutually illuminating comparison with Nabokov and Sebald in both their differences and commonalities, not the least of which is the authorial-narratorial relationship with her/his mother (and father) in their respective relation to mnemic inspiration.

The poetics of memory Nabokov outlines in *Speak, Memory*, chapter 5 (and throughout his autobiography), amounts to a method for taking control of not merely memory but of the process of *forgetting* as well. Thus the sentence "Houses have crumbled in my memory as soundlessly as they did in the mute films of yore" (Nabokov 1989, 136) is not an admission of memory's failure as much as it is the assertion of a *conscious* control over even the process of mnemic degradation against which Proust claimed to have discovered the partial and unpredictable defense of involuntary memory (see Nabokov 1989, 136).[14] Sebald, for his part, advances a third position vis-à-vis memory and forgetting: his "art of memory" is based on the overt principle of intermediality or, to use the older but in this case more precise term, intertextualization, the incorporation of prior texts into a new one in order to dialectically produce a new meaning (see Foster 1993, x). In Sebald, memory never avoids an acute self-awareness of its own limitations, not least those produced by modern memory's irreducible reliance upon preexisting cultural forms and especially technologies of representation, which provide not only the metaphors by which we conceive of memory[15] but also the very materiality of memory in what Walter Benjamin calls the age of technological reproducibility. For example, early on in the eponymous narrative Austerlitz describes to the narrator his "first experiments with photography" as a teenage schoolboy in Wales: "In my photographic work I was always especially entranced, said Austerlitz, by the moment when the shadows of reality, so to speak, emerge out of nothing on the exposed paper, as memories do in the middle of the night, darkening again if you try to cling to them, just like a photographic print left in the developing bath too long" (Sebald 2001, 77). Austerlitz metaphorizes the process of photographic development for the subject's passivity in the face of memory's vagaries: as if the photographer had no power to intervene or control the process; as if the image emerged or faded into oblivion of its own accord.[16]

Sebald notes in *Speak, Memory*'s fifth chapter the following passage: "That particular return to Russia, my first *conscious* return, seems to me now, sixty years later, a rehearsal—not of the grand homecoming that will never take place, but of its constant dream in my long years of exile" (Nabokov 1989, 97 [76]). As Nabokov puts it in a subsequent passage, "One is always at home in one's past" (1989, 116)—a claim he is uniquely positioned to make having escaped with his family both Russia and, later, with his new family, France, each time shortly before it was too late. Referring here to Russia as "motherland" (96), Nabokov admits that "he could not help being affected in some way . . . by a mother's nostalgia and a father's patriotism" (97).[17] At first lacking any knowledge of his real parents, Austerlitz, for most of his life, has no home to return to and therefore no coherent identity; his identity when the narrator first meets him is grounded in what Wood (1994, 95) in another context calls "homelessness understood not as a banishment from an old domain but as a forlorn quest for what cannot possibly be found." Unlike other victims of the vagaries of History and memory alike, Austerlitz resists the easy compensations of either patriotism or nostalgia. (In *Vertigo,* part 4, "*Il ritorno in patria,*" for instance, Sebald refers to Germany as *Heimat*: homeland as "fatherland," ironically underscored in the Italian *patria,* lifted from Monteverdi's 1639 *Il ritorno in patria d'Ulisse*. This opera begins with a scene structurally similar to but semantically the inversion of that with which Magris's *Blindly* ends: the hero, Ulysses, awaking on a beach in Ithaca, beneath a ship's prow, turned to stone by angry gods.) As will be shown below, in *Austerlitz* Sebald negotiates the difference between those with the "gift of being remembered" and those constrained by History to forget, or to be forgotten.

Sebald notes the following passage in *Speak, Memory*'s fourth chapter: "I have also placed that tilted mirror, and the lamp, and the chandelier drops. Few things are left, many have been squandered" (80 [101]). This comes in the midst of a section in which Nabokov literalizes his art of mnemic divestment—the dialectic of memory and forgetting, giving away the "gifts" of memory—as his memoir's *non*fictional poetics. As he "gives away" discursively, as his memory is as it were depleted, the memoir grows; the "natural" archive is sacrificed to build the artificial. Paradoxically, memory cannot function without this more or less deliberate casting off of the objects of memory, *apomnesis* in contrast with mere forgetting, for these objects or attributes are not lost to oblivion. The expansive metaphor of casting off jewels or diamonds, or its contractive complement, their secretion in a velvet pouch or pocket, recurs throughout Nabokov's works, such as in the first chapter of *Speak, Memory*,[18] where it is developed more self-consciously as a kind of authorial mnemic divestment paradigmatic of all fiction making:

> How small the cosmos (a kangaroo's pouch would hold it), how paltry and puny in comparison to human consciousness, to a single human recollection, and its expression in words! I may be inordinately fond of my earliest impressions, but then I have reason to be grateful to them. They led the way to a veritable Eden of visual and tactile sensations. One night, during a trip abroad, in the fall of 1903, I recall kneeling on my (flattish) pillow at the window of a sleeping car . . . and seeing with an inexplicable pang, a handful of fabulous lights that beckoned to me from a distant hillside, and then slipped into a pocket of black velvet: diamonds that I later gave away to my characters to alleviate the burden of my wealth. (1989, 24)

This mnemic divestment, *apomnesis*—to memory what apophasis is to discourse—is central to Nabokov's poetics, where it intersects with his aesthetic, thematic, and ethical preoccupations. Nabokov recognizes forgetting as the concomitant of recollection: "The disintegrating process continues still, in a different sense, for when, nowadays, I attempt to follow in memory the winding paths from one given point to another, I notice with alarm that there are many gaps, due to oblivion or ignorance, akin to the terra incognita blanks mapmakers of old used to call 'sleeping beauties'" (136; see also 95).

As noted in chapter 4, in his copy of *Speak, Memory* Sebald underlines the first sentence in the following passage: "I confess I do not believe in time. I like to fold my magic carpet, after use, in such a way as to superimpose one part of the pattern upon another. Let visitors trip" (139 [109]). Nabokov calls this state "timelessness," which can lead to a peculiar brand of "ecstasy," a kind of unabashedly utopian aestheticization of time through memory. Nabokov here achieves "a seemingly atemporal outlook by fusing disparate moments of remembered experience to form a single image" (Foster 1993, 199). By contrast, Austerlitz's questioning of time also begins from a kind of spatialization or materialization, allowing him to place himself "outside time," in a vision very far from Nabokov's:

> Could we not claim, said Austerlitz, that time itself has been non-concurrent over the centuries and the millennia? It is not so long

ago, after all, that it began spreading out over everything . . . Even
in a metropolis ruled by time like London, said Austerlitz, it is still
possible to be outside time, a state of affairs which until recently
was almost as common in backward and forgotten areas of our own
country as it used to be in the undiscovered continents overseas. The
dead are outside time, the dying and all the sick at home or in hospi-
tals, and they are not the only ones, for a certain degree of personal
misfortune is enough to cut us off from the past and the future . . .
I have always resisted the power of time out of some internal com-
pulsion which I myself have never understood, keeping myself apart
from so-called current events in the hope, as I now think, said Austerlitz, that time will not pass away, has not passed away, that I can
turn back and go behind it, and there I shall find everything as it once
was, or more precisely I shall find that all moments of time have co-
existed simultaneously, in which case none of what history tells us
would be true, past events have not yet occurred but are waiting to
do so at the moment we think of them, although that . . . opens up
the bleak prospect of everlasting misery and neverending anguish.
(Sebald 2001, 100–101)

Austerlitz's conclusion here is one of contemporary literature's most eloquent
visions of a secular hell. This also underlines the importance of specific kinds
of spaces in the representation of subjectivity in the prose texts—in *Austerlitz*, spaces such as the disused Ladies' Waiting Room in the Liverpool
Street Station or the billiards room at Lord Ashman's Iver Grove Manor.
The latter is an example of the same seventeenth- and eighteenth-century
country houses Sebald's narrator presents in *The Rings of Saturn* as objects
of simultaneous nostalgia and regret, insofar as their rapid demolition or
museumification beginning in the 1950s signaled the passing of a particular
world in its lived authenticity. At the same time the fact of these houses'
having been constructed in the first place meant the felling of large tracts of
forest throughout the country to create the artificial prospects so beloved of
the late eighteenth and early nineteenth centuries (Sebald 1998, 262–63).
Such great country seats signify in a somewhat different sense in *Austerlitz*,
however, insofar as the later examples of such houses (the product of "new
money") represent a specific instance of the spread of the bourgeois capitalist
ideology in architectural form. Unlike Proust, to whom he owes a debt in
this respect, Sebald combines the affectively charged chronotope of memory
with a quiet ideological critique—or perhaps such a critique is germane to
the post-nineteenth-century realist novel's evocation of a world on the brink
of disappearing, the central subject of such diverse canonical texts as Proust's
In Search of Lost Time and Jean Renoir's 1939 film *The Rules of the Game.*
"It is as if time, which usually runs so irrevocably away, had stood still here,
as if the years behind us were still to come" (Sebald 1998, 108). Iver Grove

contains more than one such space, for example the nursery, hidden behind a false wall when the house was requisitioned during the war. Austerlitz's account pinpoints the emotions experienced by Lord Ashman "as he ran his finger over the long row of notches he had carved in silent fury at the age of eight on the edge of his little bedside table, the day before he was sent off to preparatory school," emotions equivalent to Austerlitz's own, and indeed to those of any small child compelled to leave family and home too soon. Without knowing how, Ashman recalls finding himself outside in "the yard behind the house, firing his rifle several times at the little clock tower on the coach house, where the marks he made are visible on the clock face to this day" (108). Ashman's furious attack upon time is precipitated by his present reexperiencing of his childhood frustration, recorded for posterity in the angry tallies on the bedside table. "Time marks" markedly different from those to which Nabokov recalls his mother's drawing his attention, in his bittersweet contribution to this transmedial genre of Old World childhood manor house nostalgia. Such a memory chronotope seems to bear out Austerlitz's theory of time as a continuous space, like a giant chessboard. But these particular spaces are devoid of people (in the proper sense), inhabited only by ghosts of the past (e.g., Vera) or by objects alone, ironic "madeleine objects,"[19] mute reminders in the present of what has been lost, what will never return except as a visible or legible trace.

Nabokovian Traces in *Austerlitz*

Among the list of Russian expatriate authors Nabokov met while in Paris in the 1930s, Sebald, in his copy of *Speak, Memory*, chapter 14, notes and circles the name Ayhenvald, described by Nabokov as "a Russian version of Walter Pater." Noted at the bottom of the page: "Mother of Austerlitz" (Nabokov 1989, 287). In Sebald's book, of course, it is Austerlitz's *father*, Maximilian, a Russian Jew from Saint Petersburg, whose surname is Aychenwald (Sebald 2001, 153). "Austerlitz," as he learns only as a teenage schoolboy, is the name the protagonist had to leave behind when he left Prague for London as a little boy in 1939 (67–68).[20]

In the same chapter of Nabokov's autobiography Sebald underlines parts of the paragraph that begins, "the composing of chess problems . . . a beautiful, complex and sterile art" (Nabokov 1989, 288). Noted at the bottom of the same page in Sebald's hand: "Austerl." It seems safe to posit that Sebald has in effect granted his protagonist certain specific traits or attributes associated with the version of his younger émigré self but without going so far as to model his character more comprehensively upon the Russian writer's—in part because of Nabokov's role as "tutelary deity" in *The Emigrants* but also because Austerlitz as a character is a composite of specific aspects of several persons, both real and fictional.[21]

As in *The Emigrants*, Sebald's tendency in transposing Nabokov is to resignify the latter's redemption of temporal exile, emphasizing the contradictory and unresolvable dimension of personal memory. In *Austerlitz*, however, as the foregoing examples show, Sebald also repeats a tactic from the last section of *The Emigrants*, in which a paragraph-length passage is incorporated into the new text with certain key changes, thereby transforming the source text's meaning. From this empirical basis I want to expand upon the fourth chapter's reading of Nabokov's central significance for Sebald, as well the latter's contribution to an oblique redemption of the exiled Russian author's reputation.

In *Austerlitz* Sebald extends this remediative technique across the entire narrative, in a fictional biography recounted through interwoven direct and indirect discursive layers. Where Luisa Lanzberg in *The Emigrants*, for instance, is allowed to speak for herself through the device of the embedded fictional memoir, in *Austerlitz* the titular protagonist's fraught relationship with both history and his own past identity is mediated through a complex, highly imbricated or "periscopic" narration.[22] Sebald imagines the ramifications of Austerlitz's sudden and traumatic recovery of his childhood memories after a lifelong, self-imposed amnesia, a response, governed by the need for self-preservation, to the primal trauma of being sent in 1939 on a *Kindertransport* from Prague to a new life with a new name and new parents in an entirely alien place—an experience depriving him in one stroke of language, country, family, and identity.[23] Eventually Austerlitz journeys to present-day Prague, where a reencounter with Vera, his childhood governess, and her recounting of the past trigger the reemergence of his own memories of his childhood and of his real parents, long since lost to the Holocaust.[24] But, as if in consonance with the photos he lacks, Austerlitz can unearth no *visual* memories of his parents, no matter how hard he searches. As per Sebald's typical formal strategy, the book includes many visual images, including photographs and film stills of various women, none of which are *provably* authentic images of Austerlitz's mother. Even the one picture his governess approves is just another *possibly* authentic trace of his mother's now-absolute absence. Once again the text emphasizes the fraught relationship between memory in some putatively authentic state and its embodiment in visual images.

Memory, Visuality, and the Productivity of Loss

As discussed in chapter 4, Nabokov's avatar puts in an appearance at a key moment in each of *The Emigrants*' four parts. In a manner as ironic as it is serious, these intertextual apparitions seem to manifest at the moment for each of Sebald's protagonists when the burden of memory comes to outweigh its pleasure, and the subject of memory must confront the cost of exile in time as well as in space. Sebald reverses the chronology of Nabokov's autobiography, which in the original is thematically motivated, moving across the book's four parts from the elderly butterfly hunter in Switzerland to the little boy on a southern German holiday. Sebald consistently inverts the value of memory he finds in his close reading of Nabokov, inflecting it in the direction of melancholic mourning. Where Nabokov typically makes good his losses, both financial and spiritual, through memory's redemptive potential, Sebald places the affective emphasis on memory's paradoxical power to return the subject to a happier time when that time—as *place*, figured in spatial terms—is long since lost.

In a famous passage in *Speak, Memory*, Nabokov's earliest memory of his parents coincides with the "awakening of his consciousness of time" (Foster 1993, 194). This, for Nabokov, as for Saint Augustine in his *Confessions*, is his "birth" into consciousness, his "baptism" into memory: "The inner knowledge that I was I and that my parents were my parents seems to have been established . . . with my discovering their age in relation to mine . . . I felt myself plunged abruptly into a radiant and mobile medium that was none other than the pure element of time" (Nabokov 1989, 21). Austerlitz's relation to his lost parents is also intimately bound up with his relation to time and memory, albeit in a radically negative sense. Ultimately, Sebald's appropriation of specific elements from *Speak, Memory* complicates as much as it illuminates Nabokov's famous denial of time in chapter 6 (1989, 109). As Wood (1994, 86) comments, however, "Death, like time, like parting, can be averted but not forgotten; it haunts even the happiest occasions of its avoidance. This haunting is the chief structural effect of *Speak, Memory*, and death and time themselves begin to look like masks for something that Nabokov and memory are reluctant to name: loss."

The other important implication of this primal scene (as Foster 1993, 207, reminds us) is that it explicitly repudiates the psychoanalytic myth of the Oedipal subject: for Nabokov, there is no *erotic* aspect to intrafamilial relations, no nascent recognition of sexual difference; the self is constituted in the dawning of the awareness of time, and, while gender difference does play a role, it manifests in terms of the difference between the self's inward orientation toward memory and its outward orientation toward social-political life. Again, Nabokov's famous anti-Freudianism is both supported and complicated in *Austerlitz*, specifically in terms of Austerlitz's relation to his mother. Sebald aligns with Nabokov in his rejection of a narrowly psychoanalytic approach to memory;[25] in *Speak, Memory* memory is theme, structure, and compositional principle, at the very core of Nabokov's self-representation. Sebald notes the following passage in chapter 3 of Nabokov's book: "The act of vividly recalling a patch of the past is something that I seem to have been performing with the utmost zest all my life, and I have reason to believe that this almost pathological keenness of the retrospective faculty is a hereditary trait" (Nabokov 1989, 75 [1987, 60]).[26] Foster (Foster 1993, 182) draws attention to the feature of Nabokov's art of memory that aligns him with a tradition stretching back through Locke to Saint Augustine:[27] "Nabokov's intense absorption with pictorial images fashioned by memory, images that capture his past so vividly that they seem to transcend time."[28] At the same time, according to Wood (1994, 87), "Nabokov will have no truck with involuntary memory, or indeed with anything involuntary. Memory is an act of will, and of the will at its most determined and lucid and courageous." Foster (1993, 206) stresses Nabokov's great "faith in conscious awareness and even effort as the key to recapturing the past, and when [in the Proustian chapter 8] he likens memory to the luminous disc of a well-focused projector, he makes this attitude even more explicit."[29] There is another crucial difference between Nabokov and Proust, moreover, in terms of their respective conceptualizations of memory: whereas for Proust the past as such is recuperable, for Nabokov you *cannot* revisit your past, once it is past, but you can always revisit the textual (mnemic-eidetic) record of the past, which it costs the artist of memory great conscious effort to (re)construct.

Central to *Speak, Memory*, and to its appropriation by Sebald in *Austerlitz*, is the self-conscious thematization of memory. Nabokov's mother is associated throughout with Mnemosyne as mother of the muses, ultimate source not of inspiration so much as a means or method of *voluntary* recollection—the conscious retention in the present of vivid mnemic images to console one's future self otherwise cut off from the past:[30]

> To love with all one's soul and leave the rest to fate, was the simple rule she heeded. "*Vot zapomni* [now remember]," she would say in conspiratorial tones as she drew my attention to this or that loved thing in Vyra—a lark ascending the curds-and-whey sky of a dull spring day, heat lightning taking pictures of a distant line of trees in the night, the palette of maple leaves on brown sand, a small bird's cuneate footprints on new snow. As if feeling that in a few years the tangible part of her world would perish, she cultivated an extraordinary consciousness of the various time marks distributed throughout our country place. She cherished her own past with the same retrospective fervor that I now do her image and my past. Thus, in a way, I inherited an exquisite simulacrum—the beauty of intangible property, unreal estate—and this proved a splendid training for the endurance of later losses. (1989, 40; underscoring by Sebald)

Nabokov does exactly as his mother says; the evidence is right here, in this paragraph. In a single phrase he enumerates the "time marks," a series of discursively rendered imagistic snapshots, capturing temporal movement as seasonal change from spring to summer to fall and winter. It is noteworthy, too, that Vyra, the "real estate" behind the "unreal estate" of these, his earliest memories, is his *mother's* property. Wood (1994, 91) contrasts Nabokov's respective treatments of his father and mother in *Speak, Memory*, pointing out how, while the book is "strongly organized around the father's death,"

"Nabokov's mother, on the other hand, is loss itself, or rather she is loss and its survival, mistress of what her son calls 'unreal estate', and the art of knowing what cannot be taken from one." "The mother is intimately associated with the writer's talent" (92), as Wood points out, but separated, I would add, from paternal political consciousness, from the overt recognition of the role of "History" in this sundering of the subject from *his* beloved past. Hence the implications of the phrase "leave the rest to fate": it is left to Sebald to transpose Nabokov's gendered sentiments into a context in which the pressures of History upon the individual cannot be ignored, and therefore memory can no longer be seen in even the highly qualified redemptive light of *Speak, Memory*.

In Nabokov's representation, his mother provides the model for his own sophisticated mnemonic poetics, in which everything of value is recuperated, taking into account his evident regret at not being present at her death. As he notes at the end of chapter 2, in her old age in a small apartment in Prague, "a soapbox covered with green cloth supported the dim little photographs she liked to have near her couch. She did not really need them, for nothing had been lost" (1989, 49). In a phrase Sebald underlines, "she had with her all that her soul had stored" (1989, 41 [1987, 50]). Reading Nabokov through Sebald, however, has the salutary effect of amplifying the irony of a statement such as "Everything is as it should be, nothing will ever change, nobody will ever die" (1989, 77). But there is more than one kind of death, as Nabokov so eloquently demonstrates, where the nonexistence of oblivion outweighs mere physical nonexistence. And then there is the life after death that is literature's gift.

"The gift of being remembered"

In his 1996 essay on Nabokov Sebald notes that his predecessor "knew, better than most of his fellow writers, that the desire to suspend time can prove its worth only in the most precise re-evocation of things long overtaken by oblivion" (2005, 145). As in *The Emigrants*, Sebald's tendency in transposing Nabokov is to resignify the latter's "redemption" of temporal exile, emphasizing the contradictory and unresolvable dimension of personal memory and giving far more weight to the dialectic of memory and History. In *Austerlitz*, however, Sebald once again appropriates a paragraph-length passage, radically transforming the source text's meaning. In Sebald's copy of *Speak, Memory*, he notes the entire page, in chapter 2, from which this passage is taken:

> On overcast afternoons, all alone in the drizzle, my mother, carrying a basket . . . would set out on a long collecting tour. Toward dinnertime, she could be seen emerging from the nebulous depths of a park alley, her small figure cloaked and hooded in greenish-brown wool, on which countless droplets of moisture made a kind of mist

all around her. As she came nearer from under the dripping trees and caught sight of me, her face would show an odd, cheerless expression, which I knew was the tense, jealously contained beatitude of the successful hunter. (1989, 44)

In the remediated scene in *Austerlitz*, the protagonist sees for the last time his friend Gerald's mother, who, during his adolescence, had become a surrogate mother to him. Tellingly, there is no accompanying photo:

> When I returned—dusk was already falling, said Austerlitz, and fine rain hung suspended in the air . . . Adela came to meet me from the misty depths of the garden, muffled up in greenish-brown tweed with millions of tiny drops of water clinging to the fine fuzz of its outline and forming a kind of silvery radiance around her. She was carrying a large bunch of rust-colored chrysanthemums in the crook of her right arm, and when we were standing in the doorway, she raised her free hand and put the hair back from my forehead, as if she knew, in this one gesture, that she had the gift of being remembered. Yes, I can still see Adela, said Austerlitz; in my mind she has remained unchanged, as beautiful as she was then. (Sebald 2001, 111)

Sebald's adaptation of this scene overtly emphasizes what is only implicit in the passage in *Speak, Memory*: Nabokov's rare ability to produce mnemic images of vivid—and therefore memorable—intensity.[31] Throughout his memoir Nabokov exhibits a comparable, characteristically playful awareness of his own capabilities as artist of memory. It is noteworthy, however, that Sebald contrives to have Austerlitz, the primary narrator, share the mnemonic agency with Adela, granting the object of the gaze an active role in the construction of the mnemic image: "I can still see Adela, said Austerlitz," "as if she knew, in this one gesture, that she had the gift of being remembered,"[32] even as she grants this capacity to the memory, the image itself. Nabokov's mnemic image powerfully represents memory's—*his* memory's—ability to preserve the past, allowing the subject in the present to revisit such a scene at will, thereby complicating Wood's assertion that the author is always covering up his preoccupation with loss, where such loss is always mitigated by memory's recuperative power. Sebald's reworking of the mnemic situation shifts the emphasis onto the specter of loss implicit in Nabokov, amplifying the irony of an image of a now absolutely absent person who at the time already knew that the viewer would retain this image in his mind—the very inverse of Magris's Maria/Medea/et al., whose only agential act is to destroy the man who subjected her to the double fate of objectification and oblivion. In both *Speak, Memory* and *Austerlitz*, the passage contains a mnemic image as miniportrait, but in Sebald's remediation memory's preservative power is always already undercut by the darker awareness of the now-absolute absence of those once present to the remembering subject's so to speak recording apparatus, in direct analogy with C. S. Peirce's semiotic analysis of the visual image as simultaneously indexical and iconic (see Kilbourn 2010). In these photographic terms, Nabokov is the artist of nostalgic iconicity, while Sebald is the artist of melancholic indexicality, manifesting in part through the relation between the verbal text and the photos scattered throughout each book.[33]

Memory and Visuality

Even more than Proust, who in his theory of involuntary memory privileged taste and texture over sight,[34] and despite his valorization of time as a medium of consciousness and the verbal-discursive nature of his mnemotechnics, Nabokov, like Sebald, privileges the visual aspect of memory, both in sensory terms and with respect to representational modality. For example, in *Speak, Memory*, chapter 4, Nabokov recalls kneeling on his bed to say his prayers, while

> a framed aquarelle showed a dusky path winding through one of those eerily dense European beechwoods . . . In an English fairy tale my mother had once read to me, a small boy stepped out of his bed into a picture and rode his hobbyhorse along a painted path between silent trees . . . I imagine the motion of climbing into the picture above my bed and plunging into that enchanted beechwood—which I did visit in due time. (1989, 86)

Retrospectively, Nabokov imagines passing into the picture, whose "enchanted beechwood" in turn becomes a figure for another beechwood in another temporal zone of his life. In *Austerlitz*, by contrast, the protagonist shifts the mediatic register, thereby raising the affective stakes, as he imagines watching the mother he cannot remember in a film about Theresienstadt he does not possess in which she probably doesn't even appear:

> I found myself unable to cast my mind back to the ghetto and picture my mother Agáta there at the time. I kept thinking that if only the film could be found I might perhaps be able to see or gain some inkling of what it was really like, and then I imagined recognizing Agáta, beyond any possibility of doubt, a young woman as she would be by comparison with me today . . . I imagined seeing her walking down the street in a summer dress and lightweight gabardine coat, said Austerlitz: among a group of ghetto residents out for a stroll, she alone seemed to make straight for me, coming closer with every step, until at last I thought I could sense her stepping out of the frame and passing over into me. (Sebald 2001, 244–45)

Speak, Memory's employment of the fairy-tale-like motif of the hero mag-ically entering into the two-dimensional world of a painting he remembers from childhood is inverted in *Austerlitz* into the ironically elegiac, cinematic "false memory" conjured by the protagonist in compensation for the authen-tic mnemic images he lacks. The recuperative dimension of the present-tense beechwood chronotope is utterly denied Austerlitz, whose visit to the actual precincts of Theresienstadt yields nothing, the city one of the many uncan-nily deserted spaces in his work, the only people he ever actually sees within its walls being those whose ghostly images are captured in the fragmentary propaganda film *Hitler Gives a City to the Jews*.

At this juncture it is necessary to acknowledge the density and complexity of the intermedial convergence in Austerlitz, especially of various thematic strands wending across the prose works. The most curious and significant of these is the coming together of the microlevel of Austerlitz's personal story of affective-emotional loss—originating in the loss of Agáta, his actual mother—and manifesting subsequently in his constitutional inability to form intimate relationships with anyone, least of all (in a strong Kafkan echo) a woman as object-of-desire. In a strange sense, the various women in Austerlitz's life—Agáta, Vera, Adela, Marie, and even his Welsh stepmother, Gwendolyn—whether caregivers or potential lovers, are all surrogate mothers, according to the unconscious logic of displacement and compensation that governs his life until the 1990s, when he begins to recount his story to the narrator. This succession of mother figures again mirrors Proust and the "going to bed" motif in *Swann's Way*. In a sense Sebald makes good on the erotic dimension latent in Marcel's relationship with his mother, but ironically so; after all, whereas Marcel still has his mother, despite his grief at her nightly disap-pearance (and that of her kiss), Austerlitz has always already lost his mother, in the sense that he cannot remember her at all, instead filling this void with surrogate mothers (Gwendolyn, Adela) as well as a woman such as Marie de Verneuil, who according to a certain logic cannot take her place because she is a potential lover, not his mother, even if he can only imagine his mother as a comparably youthful and beautiful—and therefore desirable—woman. To an extent Gerald's mother, Adela, is the closest in Austerlitz's experience to a woman who fulfills all the roles at once: she is both motherly and (somewhat problematically) an object of desire. In terms of either role, however, he is doomed to lose her, as he loses all the others, with the exception of Vera, a very elderly and still beautiful woman when he locates her again in Prague, sixty years after leaving on the *Kindertransport* (Sebald 2001, 105, 157). Adela, like Austerlitz himself, is also figuratively aligned in the narrative with the category of the victims of history epitomized by the Jews, often invoked obliquely in the pseudo-orientalist image of a desert caravan: "I remember, said Austerlitz, as we gazed together at this slowly fading world [in the shad-ows cast by the waning sunlight upon the wall of the ballroom of Andromeda Lodge], Adela leaned toward me and asked: Do you see the fronds of the palm trees, do you see the caravan coming through the dunes over there?" (112). Personal loss thus converges in *Austerlitz* with general, historical loss: exile, diaspora, wandering, death—the reality of redemption forever withheld.

The Productivity of Loss: The Writer and His Mother(s)

Proust is arguably the modern original for the literary topos of "the writer and his/her mother."[35] In *Speak, Memory*, chapter 4, Nabokov offers the scene of his childish self being put to bed by his beloved mother: "I next see my mother leading me bedward through the enormous hall, where a central flight of stairs swept up and up" (83). This would seem to allude (perhaps coincidentally) to the bedtime scenes in the first volume of *In Search of Lost Time*. But where Marcel might come across as the paradigmatic Oedipal "mama's boy," pining in his bedroom for his mother, longing for one last good-night kiss (see, e.g., Proust 1996, 12–13), Nabokov grants to his boyhood self the healthy, neurosis-free relationship of which Proust can only dream, and which in *Austerlitz* operates as a fundamental but unnamed present absence at the heart of the book's reconstructed narrative of a long-lost Central European identity. Like Roland Barthes (in *Camera Lucida*), Jacques Derrida (in "Circumfession"), and, ultimately, Saint Augustine (in book 9 of *Confessions*), therefore, Sebald has contributed in more than one text to what I call the mother's death subseries of the "writer-and-his/her-mother" topos.[36] This aspect of the prose texts is well illustrated in the latter section of *The Emigrants*, part 4, in which Max Ferber gives to the narrator his mother's memoirs, handwritten between 1939 and 1941, when it was no longer possible for Luisa Lanzberg and her husband to emigrate from occupied Germany (Sebald 1996, 192). Since I dwelt at length on this episode in chapter 4, I will refrain from doing so here.

Nabokov's mother may be his muse of memory, but, as Michael Wood (1994, 99) reminds us, the rhetorical addressee of *Speak, Memory* changes halfway through to a second person "you," who is, of course, Nabokov's wife, Vera. So in *Austerlitz*, the protagonist's mother is the primary absent figure or object of his quest in time and space, the face he wishes to be able to put upon the past of which he was dispossessed. Austerlitz never really finds his mother for certain, which is to say he never retraces her specific fate as a victim of the Holocaust, but he is reunited with another Vera, the nanny of his early childhood, who becomes the only direct conduit to the past and people, or their mnemic images, he seeks to rediscover: "No sooner had I arrived in Prague than I found myself back among the scenes of my early childhood, every trace of which had been expunged from my memory for as long as I could recollect" (Sebald 2001, 150).

Vera's discourse, recounted at second and third hand by a nameless narrator, triggers in Austerlitz a particular and peculiar memory of his real mother,

Agáta. This scene is emblematic of the synesthetic complexity of Sebald's representation of the very process of remembering as the uncovering of *lack* as much as the recuperation of some positive, *visualizable* mnemic content. Austerlitz recounts to the narrator how, while in Prague, he "suddenly remembered that [he] had been filled by a grief previously unknown to me" (161). As the adult Austerlitz recalls, his childhood fear that his mother, an opera singer, has changed into someone else, "a complete stranger," is ironically borne out in the vertiginous temporality of memory:

> "I . . . suddenly remembered that I had been filled by a grief previously unknown to me, when, long past my usual bedtime, I lay with my eyes wide open in the dark . . . listening to the church clocks strike the quarter hours and waiting for Agáta to come home, waiting to hear the car bringing her back from that other world stop outside the gate, waiting for her to come into the room at last and sit down beside me, enveloped by a strange theatrical odor in which dust and drifts of perfume mingled. I see her wearing an ashen-gray silk bodice laced up in front," he says, "but I cannot make out her face, only an iridescent veil of pale, cloudy milkiness wafting close to her skin, and then, said Austerlitz, I see the scarf slip from her right shoulder as she lays her hand on my forehead." (162)

As Derrida (2001, 46) remarks of his friendship with Roland Barthes, his mourning for the latter began while he was still alive, "even before the unqualifiable event called death."[37] In this memory-image Austerlitz recalls his younger self already mourning the loss of his mother while she is still alive, grieving the future absence of the loved one. His failure to recall her face bears out this fear and this grief, before the fact, from a present otherwise sundered from this remembered past, the memory-image pointing here beyond its beautiful mimetic surface toward its terribly ironic indexical meaning as a sign of a presence now absolutely past, of a being who was there but who will now never be "resurrected" in the image.[38] With neither photograph nor second-order memory-image, Austerlitz cannot hope to recover anything more than the knowledge that, although she was once present, his mother has for him always been absent—a temporality that cannot be represented photographically. Austerlitz's psychoaffective condition here contrasts meaningfully with Nabokov, for whom such a paradoxical state of mourning becomes the basis of an aesthetic principle.

Derrida's notion of mourning as a uniquely ethical basis of the self-other relation—because it respects the other's unique alterity—sheds light on Marcel's childish obsession with his mother's bedtime kiss in the first volume of Proust's magnum opus. This is a nonpsychoanalytic interpretation when read retrospectively, in light of the adult Austerlitz's reimagining of his childhood self's fear that his mother will never return home, or that she will transform into a different person—both of which in a sense come true.[39] That is, the child Marcel is already "mourning" his mother's inevitable future absence from his life—where her only lingering "presence" is in the form of Proust's vivid memory-images—precisely the positive traces that Austerlitz lacks.

Midway through the narrative, in his conversations with Vera, Austerlitz is given an old photograph of himself as a four-year-old, dressed as a page boy for a costume ball. The picture was purportedly taken in 1939, some six months before he was to leave Prague for good:

> Hard as I tried both that evening and later, I could not recollect myself in the part . . . All memory was extinguished in me by an overwhelming sense of the long years that had passed . . . I always felt the piercing, inquiring gaze of the page boy who had come to demand his dues, who was waiting in the gray light of dawn on the empty field for me to accept the challenge and avert the misfortune lying ahead of him. (Sebald 2001, 184)

The misfortune, in a terrible irony, of having escaped the Holocaust, to which he lost both his parents. Austerlitz's "overwhelming" sensitivity to time has extinguished his memory of the original event to the extent that he now views his own image in the photo as that of someone else; this very sensitivity, of course, is itself the product of the loss he has incurred. This dynamic highlights the vertiginous irony of Austerlitz's position as simultaneously survivor and victim, in that his younger self has as it were come back from the dead to accuse his present self of failing to save him.[40] Austerlitz puts himself—or is put into—the position of the "influential admirer"—and therefore potential suitor—of his own mother, at whose home the ball is to be held. (The "illegitimacy" of this relation on the socioethical level is balanced by its artistic anticipation in Austerlitz's account of his relationship with Adela in Wales, a relationship equal parts filial and protoerotic. The latter is underscored by his emphasis on the concrete permanence of Adela's beauty in his mnemic image, echoed later in a purely imaginative description of his mother as "a young woman as she would be by comparison with me today" [245].) Whereas his mother's strategy of attending the ball may have resulted in Austerlitz's escape from Nazi-occupied Czechoslovakia, this fact does not shed any light on his adult self's aporetic relation to his youthful self's accusatory gaze. His sense of failure is paralleled by the failure of memory: his failure to remember and, in remembering, to somehow redeem *himself* from a metaphorical death. This failure of memory is coextensive with the ultimate (ironic) failure of the erotic-salvific paradigm as theme across the prose texts; in this regard Sebald's complication of a Freudian model of subjectivity—over against Nabokov's outright rejection of same—can be seen as the parallel on the individual level of the ultimate failure of redemption at the macrolevel of both the narrative and, by extension, history.

This passage is preceded by Austerlitz's recounting of a dream he had subsequent to his reunion with Vera in Prague, in which he returns to his parents' apartment

> after a long absence . . . I know that my parents will soon be back from their holiday, and there is something important which I must give them. I am not aware that they have been dead for years. I simply think they must be very old, around ninety or a hundred, as indeed they would be if they were still alive. But when at last they come through the door they are in their mid-thirties at the most. They enter the flat, walk round the rooms picking up this and that, sit in the drawing room for a while and talk to each other in the mysterious language of deaf-mutes. They take no notice of me. I suspect that they are about to set off again for the place somewhere in the mountains where they now live. (184–85)

The last remark refers to the ostensible source of the dream: another old photo Vera finds and shows to Austerlitz, which at first she thinks might show his parents when still together in Prague, but after all she is simply not sure; the figures are too small to be made out clearly. Then Vera adds something strange, a detail that shows how far Sebald is from Nabokov at this point in his evocation of memory. Vera points out "the mysterious quality peculiar to such photographs when they surface from oblivion. One has the impression . . . of something stirring in them . . . as if the pictures had a memory of their own and remembered us, remembered the roles that we, the survivors, and those no longer among us had played in our former lives" (182–83). It is as if those pictured in the dream, the photo, or the memory, had been granted the agency to be seen or not, to be remembered or not. To borrow a phrase, it is as though the object in question, the photograph, were not simply "staring back"[41] but, like Austerlitz's mnemic image of Adela, possessed the "gift of being remembered." In this respect Sebald offers a powerful but qualified anticipation of the twenty-first-century turn to a new materialism, in the form of object-oriented ontology as a significant manifestation of the broader, so-called nonhuman turn in critical theory and artistic practice. The salient difference in Sebald—what sets him apart utterly from such postmillennial critical-cultural shifts—is his attention to such objects within the key of elegiac memory; in short, an irreducibly "human" register, for better or worse. The other fact to which this passage draws us, and which "OOO" (as its adherents call it) seems to have completely overlooked, is that images are objects too, and that in the hierarchy of nonhuman "man-made" objects that surround us images are perhaps still deserving of the degree of attention they have historically received, over against other such objects, or as compared with other nonhuman "natural" objects. After all, how do we become aware or how is our attention drawn to the latter—nonhuman natural objects—other than through the mediating power of images?[42]

The attribution of ethical properties to an image-object recurs in somewhat different form a little later, when Austerlitz is making his second train journey from Prague through Germany to England, and the train stops briefly in the town of Pilsen, on the Czech border. Austerlitz gets down in order to take a photo of a cast iron column in the station, a photo that is not reproduced in the text.

> What made me uneasy at the sight of it . . . was not the question whether the [column] . . . had really impressed itself on my mind when I passed through Pilsen with the children's transport in the summer of 1939, but the idea, ridiculous in itself, that this cast-iron column, which with its scaly surface seemed to almost approach the nature of a living being, might remember me and was, if I may so put it, said Austerlitz, a witness to what I could no longer recollect for myself" (221).

Suggesting that the task of witnessing might be served as well by nonhuman objects, or better by photographs of such objects, underscores the significance of the object-world vis-à-vis the human, but in a way that challenges the precepts of object-oriented ontology, or speculative realism, or other manifestations of the nonhuman turn in current critical theory. These passages make clear among other things the difficulty, if not the impossibility, of thinking of objects on their own terms, completely divorced from any subjective or affective considerations, just as it is difficult, if not impossible, to think without objects in the first place. Such objects, then—and this is most significant in the case of the photos, which often exist in Sebald only as verbal descriptions—cease to function as Proustian "madeleine objects," prompts to memory's retrieval; rather, their function here as "witness" to a human past represents no solace whatsoever to the subject of memory's unpredictability.

In between these episodes comes the even more explicit scene when Austerlitz travels to the Czech town of Terezín, site of Theresienstadt, the former Nazi transit camp, in which, he had learned from Vera, Agáta had been interned from 1941 until her deportation farther east in 1944. The town is uncannily empty of people, in an intratextual echo of the many empty public spaces through which the narrator sojourns during his pilgrimage along England's southern coast in *The Rings of Saturn*. Here the emptiness signifies in a highly specific way, given the town's wartime function as way station for thousands of Czech Jews en route to extermination camps from which most would never return. During his visit he stands outside the display windows of the "Antikos Bazaar," seemingly the only store in the town. The four large windows contain a plethora of objects, meticulously listed by Austerlitz, for they "exerted such a power of attraction on me that it was a long time before I could tear myself away from staring at the hundreds of different objects . . . as if one of them or their relationship with each other must provide an unequivocal answer to the many questions I found it impossible to ask in my mind"

(Sebald 2001, 195). These objects, presumably once the property of the former inhabitants of Theresienstadt, "for reasons one could never know had outlived their former owners and survived the process of destruction" (197). What was the meaning, for instance, "of the ivory-colored porcelain group of a hero on horseback turning to look back, as his steed rears up on its hindquarters, in order to raise up with his outstretched arm an innocent girl already bereft of her last hope, and save her from a cruel fate not revealed to the observer?" (197). All the objects are "just as timeless as that moment of rescue, perpetuated but forever occurring," like Titorelli's painting (in Kafka's *The Trial*) of the ambiguously gendered allegorical figure of the "Triumph of Justice" as a Fury or avenging angel, whose ambivalent meaning is implicitly echoed in Titorelli's rendering of the attitude of the judges: at once menacing, ready to pounce, and yet maddeningly passive, sitting in judgment, as if "the Day of Judgment [were] a summary court in perpetual session."[43]

Conclusion: Affect + Memory = Nostalgia

Svetlana Boym (2001, 53) understands "collective memory" as "the common landmarks of everyday life . . . constitut[ing] shared social frameworks of individual recollections," and nostalgia plays a crucial role, remaining "an intermediary between collective and individual memory" (54). Boym's complex theory of nostalgia updates Maurice Halbwachs's notion of collective memory in a manner highly relevant to my readings of Sebald and Nabokov by taking into account the impact of emotion upon the formation of social as well as individual memory:[44] "One remembers best what is colored by emotion. Moreover, in the emotional topography of memory, personal and historical events tend to be conflated" (Boym 2001, 52). Boym's formulation of reflective nostalgia (to be explored in the next chapter), especially, "reveals that longing and critical thinking are not opposed to one another, as affective memories do not absolve one from compassion, judgment or critical reflection" (49–50). So must any theory of collective or social memory take into account how affect inflects or determines memory's ethical dimension. With respect to nostalgia as symptomatic of collective and individual memory in late modernity—and in light of the texts under consideration here—the most significant affective state would seem to be mourning. "One becomes aware of the collective frameworks of memories when one distances oneself from one's community or when that community itself enters the moment of twilight. Collective frameworks of memory are rediscovered in mourning" (55). This is certainly true of a text such as *Austerlitz*, which combines a preoccupation with memory, mourning, and, to a certain extent, melodrama in a unique manner, as will be explored in the coda. And, as suggested in previous chapters, it is Sebald who, in intertextualizing Nabokov, shifts the latter's mnemonic poetics into the key of mourning, emphasizing the more sober side of reflective nostalgia.

In both *Vertigo* and *The Emigrants* Sebald, in his more Kafkan mode, resists the Nabokovian resort to an ironically metafictional solution. Nevertheless, the later novel offers a subtly but significantly different response to the possibility of redemption held out to the victim of traumatic memory—a possibility embodied in what a Nabokovian fictional poetics presents as memory's collapsing of spatiotemporal depth. In *Austerlitz* Sebald weaves a narrative that is concerned in part with the representation of a particular subjectivity coming into a new, more deeply negative and therefore ironic, self-awareness through memory. This is accomplished, though, only after the protagonist has worked through and eventually abandoned a model of time figured subjectively, based in (generally) spatial metaphors of memory; metaphors whose figurative status is lost, folded into the erstwhile virtual reality of represented space transformed by the enormous pressure exerted by the past upon the present. This is accomplished in the book by means of what I call the chronotope of memory: a specific spatiotemporal relation within the text in which Austerlitz encounters an actual three-dimensional space in which (for him, at least) time has stopped, both literally and metaphorically; a space in which epistemology and eschatology are indistinguishable, in the sense that any afterlife is coterminous with this life, and that any possible salvation lies elsewhere, back in the past or ahead in the future, but never here.

Chapter 7

"One Is Always at Home in One's Past"

Austerlitz and *The View from Castle Rock*

A story, a poem, a history, a life, a river: "Meneseteung" becomes
all things female, all things generative, all things that can never
be absolute.
> —Pam Houston, "A Hopeful Sign: The Making of
> Metonymic Meaning in Munro's 'Meneseteung'"

Longing and critical thinking are not opposed to one another,
as affective memories do not absolve one from compassion,
judgment or critical reflection.
> —Svetlana Boym, *The Future of Nostalgia*

Introduction: "Something like Stories"

Sebald's presentation of the subject of memory *subjected by memory* exemplifies a more radically modernist—or postmodernist—outlook than a predecessor such as Nabokov or Kafka. Nevertheless, he does not go as far toward a deconstruction of subjectivity via the relentless excavation of language as in Beckett or Thomas Bernhard, for instance—or, for that matter, as Claudio Magris does in a novel such as *Blindly*. Like Nabokov's, Sebald's protagonists move through geographies of memory, history, and imagination whose metaphysical laws are those of a discursively constituted consciousness. The representation of this consciousness, however, is inflected by a self-reflexive oscillation between a melancholic-nostalgic affectivity and a critical perspective upon the same. Sebald's particular later twentieth-century, ironically elegiac tonality, which sets him apart stylistically from either the ironic despair one finds in Beckett or Kafka or the contrastingly positive self-awareness of Nabokov, aligns him with another contemporary writer with whom he is rarely, if ever, compared: Canadian author Alice Munro.[1] All three works discussed in this chapter—*Speak, Memory, Austerlitz*, and Munro's *The View from Castle Rock*—are, however, linked on the broad thematic level insofar as each exploits the conventions of (auto)biography in a narrative of emigration and the formation of a certain kind of diasporic identity. (It should be noted at the outset that the difference between fiction and fact in this context is irrelevant; on the level of affectively charged memory and its value for the narrative it makes no difference that "Austerlitz" is a fictional composite while "Nabokov" and "Munro" are avatars of actual historical personages.)

In the words of tenth Canadian prime minister William Lyon Mackenzie, countries such as England, Germany, and Russia have "too much history," while Canada (at least in 1936, when Mackenzie gave his speech in the House of Commons), has "too much geography" (Duffy 2010, 197). This may in part account for the very different manner in which Munro marshals specific chronotopes in her work in order to represent the experience of growing up and making a life in highly particularized regions of Canada's vast and multifarious landscape.[2] In her 2006 story cycle *The View from Castle Rock*, Munro offers an alternative vision of the intersection of time and space in a geographically and geologically specific revisioning of Bakhtin's chronotope. As in Sebald and Nabokov, the chronotope in Munro is a textual-discursive construct signifying a specific diegetic time and place. The difference is that, rather than a bourgeois or aristocratic space or setting, in her Ontario-set stories Munro tends to focus on domestic interiors (and exteriors) of a distinctly rural or lower class, coupled with a very different relation to nature, or "Nature." The latter functions with comparable significance in the determination of a very different narrative subject. Of principal interest here, however, alongside Munro's use of specific Scots-Presbyterian cultural materials, is her distinctive approach to representing landscape in relation to the significance of memory as a ground of subjectivity. Like Magris, Munro represents another instance of a writer who takes Sebald's arguments on history and eschatology a step further from his liminal position between modernism and postmodernism.

Despite his death in the Soviet Union in 1975, and his close subsequent association with certain tenets of poststructuralist theory in its 1980s heyday, Mikhail Bakhtin anticipated many of contemporary critical theory's abiding preoccupations, most notably certain fundamental aspects of what is known as the new materialism in literary studies. I refer, for example, to his insistence on a language-centered, anti-psychologistic and intersubjective dialogical theory of literary discourse, his notion of carnival with its quasi-Eucharistic emphasis on the body's immanence in popular culture, and the concept of the chronotope. As Alastair Renfrew (2014, 122) puts it, "The theory of the chronotope is more than an attempt to concretize literary time; it is an attempt to conceive of history itself in concrete and material terms, but without effacing the value and importance of the particular that such an ostensible generalization might imply." In comparison with either Sebald or Nabokov, Munro's style comes the closest to a kind of realism conceived in terms of the early twentieth-century European novel, but looking back especially to the command of free indirect style one finds in Jane Austen.[3] Ironically, of course, Munro's fame rests on her mastery of not the novel but the short story.

Unlike Sebald and Nabokov, there is no comparable relationship of influence between Sebald and Munro, apart from the thematic and structural one I elaborate here. Nonetheless, all three writers are engaged in comparable projects of "writing the self," whether fictional, factual, or something in between. *The View from Castle Rock* exemplifies what Robert Thacker (2008, 134) pinpoints as the signal shift in the focus of Munro's fictions after 1973, when she moved back to Ontario's Huron County from Vancouver, British Columbia.[4] This shift toward a "research-based" approach to writing fiction was instigated "by Munro's imaginative confrontation with the legacies of her family inheritances, seen in a new light by the changed perspective brought about by her return to Ontario, a recognized writer in her early forties" (134). Beginning in the mid-1970s, Munro draws on not only the imaginative reworking of material in her own memory but also historical materials unearthed in archives and on research trips (136).[5] Indeed, *Castle Rock* quietly challenges generic convention, blending "fiction, personal experience, and historical reconstruction" (Duffy 2010, 199).[6] Munro's symbolic *ritorno in patria* at the outset of *Castle Rock* could not be much further from Sebald's fictionalized account of his return to "W" in the fourth part of *Vertigo*. Munro undertakes this research trip to Ettrick on the Scottish borderlands in order to verify or debunk her archival research: "The old country is a matter of belief and unbelief, recovered only via correspondence with the 'stored knowledge' of texts" (Hames 2012, 75). One of the results of this change in Munro's approach, if not its motivation, is a unique contribution to the long-standing effort in Canadian literature "to construct a national imaginary" (73). Yet Munro's achievement lies precisely in her avoidance of anything like a conventional allegory of national identity. According to Duffy (2010, 201), this is in part attributable to her rewriting of the (masculinist) genre of historical fiction:

> From the forefather [Sir Walter] Scott onward, the historical novel as he and others following him conceived it strove for two goals. First, it sought to fabricate a continuous and teleological narrative out of the chaos of the perceivable past. Then, it aimed at propelling that narrative toward both the completion of a private romantic quest, and toward discernment of a historically progressive movement (often conceived as a moment in a national genesis).

By tracing her Scottish ancestors' journey to southwestern Ontario and laying the ground for a renewed exploration of her formation as a particular kind of woman, Munro traces "the problem of Canadian identity 'elsewhere', along settler folkways which bypass the influence of the United States" (Hames 2012, 73).[7] Across *Castle Rock*'s twelve interconnected stories, Munro exploits the transition from the subjectively grounded fabulations of her Scottish ancestors to ever more factually grounded narratives of uprooting, emigration, and

the establishment of new lives in a new land. Within the space of five generations of her father's side of the family tree, *Castle Rock*'s stories track the shift
from a culturally specific worldview rooted in Scottish folk and fairy tales to
one based in an increasingly objective and transhuman frame of reference.
This gradually opens out, across the final stories, into a radically expansive
vision of history understood in terms of geological time, an account of her
own emergence as unique mid-twentieth-century feminine subject against this
grand sweeping backdrop of the history of the very land in which such stories
unfold. Here Munro is on the way to elaborating by example a kind of posthumanist subjectivity (in Rosi Braidotti's postfeminist sense[8]) that contrasts in
mutually revealing ways with the Sebaldian subject traced across the latter's
four prose works. As the previous chapters imply, Sebald's masculine subject
instantiates itself in the gap between an older, Humanist model of subjectivity
and newer, more progressive avatars of selfhood, as exemplified in Munro.
The in-between and epigonal quality of the Sebaldian subject conditions its
mournful, melancholic, and yet ironical character, insofar as it is constituted
by a dualistic and affectively complex perspective: on the one hand, toward
the past in a combination of nostalgic regret and the melancholic desire for
oblivion and, on the other, toward the future in a kind of anxious resigna-
tion. The latter marks Sebald as a Nietzsche- or Cassandra-like critic of his
times, the predictive dimension of his memory-work sounding less and less
like the ranting of an eloquent curmudgeon and increasingly like a prescient
warning about a near-future that is now the present, a warning that, for the
most part, continues to go unheeded. This comparison, it goes without saying,
also points up the significance of gender in either writer's fictive staging of
subjectivity in relation to space/place and time.

In this chapter I read the chronotopes of memory in *Castle Rock* in the
broader comparative context represented by Nabokov and Sebald, partly in
order to broach a critique of the new materialist tendency in the humanities
and social sciences. Across this text Munro traces the history of her family as
it emigrates from Scotland in 1818, working her way forward to her parents' and, finally, her own story. The dominant voice throughout is that of the
author-narrator, however. In the final chapters Munro shifts focus from fictionalized history and thinly veiled memoir to the vast expanse of geological time,
acknowledging the relative inconsequentiality of the human in the unfolding of
elementary and fundamental forces, even as a space is opened up for a new, more
tempered notion of "posthuman" selfhood that privileges neither consciousness
nor subjectivity in any traditional sense. The "self" in *Castle Rock* is predicated
rather upon the dynamic and dialogic relation between and among historical,
autobiographical, geological, and cosmic perspectives. These are themselves
subordinated, however, to a narrative discourse in which "storytelling" is the
primary mediating and organizing structure and in which all such tempo-
ralities, spaces, and subjectivities—in short, such chronotopes—are always
already mediated, materialized, by voice, discourse, textuality, language. *The*

View from Castle Rock not only manifests literary chronotopes specific to this historical epoch—beginning with the ironically overdetermined vantage point identified in the title[9]—but also demonstrates that the current new materialist epoch is itself a specific historico-ideological chronotope critically and self-reflexively embodied in the text.[10] It is in terms of memory, however, that Munro's text's implicit critique of the new materialist paradigm becomes apparent. For, whatever contemporary memory science might say about memory or recollection being a series of biochemical or neurological processes, the fact remains that the content and the form of memory in literature continue to be a matter of narrative schemata, more commonly known as *stories*, which is precisely Munro's jumping-off point. Describing the intersection of family history and personal memoir, "these are stories," she writes (2006a, xx), that, in objectified, externalized, *material* form, remain susceptible to reproduction, appropriation, and commodification (see also 204, 259). Attitudes to the value of storytelling vary from her ancestor Margaret Laidlaw, angered at her decision to allow her son, James Hogg, to let Walter Scott produce a collection of her traditional ballads "which had never been written down" (17)—"'They were made for singin' and no for prentin', she is supposed to have said. 'And noo they'll never be sung mair'" 17)—to Walter Laidlaw's concern on the boat to Canada that his journal of the voyage record only "what happens," so that he may write a letter home. He has no grander aspirations to preserve their story for posterity, let alone to commodify or rather to monetize it, in the manner of Scott's collection of border balladry (47). Munro's ancestors' aversion to print culture[11] is the ironic obverse of the fetishization of books and the subversive value of reading thematized throughout *Castle Rock* (e.g., 103, 158). Munro is acutely aware of this danger and spends much of the text examining its consequences for identity both personal and social. What new materialist approaches seem willing to overlook, ironically, is that if such interior processes as memory, dream, or emotion are to be rendered legible to others, they must be given material form: "In the literary-artistic *chronotope*, spatial and temporal indicators are fused into one carefully thought-out, concrete whole. Time, as it were, thickens, takes on flesh, becomes artistically visible; likewise, space becomes charged and responsive to the movements of time, plot and history. This intersection of axes and fusion of indicators characterizes the artistic chronotope" (Bakhtin 1981, 84).[12] Rather than representation as such, Bakhtin foregrounds the artistic stylization of oral language requisite for literary production and the irreducible alterity of language itself as dialogic interface, whether face-to-face or mediated in a text.

In the titular story "The View from Castle Rock," Munro quotes from an actual letter written by her great-great-great-grandfather James Laidlaw some years after his arrival with his family in Esquesing Township in Halton County, Ontario. Munro notes that she is able to cite this letter because it was reproduced in England in *The Colonial Advocate* newspaper in response to an earlier letter sent by Laidlaw to his son Robert back home in Scotland:

> Now sir I could tell you a bit of Stories but I am afraid you will put
> me in your Colonial Advocate I do not Like to be put in prent I once
> wrote a bit of a letter to my Son Robert in Scotland and my friend
> James Hogg the Poet put it in Blackwoods Magazine and had me all
> through North America before I knew my letter was gone Home . . .
> Hogg poor man has spent most of his life in conning Lies and if I read
> the Bible right I think it says that all Liars' is to have there pairt in the
> Lake that Burns with Fire and Brimstone . . . (2006a, 65)

"And I am surely one of the liars the old man talks about," adds Munro,
"in what I have written about the voyage. Except for Walter's journal, and
the letters, the story is full of my invention" (65). James's letter ironically
underlines the self-reflexive thematization of books and reading throughout
Castle Rock. But running alongside is the critique of the writer as liar, and as
salesman, one who sells stories appropriated and put into "prent" in order
to sell magazines and books: the *word* commodified. The implicit response is
the idea that stories, constituted by reified bits of experience mixed up with
wholly fabricated events, are necessarily objectified in order for such material
to find expression, to be communicated, shared, "given away," in Nabokov's
metaphor. But they—or their mnemic content—are also negated in the process. As Nabokov remarks at the outset of *Speak, Memory*'s fifth chapter,

> I have often noticed that after I bestowed on the characters of my
> novels some treasured item of my past, it would pine away in the
> artificial world where I had so abruptly placed it. Although it lin-
> gered on in my mind, its personal warmth, its retrospective appeal
> had gone and, presently, it became more closely identified with my
> novel than with my former self, where it had seemed to be so safe
> from the intrusion of the artist. Houses have crumbled in my memory
> as soundlessly as they did in the mute films of yore. (1989, 94)[13]

Here, the negation of "donated" memories takes the specific form of an
increasingly attenuated affective value. Munro's approach to these questions
in *Castle Rock* is similar but generally lacking the overt transmediation of
place and the preoccupation with ownership. As she writes in "Home" of a
visit to her childhood town, "The town, unlike the house, stays very much
the same—nobody is renovating or changing it. Nevertheless it has changed
for me. I have written about it and used it up. Here are more or less the same
banks and hardware and grocery stores and the barbershop and the Town
Hall tower, but all their secret, plentiful messages for me have drained away"
(239). Through the process of instantiating the objects of memory in writing,
place is revealed as an expression of self via memory. In each of these texts
there is some kind of stable self negotiating between the process of "giving
away" as the basis of creative production and the represented experience of

the human being's loss of memory—or rather of a specific mnemonic affective content, the emotional value of a given memory, which proves far less indelible than the memory image itself.

Reflective Nostalgia: Irony and Affect in Sebald, Nabokov, and Munro

Munro (2006a, xix–xx) elucidates her compositional principles in her preface: "I put all this material together over the years, and almost without my noticing what was happening, it began to shape itself, here and there, into something like stories. Some of the characters gave themselves to me in their own words, others rose out of their situations. Their words and my words, a curious re-creation of lives, in a given setting that was as truthful as our notion of the past can ever be." According to Munro, fictional "truth" = "stories" + "family history." If the critical orthodoxy is correct, Munro's literary project as a whole represents an approach to writing the self that is open-ended, flowing, ateological, a state of becoming rather than one of being. In Sebald, Nabokov, and Munro alike the principal function of the literary chronotope is to represent or capture both the appearance and the operation of memory. For all three, memory is theme, object, and aspect of her/his poetics. The chronotope therefore has the crucial function of concretizing—spatializing, materializing—each text's otherwise unique approach to a discursive imaging of the past. More than in other examples, these chronotopes exemplify Bakhtin's assertion that no chronotope is an inert narrative structure or building block. Rather, every chronotope is affectively charged, discursively constituting the subjective point of view of the author-narrator or character before connecting (in some cases) with the larger, objective, historical-cultural level of the story. The degree in which the social-collective is inflected (contaminated?) by the personal-individual affective level of memory is foregrounded in particular in the case of nostalgia. As Pam Cook (2005, 4) shows in her analysis of the transnational phenomenon of cinematic melodrama, *nostalgia* is a helpful term for understanding the affective relation of the self to time and place in any given narrative.

Nostalgia is still often invoked in popular discourse in a pejorative sense, a reputation that has influenced popular thinking about memory itself. "Memory is not commonly imagined as a site of possibility for progressive politics," writes Alison Landsberg (2003, 144). "More often, memory, particularly in the form of *nostalgia*, is condemned for its *solipsistic* nature, for its tendency to draw people into the past instead of the present." As with Sebald and Nabokov, Munro's approach to the representation of the subjective experience of time and memory is much more complex. Nostalgia's pejorative status belies its history, however, and its connection to the history of thinking about affect (in the form of emotions, sentiment, etc.) and the emergence of modern subjective interiority.

Nostalgia always implies emotion, and a major irony manifests itself when one considers Munro in the light of the contemporary affection for affect. After all, it is difficult to imagine a contemporary writer who is *less* sentimental, less given to giving in to overt emotionality or melodrama.[14] This feature of her prose is directly linked to the thematic preoccupation across the stories with books and reading versus storytelling. Moreover,

> because they have not been interrogated, assumptions about [the complex interplay of orality and print] have contributed to misreadings of Munro that categorize her as a writer of realism that is somehow both grim and nostalgic. The Scottish connection is important on a deeper level, one that ultimately aligns her not with that kind of realism but with what Mikhail Bakhtin has called "grotesque realism" . . . Her response to the Scottish experience enables her to resist even as she acknowledges the power of nostalgia." (Redekop 1999, 25)[15]

There is a deeper reason still for Munro's resistance to nostalgic sentiment in her approach to representing the complex interrelation of past and present in the subjective experience of memory. An allergy to the open display of emotion is encoded into Munro's discourse at the genetic level. By this I do not mean that there are no characters who display strong emotions in word or action, for this certainly does happen; rather, I mean that on the level of the narrative discourse itself Munro's default position is an ironic, laconic, even apotropaic style.[16] This is a formal response to the aspect of theme or content often remarked upon by critics, the legacy of Munro's Scottish Presbyterian background, which in *Castle Rock* she confronts and exploits more directly and more self-consciously than in any other work. This stylistic-thematic tendency is countered, balanced, or complemented by its opposite—the equally powerful interest displayed in her writing toward subjectivities that resist this model in the form of characters or personages such as her ancestors in the Ettrick Valley: "the sort of men who do not take easily to anonymity and quiet lives" (Munro 2006a, 16), and with whom she seems to feel a tacit solidarity in her literary self-fashioning.

It is a critical commonplace that mother-daughter relations occupy a central place in Munro's fictional universe. Since her 1968 debut, *Dance of the Happy Shades*, Munro's treatment of the mother figure is a paradigmatic instance of what can be called the sick and bedridden mother topos, another subset of the writer and her/his mother series, broached in chapter 6 in relation to the mother's death. Even though these stories were written long after the author's actual mother's death, the marked lack of a mournful or elegiac tone, or any related sentiment (not to speak of melodrama), is a consistent feature of Munro's treatment of this theme. At the same time, however, her handling of the mother figure represents the logical culmination of what can be called *Castle Rock*'s macronarrative, from its opening setting in a "primordial" Scottish Highlands several generations before the appearance in six of the twelve stories of either her mother and father or the quasi-autobiographical figure of Munro herself.

On the one hand, Munro's unsentimental treatment across her body of work of her mother's struggle with Parkinson's disease is the logical extension of anything resembling a conventional tone of recuperative nostalgia such as one detects in Nabokov's evocation of his "perfect" early childhood (1989, 24). On the other hand, it also evokes a diffuse yearning, such as that displayed by Austerlitz in his quest to recover the image of his lost mother. For Caitlin Charman (2012, 263), "the memoirs in *The View from Castle Rock* . . . illustrate Munro moving from sentimental, romantic notions of place, like those exemplified in 'Lying under the Apple Tree,' to what Svetlana Boym calls 'reflective nostalgia.'" According to Boym (2001, 41), "Longing might be what we share as human beings, but that doesn't prevent us from telling very different stories of belonging and nonbelonging . . . two kinds of nostalgia characterize one's relationship to the past, to the imagined community, to home, to one's self-perception: restorative and reflective." Boym's nuanced delineation of nostalgia along reflective and restorative axes illuminates a reading of Munro in the context of Sebald and Nabokov as artists of memory. The "two kinds of nostalgia are not absolute types, but rather tendencies, ways of giving shape and meaning to longing. Restorative nostalgia puts emphasis on *nostos* and proposes to rebuild the lost home and patch up the memory gaps. Reflective nostalgia dwells in *algia*, in longing and loss, the imperfect process of remembrance" (Boym 2001, 4). There is thus to restorative nostalgia an uncritical naïveté that is missing from the reflective kind; the former, restorative, is thereby a constitutive feature of many contemporary popular cultural narratives. Rather than a historical consciousness that might allow for individually and socially progressive political action, therefore, postmodern pop culture gives us collective memory as often as not packaged in nostalgic terms:[17]

> Restoration . . . signifies a return to the original stasis, to the prelapsarian moment. The past for the restorative nostalgic is a value for the present; the past is not a duration but a perfect snapshot. Moreover, the past is not supposed to reveal any signs of decay; it has to be freshly painted in its "original image" and remain eternally young. Reflective nostalgia is more concerned with historical and individual time, with the irrevocability of the past and human finitude. Restorative nostalgia evokes national past and future; reflective nostalgia is more about individual and cultural memory. The two might overlap in their frames of reference, but they do not coincide in their narratives and plots of identity . . . Nostalgia of the first type gravitates toward collective pictorial symbols and oral culture. Nostalgia of the second type is more oriented toward an individual narrative that savors

details and memorial signs, perpetually deferring homecoming itself. Restorative nostalgia ends up reconstructing emblems and rituals of home and homeland in an attempt to conquer and spatialize time, reflective nostalgia cherishes shattered fragments of memory and temporalizes space. Restorative nostalgia takes itself dead seriously. Reflective nostalgia, on the other hand, can be ironic and humorous. It reveals that longing and critical thinking are not opposed to one another, as affective memories do not absolve one from compassion, judgment or critical reflection. (49–50)

In this distinction Boym articulates a theory of affectively charged recollection that, in different ways, informs each author's engagement with memory. The work of Sebald and Munro is nostalgic to the degree that it reflects critically upon the operation and affective impact of subjective memory upon the subject's relation to a past (time) and place (home) that is either beyond recovery (Sebald/Austerlitz) or, while recoverable, drained of value (Munro). For Nabokov, by contrast, "one is always at home in one's past" (1989, 116). As for Austerlitz, at first lacking any knowledge of his real parents—who, unlike Nabokov's, failed to leave in time—for most of his life he has no home to return to and therefore no coherent identity. Austerlitz's identity in the decades before he meets the narrator is grounded in what Michael Wood (1994, 95) calls "homelessness understood not as a banishment from an old domain but as a forlorn quest for what cannot possibly be found." As in *Speak, Memory*'s self-portrait, *Austerlitz* resists, or rather is denied, the easy compensations of either patriotism or nostalgia of the "restorative" variety. This denial takes place both intra- and extradiegetically, the protagonist's psychoemotional trauma informing the basic narrative logic of his story, as recounted at second and third hand, by the narrator. Although it would be wrong to claim that Austerlitz is prone to any conventional form of "nostalgia," as observed he does ponder the desirability of "spatialized time" (e.g., Sebald 2001, 136). To "spatialize time" is to negate time as conventionally understood, and yet there is no other way to represent time cinematically, for instance. The chronotope, as noted, gives a name to the very different manner in which space and time manifest in literature.

According to Boym (2001, 50), "nostalgics of the [reflective] type are aware of the gap between identity and resemblance; the home is in ruins or, on the contrary, had been just renovated and gentrified beyond recognition." This idea is exemplified in Munro's story "Home" when the protagonist, returned to her childhood home to see her elderly father, who is in the hospital for a bad heart, is led to a small epiphany of memory when she later reflects upon the fact that being back in the barn made her feel uneasy if only because the "very corner of the stable" where she had been spreading hay, and where "the beginning of panic" came on her, was "the scene of the first clear memory" of her life:

> In the scene I remember I am sitting on the first or second step watching my father milk the black-and-white cow. I know what year it was—the black-and-white cow died of pneumonia in the worst winter of my childhood, which was in 1935. Such an expensive loss is not hard to remember.
>
> And since the cow is still alive and I am wearing warm clothes, a woolen coat, and leggings, and at milking time it is already dark . . . it is probably the late fall or early winter. Maybe it was still 1934. Just before the brunt of the season hit us. (Munro 2006a, 250)

As in *Austerlitz*, the weather chimes with the emotional tenor of the remembered scene, although in Munro there is even more attention to the rhythms of the seasons as the protagonist in the book's second half grows up, like Munro, on a southern Ontario farm. As her "first clear memory," which moreover causes her present self to experience a sense of "panic," this account contrasts starkly with Nabokov's description of his first clear memory-image of himself as distinct from his parents, coextensive with the awakening of his awareness of time (1989, 21). While Munro shares with Nabokov the keen eye of retrospective recall, with particular attention to visual detail, this scene of stable and cow in winter exemplifies the chronotopic function of memory in Munro's narrative. From a position in the present the narrator recalls the earlier memory by first recognizing that in the intervening period, during her father's illness, her intermediate self was spreading hay in "the very corner of the stable" that was the scene of her earliest remembered experience. In cinematic fashion, as in Ingmar Bergman's *Wild Strawberries* (1957), for instance, the protagonist suddenly finds herself in the very location in which some significant event or formative experience occurred many years before.[18] And it is not only her affective state but also her *disposition* or bodily attitude—the manual labor in which she is engaged—that trigger the memory, recollected in tranquility at two removes: at first she merely experiences anxiety, a kind of "panic attack"; only some years later, at the time of writing, does she recall the memory in full. The Proustian complexity of the recollective structure here—present self recalls intermediate self suddenly recalling past self—aligns with the model of embodied memory that Deleuze adapts from Henri Bergson, which is behind the former's concept of the "affection-image," and which in turn inspired Brian Massumi's version of affect theory.

Where Munro's is presented as a quasi-Proustian epiphany, arising as it were involuntarily via the subject's senses and bodily disposition, Nabokov's purportedly earliest memory is presented in overtly mediated form, the result of conscious "probing" (1989, 21). There is the usual close attention to sensory detail, the establishment of a specific season (late summer) and location (the countryside), but the description quickly transforms into a typical Nabokovian chronotope, combining acute mnemonic detail with a personalized philosophical lesson: "I felt myself plunged abruptly into a radiant and mobile medium that was none other than the pure element of time . . . an environment quite different from the spatial world, which not only man but apes and butterflies can perceive . . . Indeed, from my present ridge of remote, isolated, almost uninhabited time, I see myself as celebrating, on that August day 1903, the birth of sentient life" (21–22). The passage ends with the clear privileging of time as the medium of quasi-infinite consciousness—they are virtually coterminous—and (second-class) space as the medium of bodies in all their finite limitations. But Nabokov doesn't stop here; as noted in the previous chapter, in his copy of *Speak, Memory* Sebald underlines the first line in the following passage: "I confess I do not believe in time. I like to fold my magic carpet, after use, in such a way as to superimpose one part of the pattern upon another. Let visitors trip" (1989, 139 [1987, 109]). Nabokov calls this state "timelessness," which can lead to a peculiar brand of "ecstasy," a kind of unabashedly utopian aestheticization of time through memory. He refines this idea further in *Strong Opinions*:

> I would say that imagination is a form of memory. Down, Plato, down, good dog. An image depends on the power of association, and association is supplied and prompted by memory. When we speak of a vivid individual recollection we are paying a compliment not to our capacity of retention but to Mnemosyne's mysterious foresight in having stored up this or that element which creative imagination may want to use when combining it with later recollections and inventions. In this sense, both memory and imagination are a negation of time. (1973, 78)

This would seem to be what he means by not believing in time. Paradoxically, time, as the medium of consciousness, is transcended, trumped, by memory and the vivid and indelible images it grants the fortunate mortal. Munro's memory-image chronotope, by contrast, is determined spatially as much as temporally, although it must be acknowledged that any gender-based conclusions one might draw about the different operations of memory in differently gendered subjects are always already culturally determined. (The same holds for socioeconomic difference: "Such an expensive loss is not hard to remember," admits Munro.) More specifically, it is the case that Nabokov's memory is reconstructed at an uncrossable distance in time, whereas Munro's memory is rooted in a specific concrete location, precisely because in the interim she was able to travel back to her family home and he was not. The example of *Austerlitz* shows, however, that such privileged access to the actual sites of past experience, whether remembered or not, is a much more fraught and complex process than might first appear.

In previous chapters I have discussed what I call Nabokov's art of mnemic divestment—the dialectic of memory and forgetting, giving away the "gifts" of memory—as his memoir's *non*fictional poetics. As he "gives away" discursively, as his memory is as it were depleted, the memoir grows; the "natural" archive is sacrificed to build the artificial. In a sense, memory cannot function without this more or less deliberate casting off of the objects, the "precious stones," of memory; *apomnesis* (unremembering) contrasts with mere forgetting, insofar as these objects or attributes are not lost to oblivion but transformed, transmediated (see Nabokov 1989, 24). This compares revealingly with Munro's approach to writing fiction and the peculiar relation to the past constituted in *Castle Rock*.

For Munro memory is always a visual-spatial construct, inflected by historical and cultural conventions of gender identity. In a 1987 interview she admits that when she "came back to live in Huron County, I thought I had written it out. I didn't intend to write any more about it" (Hancock 1987, 206). But the same logic applies in the other direction; Munro admits that she is blessed—or cursed—with a capacious memory:

> I remember everything. I'm oppressed by it. A huge baggage of memories.[19] I remember all this stuff about West Vancouver, where I lived when my children were growing up, that I haven't used. Sometimes I get a housewifely sense of needing to use all those scraps that are in the attic. When I feel this so vividly and can see it, can see the whole texture of that life. I haven't done much with it. I will never, never run out of things to write about, And I never have to search for a visual detail or for the way people talk or look or anything like that. (Hancock 1987, 207)

In the story "Home," in fact, Munro's narrator makes explicit the link between place and self that is also a kind of governing principle in Nabokov's memoir. In the story's opening she is visiting her aging father and his second wife in the house in which she grew up and in which they still live. Her father has modernized the house (this is a recollection of a visit in the 1970s), and he anticipates her nostalgic disappointment: "'I know how you love this place,' he says to me, apologetically yet with satisfaction. And I don't tell him that I'm not sure now whether I love any place, and that it seems to me it was myself that I loved here—some self that I have finished with, and none too soon" (231).

The link between "home" as a concrete place, whether in the present or in the form of a memory-image, and the discursively constituted self, is longstanding in Munro. In the 1987 interview, for instance, she remarks, "When I look at a house, its like looking at a person" (Hancock 1987, 211), as if to suggest that the more impersonal or third-person "house" is distinct from the "home" in its identification with self, a virtual chronotope of selfhood. The narrator of "Home" puts it this way: "For a long time, I lived more than a thousand miles away and would go for years without seeing this house. I thought of it then as a place I might never see again and I was greatly moved by the memory of it. I would walk through its rooms in my mind" (Munro

2006a, 229). The narrator recalls how, in the not-too-distant past, she would move through the virtual spaces of her childhood home within the encompassing spaces of her memory, not unlike Saint Augustine, in *Confessions*, book 10, as he imagines himself—or his mnemic avatar—strolling around in the vast precincts of his memory, meeting up with people and objects from his past.[20] Over the centuries, as technologies of literacy developed, the need for such powers of memory receded as artificially enhanced "natural" memory gave way to external technological-prosthetic supports. But the idea of memory as a vast space, a memory theater or palace, was too powerful to disappear altogether, lingering on into the modern period as one of the most persistent metaphors for human memory as a three-dimensional space, as part of the self's internal architecture. It goes without saying that this continues to be a productive model for creative writers and filmmakers alike. According to the dominant visual-cultural theory, this is the ontologized visual-spatial structure predicated on the represented spaces of Western painting since the Renaissance, viewed from an ideal subject position, as if through a transparent window or screen. This is the position of *visual* (if not material) mastery at the basis of Mary-Louise Pratt's "monarch-of-all-I-survey" view that underpins the colonialist subject (see Zilcosky 2003, 27).[21] More prosaically, this visual structure sustains the illusion of three-dimensional Cartesian space in relation to which and within which an all-knowing, rational, all-seeing subject—the subject of "Western" art history and capitalism alike—is ideally constituted as the ground of a realist aesthetic.[22] This is the subject that has subtended occidental culture for some five hundred years, and while Sebald in *Austerlitz* performs a quietly powerful critique of this structure, Munro's treatment of this key aspect of literary realism appears even more radical. In this context, forgetting, or oblivion, whether willful or not, is revealed in all its dangers. For to desire the destruction of the past, especially in terms of its physical or virtual spaces, is to be complicit in the historical forces that hinder the preservation of such spaces, which is to forestall the eternal return of the same.

In literature, according to Bakhtin (1981, 85), the primary category in the chronotope is not space but *time*: "The chronotope as a formally constitutive category determines to a significant degree the image of man [*sic*] in literature as well. The image of man is always intrinsically chronotopic." Following Bakhtin's logic, then, and leaving the issue of linguistic difference to one side, it would appear that the "image of man," or of the human person, and the subject that underpins it, in Anglophone Canadian literature, is fundamentally similar to its image, for instance, in much German-language fiction, even as this chronotopic dimension acquires a distinctive form in Munro's short stories. But the history of feminist critical theory, not to speak of the legacy of Munro's body of work, suggests that the situation is more complicated. The "strongly physical image of the body in a landscape where a personal sense of identity is grounded in a specific geographic location, is one of the hallmarks of Alice Munro's fiction" (Howells 2004, 5). The major difference in Munro, it goes without saying—apart from culture and geography—is that the gender of this subject becomes its defining attribute. In fact, gender enters into the discussion here far more explicitly as a result—not as essentialist category, to be sure, but as a crucial attribute or aspect of identity that colors or even determines the subject's relation to structures of power and the assignation of meaning vis-à-vis the means of representation—the chronotopic "image of man."

Calvinist Identities: "Of that which we cannot speak . . ."

In "No Advantages," the first story in *Castle Rock*, Munro expresses her surprise that her ancestor Will O'Phaup, "a near pagan, merry man, a brandy drinker . . . one who believes in the fairies, is bound to have listened to, and believed in, the strictures and hard hopes of [the] punishing Calvinist faith" preached by Thomas Boston, the Presbyterian minister in Ettrick at the time (12). "The past is full of contradictions and complications, perhaps equal to those of the present, though we do not usually think so" (14). Both Sebald and Munro, in a highly meaningful coincidence, take pains to establish a viable historical-cultural matrix for the contemporary subjective temperament that is their ultimate focus: a subject that has internalized and thereby secularized the Presbyterian emphasis upon keeping one's troubles to oneself, a kind of constitutive quasi-conscious repression whose origins predate Freudianism by at least two centuries.[23] The persistent tension in *Castle Rock* "between fantasy and repression . . . becomes Munro's Scottish birthright, a pair of genealogical imperatives that simultaneously broaden and limit the possibilities of her position as a writer in Canada" (Bernstein 2014, 189). Stephen Bernstein identifies the long-running theme in Munro's work of the impact upon the self's formation of a "communal disapproval of imaginative writing and other suspicious forms of attention-seeking, in favor of useful work" (189). "This sense of disapproval and limitation is an integral facet" of her stories and is not limited to *Castle Rock*, in which "these familiar forms of inhibition"—"learning, speaking, writing, and performing"—"emerge as distinctly Scottish phenomena" (191). Most relevant here is Bernstein's argument that this "problem with attention seeking," especially with respect to the question of the 'utility' of writing, is both implicitly gendered and connected with Munro's diasporic Scottish heritage (192).

Austerlitz's ironic resemblance to Ludwig Wittgenstein (e.g., Sebald 2001, 7, 40–41) is strangely motivated by the unspoken significance in the protagonist's protracted account of his life of the Austrian philosopher's Proposition 7: *Wovon man nicht sprechen kann, darüber muss man schweigen* (Of that which one cannot speak, one must remain silent). This rigorous precept also informs Munro's account of her and her family's past in *Castle Rock*. Munro extrapolates this Protestant logic of rigorous verbal-rhetorical self-control to a poetics she refines over decades of story writing. The irony is that her increasingly restrained, paratactic, pared-down style is often at odds with her protagonists' desire to express themselves as honestly as possible, even if this generally goes against prevailing social and familial norms of behavior. The title of the 1978 collection, *Who Do You Think You Are?*[24] is emblematic of this stylistic-thematic tendency.

Invoking the chronotope as an analytical tool prompts a negotiation between the verbal-discursive and the realist-mimetic axes of the text. Each of these is, of course, a dimension or expression of its materiality. *Austerlitz* and *Castle Rock* are connected in their comparable valuation of speech, the oral dimension of human relationships—at one or more removes. This is not to say, however, that both authors approach the literary-oral relation in the same manner. Munro's discourse has been characterized as a kind of "orature,"[25] which it is, but only in the sense that her stories exemplify the condition of fictional texts characterized by the stylization, or better the transmediation, of oral discourse by the written word within the broader context of print culture. Any literary genre that depends on character (voice, point of view) displays this feature to some degree.[26] By comparison, the narrative discourse in Sebald's text could not be much more self-consciously literary or "written"—largely the effect of its embedded or "periscopic" structure. It is also the case, however, that Austerlitz derives consolation in the recounting of his life to the narrator, in a kind of talking cure, despite the fact that it takes him thirty-odd years to relate his story, which remains, to be sure, unfinished, *unerzählt*. This is a literal "disburdening" of self: where Nabokov and Munro, respectively, give away or use up the contents of their memories, with no auditor "embodied" in the respective diegetic worlds, Austerlitz (within the book's fictional world) off-loads his life story, including a sizable archive of photographs, onto the narrator, who—insofar as he elides with the author, "Sebald"—transmediates this content in the form of the book we are reading. As with the others, a narrative is produced, but, unlike them, at the same time the subject is gradually reduced, eventually disappearing from the story altogether. This talking cure reaches its ironic apogee at the point when Austerlitz relates how he discovers H. G. Adler's massive tome, launching into a single unbroken five-page sentence in which he logorrhoically enumerates for his auditor the infernally simulacral world of Theresienstadt (Sebald 2001, 236–44).

The peculiar nature of this "talking cure" can be traced back to Austerlitz's past, his childhood and upbringing in Wales, to what he reveals of his foster parents and of the world in which he grew up. In the wake of the *Kindertransport* that took him out of his Czech-Jewish childhood, Austerlitz's stepparents are Calvinist Methodist, a Welsh version of the Presbyterianism that was the major form of Protestantism in England and Scotland (outside the Anglican Church) from the seventeenth to the twentieth century. This aspect of Austerlitz's character connects on the cultural-historical level to Munro's account of her ancestors leaving Scotland for Ontario in the early nineteenth century and to their subsequent moral-ethical or "spiritual" development thereafter. In the first story, "No Advantages," which is also the first chronologically, Munro reconstructs everyday life in the part of the Scottish Highlands from which her father's family emigrated in the early nineteenth century: "Every Presbyterian home in Scotland was meant to be a pious home. Constant investigations of private life and tortured reshapings of the faith went on to take care of that. There was no balm of ritual, no elegance of ceremony. Prayer was not only formal but personal, agonized. The readiness of the soul for eternal life was always in doubt and danger" (Munro 2006a, 12). By the time of the Laidlaws' emigration to North America in 1818, this "agonized" internalized faith had turned into a way of relating to others and to the world, and of bearing life's vicissitudes, a kind of secular Presbyterian stoicism. In the story "Illinois," for instance, which begins outside Chicago in the years 1839 to 1840, Andrew Laidlaw arrives in the spring following the midwinter death of his brother William. When Mary, William's widow, remarks that one of her sons is still upset over his father's death, Andrew replies that "there'd been time to get over it by now" (71), suggesting an attitude toward death and mourning equivalent to that exhibited by Elias and Gwendolyn, Austerlitz's Welsh foster parents, who exemplify the Calvinist-Methodist tendency to avoid any overt emotional display apart from righteous anger, keeping all pent up inside oneself.[27] But Andrew's laconic stoicism contrasts sharply with the almost parodically Gothic climate that prevails in Austerlitz's account of his Welsh childhood. The affective disposition manifest in "Illinois" finds its objective correlative in the protagonist's account of Gwendolyn's death in the midst of a winter so cold that the entire country of Wales "came to a standstill" (Sebald 2001, 64–65). It is as if the whole of Nature mirrored the prematurely dark and silent spiritual world into which Elias and his dying wife had permanently descended, a death-within-life, outside time. "What was it that so darkened our world?," she asks her husband 64–65), and after Gwendolyn dies it is as if "the unhappiness building up inside" Elias for so long "had destroyed his faith just when he needed it most" (65). This pseudo-Gothic despair translates historically in *Castle Rock* into the moral-ethical straitjacket worn by the first Scotts-Irish settlers, of whom Munro's father remarks, "The nerve it took, to pick up and cross the ocean. What was it squashed their spirits? So soon" (99). This aspect of the story also aligns thematically with Munro's ironically laconic, even apotropaic, late style.

The New World–Old World distinction in setting is the key to this difference between the two texts. As Munro's "Illinois" shows, one of the less obvious but most significant alterations in daily life that occurs in the wake of emigration from Calvinist Scotland to the American Midwest and what would become southern Ontario is the shift from a world in which if not religion then some sort of "spirituality" is replaced by a New World materialism.[28] In Munro's characteristic free indirect style we learn that "one thing there was no word of here was religion—unless you wanted to count the revival meeting, and Mary did not. No fierce arguments about doctrine. No mention of ghosts or weird visitors, as in the old days in Ettrick. Here it was all down-to-earth, it was all about what you could find and do and understand about the real world under your feet" (65–66). Ironically, in the later, present-day stories, the narrator comes to her own, wholly different understanding of "the 'real world' under her feet"—a "real world" that transforms the objective expression of a still-Romantic self (e.g., "Lying under the Apple Tree") into the wholly nonhuman materiality of a landscape forged by forces across a period beyond human comprehension.

The principal effect of Munro's focus on Scottish Presbyterianism in *Castle Rock*—not to speak of its palpable thematic presence going back to the 1970s stories—comes down to the importance of Scottish Reformation history to Munro's literary exploration of place and self.[29] Here the secularizing and modernizing impact of the Reformation combines with the lingering effects of Calvinism in the form of specific values, including "fortitude, self-reliance, hard work" (Munro 2006a, 99)—not to mention increased literacy rates and (despite Calvinism's otherwise conservative nature) an attitude of skeptical suspicion toward authority and pretense alike. These values or beliefs, as Somacarrera (2015, 105) argues, are in Munro systematically disconnected from their metaphysical counterparts in the main points of Calvinist doctrine: "predestination, salvation, and grace," which in *Castle Rock* (as in many other stories) come in only for ironic treatment. As an aspect of her quietly audacious approach to a critical literary feminism, Munro exploits the rhetorical logic of Scottish Calvinism in order to deconstruct its moral-ethical logic.

Conclusion: The Physiography of Memory

Munro's employment of the literary chronotope is at its most original in *Castle Rock*'s later stories, when she acknowledges the deep historical and geophysical dimensions of the southwestern Ontario landscape. Critics generally concur that Munro's turn to objective scientific knowledge of the landscape's geophysical formation over millennia seems to underline and amplify her treatment of character and theme. According to A. O. Scott, for instance, "the particular and varied features of the terrain can't help influencing the patterns of human behavior enacted upon it . . . The deep—one might say the geological—subject of her book is how the world changes, at a pace that is both glacial and ferocious, beyond all recognition, while still retaining traces of what came before" (Scott 2006, 2). For Adam Mars-Jones (2006, 2), "Munro refers to the 'glacial geography' of Canada and the existence of maps that show how the Ice Ages shaped the landscape. She is undertaking something similar on the level of culture, charting the remains and the permanent scouring effects of the retreating glacier known as Presbyterianism." According to Howells (2007, 166), the story "What Do You Want to Know For?" is "emblematic" of *Castle Rock* as a whole, insofar as it "include[s] the collective history of a locality as frame for a very personal narrative." But it becomes clear, with the publication of *Castle Rock*, and especially the above-named story, that Munro has moved on to an even more radical position vis-à-vis her artistic remediation of the landscape of the Canadian shield. "The landscape here is a record of ancient events, it was formed by the advancing, stationary, and retreating ice. The ice has staged its conquests and retreats here several times, withdrawing for the last time about fifteen thousand years ago. Quite recently, you might say. Quite recently now that I have got used to a certain way of reckoning history" (252–53). In this story Munro shifts to direct address, asking the reader rhetorically to look at the maps she and her second husband use on their drives along southern Ontario's back roads: "Look at just one map—a section of southern Ontario south of Georgian Bay. Roads. Towns and rivers appear . . . But look what else—patches of bright yellow, fresh green, battleship gray, and a darker mud gray, and a very pale gray . . . What is all this?" (253–54). This is a version of the natural world—"Nature"—about which Munro admits she did not learn in school or from books. Hers is an understanding of the landscape that affords her a "naïve and particular pleasure," derived from the use of special physiographic maps. This is a landscape whose only secrets are those of its own origins, which have nothing whatsoever to do with the immigrants that arrived here subsequently, including Munro's forebears, quickly spreading over the land, inadvertently framing even the unpopulated portions within a thoroughly human perspective. The latter is the perspective whose apotheosis is Sebald's "synoptic view": "Through this view from above, the traveler can gain a better sense of the land's specificities, his own point-of-view, and, finally, his 'self'" (Zilcosky 2003, 27). In her invocation of the physiographic maps Munro succeeds in suggesting a point of view on the landscape free of such hypostatized humanistic limitations.

And in fact by the book's epilogue, "Messenger," the narrative has pushed back to a more "human" sense of scale, both temporally and spatially, exchanging the vast, transhuman perspective of the previous story ("What Do You Want to Know For?") for a vantage point on the southwestern Ontario landscape that ironically echoes and updates for a North American context Sebald's critique in *The Rings of Saturn* of the "Torricelli-like emptiness" occasioned by the felling of large tracts of trees in England in the eighteenth century (Sebald 1998, 262–63): "The removal of so many of the fences, and of orchards and houses and barns seems to me to have had the effect of making the countryside look smaller, instead of larger—the way the space once occupied by a house looks astonishingly small, once you see only the foundation . . . As if you could see more then, though now you can see farther" (Munro 2006a, 274). This is the salient difference between them and us, between then and now: "then" there was less past and more space, nothing but possibility; "now" there is more past, but less space. Time is running out. And yet the writer's task, always futile, seems paradoxically even more crucial, for as always it is on the side of the living: "We can't resist this rifling around in the past, sifting the untrustworthy evidence, linking stray names and questionable dates and anecdotes together, hanging on to threads, insisting on being joined to dead people and therefore to life" (276). Much more than a justification of death, Munro's credo shows an awareness of the productivity of negation, connecting death not to oblivion but to an insatiable memory.

Coda

"In the Name of the Victims"

Memory, Redemption, Restitution

Pleasant it is, when over a great sea the winds trouble the
waters, to gaze from the shore upon another's great tribulation.

—Lucretius 2007 (II.1)

Introduction: The Literature of Modern Catastrophic Subjectivity

As observed in chapter 5, identity and agency are together the central preoccupation of modernist cultural exploration and perhaps modernity per se. But
such questions must be addressed in a moral-ethical framework in order for
their full significance to be appreciated. And as the contemporary resurgence
of identitarian politics at the level of popular discourse demonstrates, the
cultural mediation of identity remains a fundamental dimension of social-
political life. In other words, fictional narrative, especially in the form of the
novel, continues to play a crucial role in our navigation through the world
and the negotiation of our relations with others. But like any genre the novel
also addresses collective identities. Nevertheless, as the modern narrative form
par excellence the novel by definition can never fulfill the function of what
Jan Assmann (2006, 38) calls a *normative* sacred text, whose purpose is to
answer for a specific people in a specific cultural context the question, "What
do I do?"[1] As noted, the counterpart to the normative text's moral-ethical
role is the *formative* text, which answers the question, "Who am I?" (38)—a
question of far greater relevance to a postethical era. Kafka's "failure" to write
such a text for a secular age, for instance—one that anticipates the social
purpose of many modern novels—is compensated for by his many attempts
to do so. The modernist tradition that issues in Beckett's ironically postsecular
excavations of subjectivity is another approach to this question; his radically
apophatic stripping down of the self to nothing but a ceaselessly speaking
voice, however, precludes the kind of ethical and political engagement called
for in the twenty-first-century context. In sum, where modernist literature
at its most radical traced the self's dissolution, popular taste in the second
half of the twentieth century continued to demand literary and cinematic
narratives focused around a clearly defined subject. At the same time, the

contemporary equivalent of the late nineteenth-century realism exemplified in Conrad's novels continues to thrive despite a century or more of avant-garde formalist experimentation. It would seem that there is still a need for the kind of realism construed in terms of a fictional text's aesthetic mediation of an ethical stance toward the world. In the interval, the task of addressing a postsecular world through writing long-form fictional narrative has been taken up by numerous others, of whom Sebald, Magris, and Munro's recent contributions are among the more significant. I call this the literature of modern catastrophic subjectivity.

Some of the most artistically (if not politically) effective novels in the twentieth century have been books that were not written as novels. In his memoir, for instance, Vladimir Nabokov treats memory ultimately from his own perspective, or that of his past experience, which shaped who he was in the present of the 1960s as he sat composing the narrative of his life. This is no straightforwardly narcissistic exercise, however, since this focus on the self is predicated upon specific, vivid, and indelible mnemic images originating with his mother's deliberate instillation in him of a conscious art of memory, the better to shore up such vividly visual fragments against a future ruin resulting from the events in Russia and Europe after 1917, one of those dates that in retrospect is seen to constitute an absolute break with the past. As noted, however, the fact that Nabokov grounds his self-conscious account of his conscious coming-into-being in his relationships with both mother and father doesn't change the book's irreducible focus on the narrating I's quasi-transcendent point of view.

In comparison with Nabokov and Munro, Sebald might appear to be the most radical in his relation to memory, insofar as he manages to imagine himself into the discursively constituted mental-experiential-affective spaces of wholly other subjectivities—most extensively in *Austerlitz*, of course. This technique is already clearly in place in *The Emigrants*, however, especially in the Luisa Lanzberg sections of "Max Ferber," in which Sebald the author ventriloquizes Ferber's long-dead mother's memoirs, a fictional text whose paradoxical effect is to bring the reader face-to-face with one particular victim (before she became a victim) of modern European history. This is also achieved on a far grander scale in *Austerlitz*, but rather than the double shift in gender and ethno-cultural background entailed in Sebald's portrait of Lanzberg, in *Austerlitz* the emphasis is placed even more overtly on the character's Jewishness, with gender shunted aside, or rather transposed artistically onto the various female characters in the book: Agáta, Adela, Vera, and others—of which only Vera is revealed with comparable attention to her inner life as an ordinary, non-Jewish woman coping with the Holocaust's lasting impact on her life. In this respect, then, the effect in *Austerlitz* is not dissimilar to that of *Speak, Memory*, to the extent that the former also seems to subordinate an understanding of History per se, not to speak of Time "itself," to the microscopic, and often inscrutable, operations of individual memory.

Munro emerges from these comparisons as the most progressive in her treatment of memory as theme and narrative device, mainly for her insistent attention to the linked questions of gender and genre in the literature of modern catastrophic subjectivity. Unlike either Nabokov or Sebald, Munro merges her reconstructed family history with fictionalized snapshots from her own life story. In the second section of *Castle Rock*, "Munro's family history moves closer into the spaces of personal memory . . . only to open out toward the end into the local history and prehistory of her home territory in southwestern Ontario" (Howells 2007, 166). In this respect Munro's text as genre-bending memory work is unique in daring to envision such a family history-cum-memoir as being, in the end, not about the narrative subject per se but about the grander objective environment in which she finds herself at this late stage in her life. This larger transindividual context is presented moreover in neither a Romantic nor an anthropomorphic fashion; Munro's recourse to the "hard" scientific knowledge of southwestern Ontario's geological formation many thousands of years past ensures such a dispassionate and (generically speaking) counterintuitive deprivileging of the self. More than this, Munro's narrator's focus in "What Do You Want to Know For?" on the special physiographic maps of rural southwestern Ontario tacitly acknowledges as it obliquely celebrates her "lack" of a comparable Central (Austerlitz) or Northern (Nabokov) European upbringing—that rare and, in the latter's case (like Proust's) privileged sort of haute bourgeois or aristocratic childhood. In each of these cases, with Proust as a template (and with Beckett's *Molloy* as comparative *reductio ad absurdum*), this "golden" childhood is irretrievably lost, whether to memory alone or in a more absolute sense. Curiously, while Munro's narrator—like any one of her imagined family members—can look back upon a childhood and young adulthood of what can at best be called respectable poverty, she seems to be in no danger of losing her past, whether through forgetting or other, more material, catastrophe. This security is attributable partly to the author's avowedly capacious memory and partly to her appreciation of her position vis-à-vis a world that takes an interest in the kind of woman she typically depicts only when that woman is, quite precisely, a fictional character.

The three-way comparison of Sebald, Nabokov, and Munro in the previous chapters charted the shift in Sebald's text from an Oedipal-paternal relation and its dependence on eroto-salvific redemption to the maternal influence, particularly in terms of the centrality of memory to the writer's approach to the task of writing. This culminates in Munro's rewriting of the "writer and 'his' mother" topos, which has its locus classicus for modern literature in Proust. At the same time, I have forwarded a reading of Munro as the most politically progressive of the three insofar as she is willing to forgo a hypostatized adherence to the post-Enlightenment faith in humankind and embrace the possibility of nonhuman timescales and the recognition of nonhuman modes of being, advocating for an indiosyncratically Canadian materialist epistemology. What Munro's work implies, in the end, is that the archetypal subject of the literature of modern catastrophic subjectivity, the spectator who is at once looking on *and* in the midst of the slowly unfolding catastrophe of modern life—this subject, in its most representative form, is a woman. Or if not literally a woman then someone who occupies this subject position, with all its attributes and desires, its relative powers and weaknesses. This is in large part because of woman's historical role as the victim of a hegemonic masculinist patriarchy—a victim status complicated by the fact that Munro's point is anticipated in the work of certain late twentieth- and early twenty-first-century male writers. This is the equivalent set of issues raised in the debate around postmemory as a special instance of "appropriation of voice." But rather than non-Jewish writers and filmmakers—or, for that matter, spectator-consumers—appropriating the experience preserved in the individual and collective memories of Jewish victims of the Holocaust, this is a shift to the appropriation of an even larger-scale, longer-term history of subjection—a subjection whose ultimate result is the denial of an empowered and autonomous subjectivity. Heiner Müller (1984, 58), for instance, applies a highly intermedial Brechtian approach in an avant-garde theatrical critique of later twentieth-century political life in which Shakespeare's Ophelia is conflated with Sophocles's tragic heroine in a postapocalyptic feminist vision of impossible subjectivity (I quote this passage again to refresh the reader's memory):

> This is Electra speaking. In the heart of darkness. Under the sun of torture. To the capitals of the world. In the name of the victims. I eject all the sperm I have received. I turn the milk of my breasts into a lethal poison. I take back the world I gave birth to. I choke between my thighs the world I gave birth to. I bury it in my womb. Down with the happiness of submission. Long live hate and contempt, rebellion and death. When she walks through your bedrooms carrying butcher knives you'll know the truth.
>   *The men exit. Ophelia remains on stage, motionless in her white wrappings.*

Müller's complex intertextual collage manages to express a feminist outrage at decades or centuries of misogynistic prejudice without suggesting a positive course of action or any possible *écriture féminine* beyond the author's trademark patchwork of found texts, from Conrad to the Manson family. Electra's tirade culminates in a reputed quote from the courtroom testimony of Sadie Mae Glutz (Susan Atkins), on trial for her part in the 1969 Manson family murders of Sharon Tate and others near Los Angeles. Glutz/Atkins, like the other female members of Manson's "family," can hardly be said to represent an ideal of feminist autonomy and agency. On top of this, Müller's hybrid of Ophelia/Electra is last seen immobilized onstage, as if at the bottom of the sea, "in the heart of darkness," offering a visual contradiction to the violence implicit in her final, unoriginal, words. In a very different manner, Magris in *Blindly* also anticipates the female subject of catastrophic spectatorship by giving form to the paradox of Maria/Medea, a voiceless woman who nevertheless, "under the sun of torture," manages to destroy the man who is guilty of denying her subjectivity in the first place. In comparison with these antecedents in the literature of modern catastrophic subjectivity, Munro appears radically innovative, not least because she eschews violence as a final solution to her protagonist's ontological and epistemological crises.

In contrast to the foregoing, and as argued in the introduction, Sebald's perspective across his prose narratives represents the best possible literary-philosophical alternative to a generation unwilling to forgo the autocritical dimension of the Humanist tradition—a highly ethical posthumanist epistemology—which, through a postsecular critique of indelible cultural tropes such as redemption, presents the most likely avenue of humankind's "salvation" at this time and on this earth. In Sebald, the literature of modern catastrophic subjectivity acquires what is perhaps its most important (masculine) European voice.

Postmemorial Sebald: Revaluing Redemption, Redeeming Memory

Tracing the red thread of redemption across all four of Sebald's prose texts reveals a consistent approach. Redemption as theme, trope, or structure in Sebald is always already ironically predetermined. In short, redemption—or the even more overtly theological *salvation*—remains a theoretical possibility only in the most elegiac modernist sense, subtly formulated by Benjamin in his notion of a modern postsecular messianicity, holding out the ever-present possibility of the "redemption of every moment in its capacity to name itself as that instant," the salutary shock of the Now, the *Jetztzeit* that frees or saves us, momentarily, from the ongoing unfolding of the story that is the catastrophe of "History" (Cacciari 1994). We are thereby reminded of the deeply premodern roots of Sebald's postmodernity. One of the most significant manifestations of this aspect is his complex critical and artistic engagement with memory, both individual and collective, as a fundamental framework within which to negotiate an ethical relation to the world. Therefore, postmemory, the creative appropriation of another's experience,[2] emerges as the most relevant category by which to judge Sebald's contribution in this respect.

This focus on the postmemorial dimension in relation to what I call the memory chronotope in *Austerlitz* opens the door to illuminating comparisons with both Munro and Nabokov as writers of memory. For all his protopostmodernism, the category of postmemory cannot meaningfully be applied to Nabokov, insofar as the past he recaptures in prose is his own. Therefore, that of which Nabokov (or his memory) *avoids* speaking takes a very different form. Because he was not present at the deaths of either his mother or his brother Sergey (the first in Prague, on the eve of World War II, the latter in a German concentration camp [Nabokov 1989, 49; 258]), Nabokov logically refrains from anything other than the tersest mention of these, obviously autobiographically significant, events (e.g., Nabokov 1989, 193). Nabokov's affectively charged recollection of his mother before her death "on the eve of World War Two" (Nabokov 1989, 49), living with her daughters' former governess in Prague, evokes the image of Vera, Austerlitz's former nanny, who lived on in the adjacent apartment decades after his mother's deportation to what he imagines may have been Theresienstadt. Austerlitz recounts how he was eventually able to retrace his steps back to Prague, his place of birth, of which he has retained no conscious memories. After visiting Vera, Austerlitz resolves for reasons not entirely clear to him to make the return journey to England by train, from Prague across the length of Germany. He has of course since learned that this is the second time in his life he has made this trip, the first being all those years before, during the war, when as a little boy he traveled from Prague to London on the *Kindertransport* (hence Auster-litz's childhood fascination with trains and railroads, both after his arrival in Wales and, uncannily, even before his departure from Prague). As in Sebald's other books the act of traveling is combined with the acts of dreaming and recollecting, often simultaneously, the memory of a dream: "As I gazed out [the train window], a distant memory came to me of a dream I often had both in the manse at Bala and later, a dream of a nameless land without borders and entirely overgrown by dark forests, which I had to cross without any idea where I was going, and it dawned upon me, said Austerlitz, that what I now saw going past outside the train was the original of the images that had haunted me for so many years" (Sebald 2001, 224). Sebald here intertextualizes Nabokov's account in *Speak, Memory*, chapter 7, in which he recounts a train trip from Russia through Germany to the Riviera, and in which Nabokov lovingly recaptures his childish sense of wonder as in his imagination he put himself "in the place of some passer-by who . . . was moved as I would be moved myself to see the long, romantic, auburn cars, with their intervestibular connecting curtains as black as bat wings and their metal lettering copper-bright cross an everyday thoroughfare and then turn, with all windows suddenly ablaze, around a last block of houses" (1989, 144).[3] Where Nabokov from his position in the later twentieth century recol-lects a romantic image of Europe's trains from long before World War II and the Final Solution, in these remediated passages in *Austerlitz* Sebald retro-actively augments (and complicates) Nabokov's rich textures with the latent meanings of collective cultural memory.

Austerlitz's dream-memory continues, informed by a pervasive subcurrent, an affectively charged intertextual thread running across the four prose texts: "Then I recollected another idea which had obsessed me over a long period: the image of a twin brother who had been with me on that long journey, sitting motionless by the window of the compartment, staring out into the dark. I knew nothing about him, not even his name, and I had never exchanged so much as a word with him, but whenever I thought of him I was tormented by the notion that towards the end of the journey he had died of consumption and was stowed in the baggage net with the rest of our belongings" (Sebald 2001, 224–25). This spectral "twin" first appears much earlier in the narrative, in Austerlitz's recounting to the narrator of his childhood in Wales, but in a more overtly metaphysical context: "It is a fact that through all the years I spent at the manse in Bala I never shook off the feeling that something very obvious, very manifest in itself was hidden from me. Sometimes . . . I felt as if an invisible twin brother were walking beside me, the reverse of a shadow, so to speak" (54–55). Nabokov's account of the original train journey offers only these lines, underlined by Sebald in his copy of *Speak, Memory*: "From my bed under my brother's bunk (Was he asleep? Was he there at all?)" (Nabokov 1989, 145 [1987, 114]). The difference Sebald introduces is that, where in *Speak, Memory* Sergey is Nabokov's actual brother (to be discussed below), in *Austerlitz* the "twin brother" is an avatar of the protagonist himself, the self he had to leave behind, in the past.[4]

I address this intertextual nexus in order to underline my aim in this concluding chapter, which is to set the "queer" Sebaldian subject elaborated by Helen Finch (2013) (and others) into a larger postsecular context in relation to the politics of redemption per se. For whatever queering of preexisting historical, biographical, and literary material Sebald performs is always a transgressive reworking born of the text itself. In chapter 3 of *Speak, Memory*, for instance, Sebald notes Nabokov's description of his maternal uncle Ruka, whose wealth and properties the author inherited when the former died in 1916, meaning that he possessed this inheritance for just one year, until the Bolshevik Revolution swept it all away, as if overnight. But Nabokov's point in writing this section is to express the retrospective mixture of regret and ingratitude he felt as he looks "back across the transparent abyss" and recognizes his participation in a general condescension toward an eccentric uncle who, in a more contemporary parlance, was likely to have been gay. With his physical resemblance to Proust, Uncle Ruka is the hypersensitive composer of a single musical piece, a "romance" whose sole fan appears to have been Nabokov's brother Sergey (his name circled by Sebald), who, Nabokov admits, in parenthesis, is "the only person who memorized the music and all the words . . . whom [Uncle Ruka] hardly ever noticed, [underlined from here] who also stammered, and who is also now dead" (1989, 74). Sergey, also gay it seems,[5] is the one person of whom Nabokov has the greatest difficulty speaking (1989, 257–58). His death in a camp in January 1945 prompts one of Nabokov's most candid admissions: "It was one of those lives that hopelessly claim a belated something—compassion, understanding, no matter what—which the mere recognition of such a want can neither replace nor redeem" (258). The various examples of secretly or unconsciously gay men and unrequited queer desire in *The Emigrants*, *The Rings of Saturn*, *Vertigo*, and *Austerlitz* can be revealingly compared with the various examples of comparably doomed, unrequited heterosexual attraction in the same books.[6] According to Finch (2013),[7] "alternative masculinities subvert catastrophe in Sebald's works. From the schizophrenic poet Ernst Herbeck to the alluring shade of Kafka in Venice, the figure of the bachelor offers a form of resistance to the destructive course of history throughout Sebald's critical and literary writing." While I agree in general, I would add that while they do represent forms of resistance or even subversion, these subjectivities can only *fail* to prevent catastrophe.[8] What they achieve, of course, is a form of *deferral* of catastrophe. In the first instance, these men and their relationships seem to stand for all those dispossessed and disenfranchised by history, while also affording a poignant case of the necessity of respecting alternative alterities.[9] Second, Sebald seems to be at once conceding to literary tradition while ironically undermining the tropes of romantic desire, fateful longing, and, above all, erotic redemption. After all, to the best of my knowledge the only sex scene as such in any of the four prose texts is the one in *The Rings of Saturn*, to which the narrator is only an accidental, passive witness, a spectator of an allegory of the catastrophe of heteronormative desire:

> I thought I saw something of an odd, pallid colour move on the shoreline. I crouched down and, overcome by a sudden panic, looked over the edge [of the cliff]. A couple lay there, at the bottom of the pit, as I thought: a man stretched full length over another body of which nothing was visible but the legs, spread and angled. In the startled moment when that image went through me, which lasted an eternity, it seemed as if the man's feet twitched like those of one just hanged. Now, though, he lay still, and the woman too was still and motionless. Misshapen, like some great mollusc washed ashore, they lay there, to all appearances a single being, a many-limbed, two-headed monster that had drifted in from far out at sea, the last of a prodigious species, its life ebbing from it with each breath expired through its nostrils. (68)

The scene reads like an ironic inversion of Sebald's appropriation, in *The Rings of Saturn*'s opening, of the episode in Kafka's "Metamorphosis" of the insectile Samsa peering out the window at the gray and disappearing world.[10] It should not be overlooked that the narrator here is not sure whether his Caliban-like vision of the intermingled couple on the beach, which he refers to as "the pale sea monster at the foot of the Covehithe cliffs" (69), is one that he really saw or perhaps only imagined as he perched vertiginously on the edge of the precipice.[11]

Gender, Genre, and "Holocaust Melodrama"

In the end, this is a book about Sebald's prose works in relation to the persistence of tropes such as redemption and their significance for narratives and subjectivities in the postsecular era. But it is also a study of the general problem of *Schiffbruch mit Zuschauer*, the subject-spectator, looking on to the scene of its own objectification and imminent annihilation. This is the subject of the late- or postmodern period, the human being understood as a subject without which there would be no other subjects, whether subaltern, feminist, queer, transgendered, post- or even nonhuman. This is the key modern metaphysical concept with which Sebald is unwilling to part, which sets him apart from many posthumanist thinkers, not to mention more representative postmodern writers. This is the subject as visually and discursively empowered agent, at once spectator and, despite a necessarily limited point of view, ethically motivated witness. At the same time, this subject, and all the mnemic, affective, and other forces and intensities by which it is shaped, is accessible only through the mediation of a text. For, as I have argued throughout this book, questions of subjectivity, identity, and agency are never far from a consideration of *form* in Sebald, where form includes genre, cognate with gender. Even allowing for the fictional dimension, Sebald's writing is unapologetically gendered;[12] one cannot read his books without negotiating a relationship with the typical Sebaldian narrator-protagonist[13] whose ontological difference from the actual author much early criticism tended to collapse.[14] Genre in Sebald (as everywhere) is most helpfully theorized within the lexical paradigm stemming from the Latin *genus*, meaning "race," "kind," or "category."[15] After all, the markedly gendered quality of Sebald's prose fictions seems to have something to do with their origins—and an abiding fascination with Sebald the man continues to manifest in the critical literature.[16] At the risk of indulging in the very form of criticism just mentioned, it is interesting to note that in his copy of Susan Sontag's *Under the Sign of Saturn* (1983),[17] Sebald marked this passage in the essay on Canetti, "Mind as Passion": "Portraits drawn from the inside, with or without the poignant inflections of exile, have made familiar the model of itinerant intellectual. He (for the type is male, of course) is a Jew, or like a Jew; polycultural, restless, misogynistic; a collector; dedicated to self-transcendence, despising the instincts; weighed down by books and buoyed up by the euphoria of knowledge" (185). It is not difficult to see the attractions of this rather Benjaminian type for a writer such as Sebald, or rather for the typical Sebaldian narrator persona (since only those who knew "Max" intimately could say for sure)—not to speak of a character such as Austerlitz, so tempting to identify with the author, who seems to share in a number of the traits of this "itinerant intellectual." That these traits do not include Jewishness is a highly significant difference when considering the prose works under the rubric of postmemorial, post-Holocaust literature.[18]

It is Sebald's "perspective as an expatriate German writer which accounts for his own, unique approach to the experience of the Holocaust" (Fischer 2009, 20). How does this square with Sebald's peculiar literary postmodernism? According to David Duff (2000, 1), "the modern period has been . . . typically characterized by a steady erosion of the perception of genre, and by the emergence of aesthetic programmes which have sought to dispense altogether with the doctrine of literary kinds or genres," hence the recurring definition of postmodern fictional narrative as open to, or indeed obsessed with, play with preestablished genre forms. "This may have something to do with the elevation of popular culture which is so conspicuous a feature of Postmodernism, involving as it does a recognition that a much more favourable estimate of the value of genre has always prevailed in the popular sphere, despite the apparent rejection of the concept by the literary avant-garde" (2). Duff's insight illuminates our understanding of Sebald, positioned so complexly between modernist nostalgia for past forms and practices (not least of which is the novel itself, notwithstanding Sebald's disavowals about genre) and, inevitably, something more self-reflexively innovative, even radically so—in terms of content, style, form, and structure. Sebald "cannot work with traditional genres of closure. He can neither return to his 'Heimat' after what has happened, nor can he articulate his relationship to his national history in active terms, whether tragic or otherwise" (Morgan 2005, 82). Just as Sebald's modernism, in other words, conditions his relation to history, which is to say the writing of history, so it does his relation to the Holocaust, which is to say to Holocaust literature. And the opposite is also true: his relation to writing about the Holocaust inflects his modernism in a radical, postmodern direction, from memory toward a kind of postmemory. In this reading, Hirsch's postmemory is the expression of memory in the later or postmodern era, characterized by the radically complicated relation between reality and its representations and by the critical destabilization of concepts such as authority, authenticity, and agency.

I acknowledge that this discussion may be another example of Fuchs and Long's (2007, 7) observation that "Anglophone critics and readers" in particular display an ongoing fascination with Sebald's writing, insofar as it "appears to give literary expression to history's unfolding catastrophes, above all to the Holocaust as a defining caesura of twentieth-century history" (quoted in Baxter, Henitiuk, and Hutchinson 2013, 2–3). (This is the macrohistorical version of Finch's more focused critique of the critical tendency to read Sebald as a melancholic prophet of apocalyptic doom while failing to acknowledge the extent of his contribution to a critique of subjectivity in later twentieth-century European modernity.) While acknowledging that Sebald "loathes the term 'Holocaust literature' ('it's a dreadful idea that you can have a sub-genre and make a specialty out of it; it's grotesque')" (Jaggi 2001, 8),[19] in John Zilcosky's (2006, 693) reading *Austerlitz* is nevertheless identifiable as Sebald's first "Holocaust novel." Ruth Franklin (2011, 186) qualifies this position, however, arguing that "Sebald's concern is not the actual events [of the Holo-caust] so much as their aftereffects . . . It would be more accurate to think of Sebald as a 'post-Holocaust writer' . . . except that such a phrase implies that there is such a thing as the 'post-Holocaust', which Sebald . . . would likely have adamantly denied."[20] More critically, Zilcosky (2006, 694) argues that "Sebald comes perilously close in *Austerlitz* to the melodramatic 'impulse toward dramatization' and 'desire to express all' that he had scrupulously avoided in the earlier fictions and, what is more, had criticized in other Holo-caust representations such as [Steven Spielberg's] *Schindler's List*."[21] Citing the rehabilitative efforts of Peter Brooks and Thomas Elsaesser, Zilcosky (2006, 697) acknowledges melodrama's status as a dominant mode in contemporary popular culture.[22] The problem, of course, is that books like *Austerlitz* are not properly popular cultural objects but the product of a more serious artistic endeavor and highbrow marketing campaign. Moreover, for Sebald, coming after Adorno's famous dictum about the barbarity of "poetry," which is to say difficult, complex texts, after Auschwitz, it is a question of the appropriate language or style, the proper perspective upon or approach to representing the Holocaust, rather than its absolute unrepresentability or ineffability—the latter a position that Holocaust studies has had to move beyond.[23]

Zilcosky (2006, 695) also criticizes *Austerlitz* for displaying what Brooks identifies as "a melodramatic desire for 'total expressivity' related precisely to the 'ineffability' of his subject matter." This critique is elaborated in terms of *Austerlitz*'s famous Bernhardian "periscopic" narrative structure, in which one speaker's words are framed within as many as three others' ("Nonetheless, said Vera, Austerlitz continued, Maximilian did not in any way believe . . ." [Sebald 2001, 222]), with the nameless Sebaldian narrator at the outermost narrative layer, as it were closest to the reader's extradiegetic position. Zil-cosky (2006, 695) asks whether the melodramatic impact of specific moments in the narrative is mitigated by this multilayered, dialogic style. This is a key question, framing fundamental concerns about representing the Holocaust within more general ethical-aesthetic questions about the representation of alterity, what Sebald calls "the usurpation of another person's life" (quoted in Franklin 2011, 193). Does the text express an ethical relation to the other—respecting the other in her or his otherness, as Levinas or Derrida would say, over there, outside oneself[24]—by "periscopically" placing an account of an untranslatable experience into the mouth of a character several times removed from the narratorial-authorial and, by extension, readerly "self"?[25]

Melodrama and Postredemptive Narratives

Despite some critics' protestations, it seems most fruitful to continue to consider Sebald's so-called writerly transgressions against generic decorum, whether melodramatic or otherwise, from the perspective of Hirsch's notion of postmemory, as several have done before,[26] and as I have done in a qualified way throughout this book. For these melodramatic—which is to say affectively charged—touches are also the result of Sebald's imaginative labor on the part of the other, the victim or victim's child or grandchild;[27] a subject, often but not always Jewish, whose experience, voice, or point of view, whether first- or secondhand, Sebald the historical personage clearly does not share but which the author imaginatively, affiliatively, appropriates.[28] For instance, in the first part of the book, Austerlitz recounts his second childhood in Wales after being sent as a little boy on a *Kindertransport* that saved him even as it severed him from himself. At one point he tells the narrator of his illustrated children's Bible, which he possessed presumably because Elias, his foster father, was a Calvinist Methodist minister,

> I particularly liked the episode where the children of Israel cross a terrible wilderness, many days' journey long and wide, with nothing in sight but sky and sand as far as the eye can see. I . . . immersed myself, forgetting all around me, in a full-page illustration showing the desert of Sinai looking just like the part of Wales where I grew up, with bare mountains crowding close together and a gray-hatched background, which I took sometimes for the sea and sometimes for the air above it. And indeed, said Austerlitz on a later occasion when he showed me his Welsh children's Bible, I knew that my proper place was among the tiny figures populating the camp. (Sebald 2001, 55)

Ironies of individual identification and of accidental appropriation of voice align here with Sebald's larger project of a typological hermeneutic anticipated at intervals in his first three prose texts and thematically fundamental to the network of postmemorial meanings in play in *Austerlitz*. Sebald develops across his oeuvre a nuanced treatment of the Old Testament trope of the "Chosen People."[29] In *The Rings of Saturn*, for instance, the narrator's state of hypnagogic alienation from others and from his environment is borne home to the reader as he introduces the theme of the Promised Land, in a clear echo of the kitschy desert-caravan fresco he had seen on a dilapidated building in an "extraterritorial" Middle Eastern enclave in Amsterdam a day or two before (Sebald 1998, 80–81): "half dreaming . . . for the first time in my life [I] believed I had arrived, and was home. Even when I awoke it seemed to me for a moment that my people were resting all around me as we made our way across the desert" (85). This half dream is automatically contrasted with the scene that immediately follows of a "beatifically beaming couple surrounded by the motley host of their grandchildren, celebrating some family or holiday occasion in a cafeteria otherwise deserted," their "people all around them" (85). This ironically orientalist reference to a "promised land" is not out of place, of course, in the overall journey structure of the narrative. More than this, though, is the connection that develops across the prose texts between a literary remediation of a folk-cultural belief in life after death—where the experience of death somehow diminishes the subject, as if she/he had gone off to a distant place or even become physically smaller in size[30]—and the trajectory of Europe's Jewish population, where the Final Solution under Hitler can be seen retrospectively as the infernally ironic fulfillment of the Exodus narrative of wandering in the wilderness. The danger here, of course—and this is really the crux of any critique of postmemory as a concept—is that the specifically Jewish victim-subject, shaped by the Holocaust, becomes the model for other, non-Jewish, nonvictim subjects more generally—the subject as memory tourist, if you will. This is a danger Sebald assiduously avoided.

In his fictional output Sebald is interested in negotiating the liminal space between the different extremes of German postwar literary (and filmic) engagement with the Holocaust rather than adopting one position or another, as he does in the "Air War" lectures. In the prose texts his treatment of such tropes and the ironies of such postmodern typologies remains remarkably ambivalent, despite his obvious (and understandable) predilection for the subject, usually but not always masculine, marked by "Jewishness" as a modernist signifier of seemingly endless passive suffering à la Kafka but mitigated with what might be called a will to salvation even in the face of its impossibility, and even if the person or character in question is not literally Jewish. This is the individual subject dispossessed, displaced, oppressed, or subjected by forces beyond his or her control, in particular the forces and pressures of memory and history. This is especially true of all five (including Luisa Lanzberg) protagonists of *The Emigrants* and is a consistent feature of all four of the prose works. In other words, the "sin" here is not so much succumbing to melodrama as to the (neocolonialist, Eurocentric) arrogance of the—in this case—male writer, creatively imagining himself into situations, times, experiences, memories, subjectivities, and affectivities not properly his own. In this light, in the microhistorical approach of the fictional biography Sebald in fact succeeds in representing the underside of history, "especially with regard to the problem of representing the Holocaust. *Austerlitz*, by focusing on one individual, demonstrates Sebald's . . . assertion that only in literature is any attempt at restitution possible" (Wolff 2009, 329). The literature of restitution in Sebald's view "attempts to restore agency to marginalized historical subjects without seeking to intervene either physically or metaphysically, without prejudicing their alterity" (Baxter, Henitiuk, and Hutchinson 2013, 2). He succeeds in this, arguably, not by avoiding but precisely by exploiting the cultural expression of bourgeois capitalism in its propensity to privilege the individual over the collective, the personal over the social, particularly in moral-ideological terms. *Austerlitz* is no melodrama, in the end, at least not in the implicitly pejorative sense to which many critics still adhere, because the protagonist's affective capacity—like his capacity for self-knowledge for the first fifty-odd years of his life—is so stunted that, in the end, the effect on the reader is precisely the opposite of what is granted by a more conventional narrative on the same themes: neither emotionally nor intellectually is any catharsis or closure provided; while fundamental ethical questions are posed, at the end no clear "moral legibility" emerges.[31] The founding absence of what Peter Brooks calls a "post-sacred" society is only emphasized, and Sebald's postmodernism is revealed in all its radical bleakness. With no clear emotional basis no clear morality can manifest itself to take the place of a "metaphysical system of transcendent values" (Gledhill 1987, 31).

In *On the Natural History of Destruction* (reproducing the metaphor from his 1996 Nabokov essay), Sebald (2003, 25–26) remarks that "the accounts of individual eyewitnesses . . . are of only qualified value, and need to be supplemented by what a synoptic and artificial view reveals."[32] A potential problem, as Julia Hell (2003, 35) points out, is the highly gendered nature of this gaze,[33] which in her persuasive reading becomes emblematic of a cultural discourse that transcends "personal trauma" in order to write "postwar history . . . as a melo-traumatic story of German non-Jewish authorship." But, as the example of *Austerlitz* makes clear, Sebald's formulation of the "synoptic view" is thoroughly conscious of its own paradoxical, nontranscendent, discursively "embodied" status (Sontag [1983, 185]: "for the type is male, of course").[34] After Bakhtin we can say that it is genre itself as an "organ of memory" that conditions the text's dialogic relation to representing the other (Morson and Emerson 1990, 288). In this sense even a so to speak generic genre like melodrama allows the other's voice to be heard, especially when it is couched in a prose narrative that is on one level a self-reflexive reflection upon the question of genre. The uniqueness of Sebald's memory work can be summed up, perhaps, as the self-conscious *failure* of a kind of "mnemonic restitution."[35]

This is in effect a constitutional and therefore necessary "failure," as Sebald writes, "to bear witness to the complexity of bearing witness" (Corngold 2008, 222).[36] This is the very purpose of literary postmemory, in a sense beyond Hirsch's original formulation, as a function of the irreducible distance necessitated by the always already second-order perspective of the non-Jewish, second- (or later) generation German writer.[37] In bearing witness in this self-aware, second-order way, such a memory struggles directly with the paradox of making good what cannot be restored, returning what has been irrecoverably lost. Sebald sought to "lend his voice to the silenced victims of history and to uncover the nature of the hegemonic systems that spawned inhumanity, [leading] him to reject specific genre attributions for his works" (Williams 2007, 51). Therefore, from the perspective of the second, and now third, generation of German writers after the war, it is not a question of a subject-victim assuming the task of representing collective catastrophe but of a third-party observer whose labor therefore will be largely imaginative, a labor of prosthetic memory interacting dialectically with what Hutchinson (2009a, 325) identifies as the melancholic inability to forget.[38] Can we apply the same logic to any writer who lives outside the place or after the events she/he chooses to explore in a prose narrative? Is it morally or artistically permissible so to speak to take the Holocaust as a particular model for the writing of postmemorial texts in general?

Conclusion: From Redemption to Restitution

I follow Franklin (2011, 193–94) (and several others[39]) in citing here Sebald's last public speech, "on the occasion of the opening of a new Literaturhaus in Stuttgart," "An Attempt at Restitution" (Ein Versuch zur Restitution): "So what is literature good for? . . . The synoptic view across the barrier of death . . . is both overshadowed and illuminated . . . by the memory of those to whom the greatest injustice was done. There are many forms of writing; only in literature, however, can there be an attempt at restitution." Is it possible to see in Sebald's prose texts the representatives of a new genre *in nuce*: the "literature of restitution"?[40] This genre might entail the literary, and therefore fictional, embodiment of the social role that I have already claimed the novel by definition could never fulfill: that of the *normative* text, whose purpose is to answer the question for a specific people in a specific cultural context, "What do I do?" (Assmann 2006, 38)—in short, a guide to forging an ethical stance toward the world that works not through didactic prescription but dialectically, through example and counterexample, the appropriation of voice and vision alike, an appropriation that is also a restitution.

As Franklin (2011, 194) explains, "The German word [*Restitution*], like its English cognate, encompasses multiple meanings, including the restoration of art (which often involves cleaning off the layers of dust left by the passage of time) and the return of anything to its rightful owner. But it also has a specific legal meaning: the restoration of not only property but also of a person's legal status, taken away in violation of international law." I read "restitution" here as a secular alternative to the more loaded concept of "redemption," which it complements, to a degree. By the same token, restitution stands in opposition to a term like "retribution," which in this context bears only pejorative connotations. For if retribution implies the adding of violence to violence in a (usually vain) attempt at restoring a semblance of order, in the process reducing the other to less than one's self, then restitution here signifies the preliminary—and purely imaginative—restoring to the other of what is most proper to it: the radical otherness of that which would otherwise remain forgotten.[41] Is it justifiable or even possible to speak of the restorative or compensatory dimension of the literary mimesis or representation of the past, of history, or of memory—not to mention the affective dimension of such structures of meaning?[42] Is it possible to speak of literature's arrogating to itself at such a late date the burden of history, of memory, of commemorating and remembering, as much as constructively forgetting, rewriting, or imagining outright? The final irony here is that retribution and redemption alike are narrative tropes that only perpetuate a masculinist, patriarchal, and heteronormative status quo, which is precisely why modernist narrative—not to speak of the contribution of poststructuralist theory—was essential in deconstructing these structures for a postsecular era that has transcended transcendence. Across his prose works, and all their ambiguous endings, Sebald's continuation and transformation of this modernist legacy is predicated upon the recognition that redemption—like reconciliation, resolution, or closure—only perpetuates the contradictions of the worldview of an order that has failed, and to whose slow demise we now bear witness, in real time.

NOTES

Introduction

Portions of this chapter first appeared in Kilbourn 2013.

1. See, e.g., Braidotti 2013.

2. See Critchley and Dews 1996; Braidotti 2013.

3. See, e.g., Arthur Williams 1998; Kilbourn 2004.

4. See Kristeva 1986.

5. See, e.g., "Discourse in the Novel" (written in the early 1930s) (Bakhtin 1981, 300).

6. On "prosaics," see Morson and Emerson 1990. See also Long 2007, 25n15.

7. See Kilbourn 2013.

8. See, e.g., Stam 2005, 3–5; Hutcheon 2006, 21–22; Sanders 2006, 1–3.

9. On this passage, see also Franklin 2011, 263.

10. On Sebald as a modernist and not postmodernist, see also Zilcosky 2003, 102–3. On Sebald as a "postmodern" writer, see, e.g., Fuchs and Long 2007, 139; Kilbourn 2006, 35; Arthur Williams 1998, 2001.

11. See also Wolff 2009, 318.

12. See, e.g., Waugh 1996, 1–19. See also Hutcheon 1988.

13. See Long 2007, 1–8; Hutchinson 2011. See also Bakhtin 1981, 11. With respect to the critical reading of Enlightenment modernity in Sebald's prose texts, I must acknowledge the groundbreaking work represented in the 2011 special issue of *The Journal of European Studies* (41, no. 3–4), including essays by Long, Hutchinson, Anderson, and other leading Sebald scholars.

14. E.g., Jameson 1999; Hutcheon 1988.

15. See Ceuppens 2004, 193. Ceuppens is one of the first critics to discuss the problem of Sebald's handling of redemption. The author's preoccupation with this theme is evidenced in the significance of Jerusalem (whether the temple alone or the city) and the "Promised Land" across all four of the prose texts.

16. See Furani 2015, 3n5, on the wide range of disciplines potentially invested in the postsecular debate.

17. On his view of history or social reality in terms of impending—or completed—catastrophe, Sebald is in tune with a general tendency beginning at least in the late 1970s. Texts in a variety of media and genres across the cultural spectrum reflect this (post)apocalyptic perspective; e.g., in film, Ridley Scott's *Blade Runner* (1982); in the novel, Don DeLillo's *White Noise* (1986); in critical theory, Derrida's "Of an Apocalyptic Tone Recently Adopted in Philosophy" (1984).

18. On the question of what comes after this classically masculinist, patriarchist, ex-nominatively determined subject—the subject of colonialism, capitalism, heteronormativity, etc.—see Braidotti 2013, whose elaboration of "posthuman" subjectivity, although ostensibly more radical because monadic and antimetaphysical,

is nevertheless predicated upon the assumption that thought cannot proceed or progress without some sort of subject as ethical focus.

19. See also Wolfe 2010, xv.

20. "Habermas's precise use of the term is an attempt to describe the reviving influence of religion in public spheres once dominated by rationalism, particularly Western, nominally secular states and their relation with rising 'fundamentalisms', such as radical Islam" (Bergstrom 2016, 196n8). See, e.g., Habermas 2003, 2008, 2010.

21. "Complexity becomes the key word, as it is clear that one single narrative does not suffice to account for secularity as an unfinished project and its relationship to Humanism and emancipatory politics" (Braidotti 2013, 34).

22. This dimension of my reading of Sebald was inspired by Anders Bergstrom's (2013) perspicacious analysis of *Melancholia* (and other postapocalyptic films).

23. Nevertheless, it could be argued that Sebald represents the literary antecedent of Richard Grusin's (2010) analysis of affect and mediality in post-9/11 culture, or of Jonathan Crary's (2013b) extension of a Debordian critique of the spectacle into the contemporary context, under "terminal capitalism," for something as fundamental to human life as sleep.

24. Sebald's reading of Kafka, however, does betray the influence of Deleuze and Guattari's book *Kafka: Toward a Minor Literature* (1986).

25. Fuery and Fuery 2003.

26. Originally published in Italian in 2006 as *Alla cieca*.

Chapter 1

Portions of this chapter first appeared in Kilbourn 2007.

1. See the introduction for a clarification of my usage of the term "subject" in this context.

2. See Bolter and Grusin 1999; Hutcheon 2006, 16–17.

3. I.e., in Jonathan Long's (2007, 49) wording, the relation of partiality to transcendence within the visual field. See also Jay 1994, 30.

4. For Amir Eshel (2003, 91), "Sebald's catastrophe . . . informed by . . . Blumenberg's notion of catastrophe as a topos of the human imagination . . . is no longer a sign of the eschatological, of divine fulfillment." I cannot agree, however, with Eshel's assertion that "Sebald's interest is focused on modern, man-made catastrophes marked by their 'paradigmatic senselessness,' by the fact that any attempt to distill sense from them would result in questionable mythological narratives" (91), unless this is to say that even the many natural disasters recounted in the narrative are subsumed within the cultural, that every catastrophe in Sebald is cultural, whether "man-made" or not.

5. See Bakhtin (1981, xxxvi, 47), for whom "voice" signifies in the limited sense of a "'semantic position,' a point of view on the world . . . one personality orienting itself among other personalities in a limited field." Thus the character as "voice" converges with the character as "subject position," where a particular viewpoint or perspective is the foremost of a relatively constant cluster of attributes.

6. "The relationship of the image and culture is far more than merely a system of orders and ideologies, and more embedded in a vast and complex set of agendas and relationships . . . A key component in this is the spectator" (Fuery and Fuery 2003, xii–xiii).

7. See Sontag 2003, 18–22: "Being a spectator of calamities taking place in another country is a quintessential modern experience . . . Something becomes real—to those who are elsewhere, following it as 'news'—by being photographed. But a catastrophe that is experienced will often seem eerily like its representation. The attack on the World Trade Center on September 11, 2001, was described as 'unreal,' 'surreal,' 'like a movie,' in many of the first accounts of those who escaped from the towers or watched from nearby. (After four decades of big-budget Hollywood disaster films, 'It felt like a movie' seems to have displaced the way survivors of a catastrophe used to express the short-term unassimilability of what they had gone through: 'It felt like a dream' . . .)."

8. In *Culture and Imperialism* (Said 1994).

9. See Presner 2010, 195, for a Hegelian reading of this dimension of Sebald's imaginative critique of the legacy of European colonialism in *The Rings of Saturn*.

10. See, e.g., Hirsch 1997, 14: "The etymological roots of *theoria* define it as an act of viewing, contemplation, consideration, insight, in other words, in terms of visuality."

11. See, e.g., Wright 2004, 3: "Our civilization, which subsumes most of its predecessors, is a great ship steaming at speed into the future. It travels faster, further, and more laden than any before. We may not be able to foresee every reef and hazard, but by reading her compass bearing and headway, by understanding her design, her safety record, and the abilities of her crew, we can, I think, plot a wise course between the narrows and bergs looming ahead. And I believe we must do this without delay, because there are too many shipwrecks behind us. The vessel we are now aboard is not merely the biggest of all time; it is also the only one left. The future of everything we have accomplished since our intelligence evolved will depend on the wisdom of our actions over the next few years. Like all creatures, humans have made their way in the world so far by trial and error; unlike other creatures, we have a presence so colossal that error is a luxury we can no longer afford. The world has grown too small to forgive us any big mistakes."

12. *Unglück*, as in Sebald's essay collection *Die Beschreibung eines Unglücks* (1994).

13. There are notable exceptions; see, e.g., *Austerlitz* (Sebald 2001, 277–78), where the new Bibliothèque Nationale in suburban Paris is compared at length to an oceangoing passenger liner, sailing through "mountainous waves," from which "one of the tiny figures, having unwisely ventured on deck, [would be] swept over the rail by a gust of wind and carried far out into the wastes of the Atlantic waters."

14. See, e.g., the double meaning of the title *Nach die Natur*, "After Nature."

15. The only explicit mention of the Holocaust (a rare occurrence in Sebald) is accompanied by a double-page photo of the piles of corpses at Bergen-Belsen: Major George Wyndham Le Strange, former owner of a Suffolk manor house, had "served in the anti-tank regiment that liberated the camp at Bergen-Belsen on the 14th of April 1945" (Sebald 1998, 59).

16. A term borrowed from Angela McRobbie's (1994, 109) appraisal of Benjamin. On Sebald and emblems, see also Theisen 2006. On Sebald's "poetics," see also Hell 2003.

17. "To remember is, more and more, not to recall a story but to be able to call up a picture. Even a writer as steeped in nineteenth-century and early modern literary solemnities as W. G. Sebald was moved to seed his lamentation-narratives

of lost lives, lost nature, lost cityscapes with photographs. Sebald was not just a militant elegist. Remembering, he wanted the reader to remember, too" (Sontag 2003, 89). See also Sontag 1979.

18. See Bond 2004, 39–44.

19. Blumenberg's (1979, 193) "shipwreck" paradigm is fully transformed, structuring Sebald's intertextual weaving that is also, as he says, in *The Emigrants*, a "remembering, reading and writing."

20. See Crary's (2013a, 20) account of perception for Benjamin as something "acutely temporal and kinetic; he makes clear how modernity subverts even the possibility of a contemplative beholder. There is never pure access to a single object; vision is always multiple, adjacent to and overlapping with other objects, desires, and vectors . . . Perception within the context of modernity, for Benjamin, never disclosed the world as presence. One mode was the observer as *flâneur*, a mobile consumer of a ceaseless succession of illusory commodity-like images."

21. In this detail *The Rings of Saturn* offers a prescient warning about the impact of global warming upon the world's overpopulated coastal regions. Ironically, at the time in which the narrator's journey takes place this particular coastal region is uncannily *under*populated.

22. Crary 2013a, 99, quotes Adorno regarding changes in modern visuality described as "the adaptation [of the observer] to the order of bourgeois rationality and, ultimately, the age of advanced industry, which was made by the eye when it accustomed itself to perceiving reality as a reality of objects and hence basically of commodities"; see also Baudrillard 1998.

23. On this subject's (obvious) masculinity, see Hell 2003.

24. "For a long while I stood on the bridge that leads to the former research establishment. Far behind me to the west, scarcely to be discerned, were the gentle slopes of the inhabited land; to the north and south, in flashes of silver, gleamed the muddy bed of a dead arm of the river . . . and ahead lay nothing but destruction" (Sebald 1998, 235). Compare the famous opening of Kafka's *The Castle* (1992a, 3): "It was late in the evening when K. arrived. The village was deep in snow. The Castle hill was hidden, veiled in mist and darkness, nor was there even a glimmer of light to show that a castle was there. On the wooden bridge leading from the main road to the village, K. stood for a long time gazing into the illusory emptiness above him."

25. See Eliot's (2010) "Unreal City" in *The Wasteland*.

26. See also *Campo Santo* (Sebald 2005). The paradigmatic instance of this synoptic gaze across space and history may be the view of the Promised Land granted Moses from the summit of Mount Nebo: "Then the Lord said to him, 'This is the land I promised on oath to Abraham, Isaac and Jacob when I said, "I will give it to your descendants." I have let you see it with your eyes, but you will not cross over into it'" (Deuteronomy 34:1–4). This is a truly objective vision of a future that is not Moses's own but that of his people.

27. See Bond 2004, 40.

28. I use the neologism "historioscopy" throughout to describe a visually determined historiography.

29. See Conrad 2003, 160.

30. I follow Finch 2013 in including in this list, as Theisen does not, homosexual and bisexual men.

31. See Hell 2004 on Benjamin's angel of history and "redemptive violence" in Sebald's "Air War" lectures.

32. See especially Achebe (rpt. Conrad 1988, 251–61).

33. On *The Rings of Saturn* and postcolonialism, see Fuchs 2004, 192.

34. *Der Verschollene*, originally published in English (by Max Brod) as *Amerika*.

35. "Kafka's realism is dynamic, even in a sense cinematic, though he detested the cinema" (Albright 1981, 143); see also Janouch 1971, 147. His "realism" possesses a slapstick quality whose provenance is most likely the Yiddish theater to which Kafka exposed himself in Prague, and yet the influence of early silent film cannot be discounted (see *Diaries* [1911]). See especially Zischler 2003.

36. "[With] the proviso that realistic art must be . . . a penetration beneath the surface, an attempt to grasp the hidden vivacity of things, Kafka is explicitly against fantasy, in favor of realism" (Albright 1981, 142); "Kafka is a realist, inventing abysses that imitate the primary abyss" (141).

37. Blanchot (1982, 82–83) draws attention to the significance for Kafka's writing of the biblical prohibition of images. The paradoxical tension Blanchot exposes is one between the demands of literature and of what might be referred to as religion. It is essentially that, in spite of everything, Kafka continued to write; in spite of not finishing works, an unwillingness to publish, and his final request that the remaining manuscripts be burned after his death, he continues to write in "the effort to make manifest, through the image, the error of the imaginary, and eventually the ungraspable, forgotten truth which hides behind this error" (82).

38. *The Treachery of Images* (1928).

39. In this light, Vladimir Nabokov's (1980, 258–60) insistence that Gregor is a three-foot-long brown domed beetle looks somewhat beside the point.

40. See Albright 1981, 128: "Self-expression is a binding of oneself to a corrupt exterior world; silence frees one from this complicity with illusion. This is why the affiliation of the law with sex is so prevalent in the novel"; "*The Trial* is the comedy of the spirit's seduction, its taking the interplay of its figments as a solid external world: and sex is a useful metaphor for this temptation into unreality [sexual temptation being equivalent with temptation per se]. It is a recapitulation of the fall of man. Indeed, it is possible that the unspecified crime that leads to K.'s arrest is mere physical existence, having a body."

41. This looks ahead, obliquely, to K.'s "locked-out" (*ausgeschlossen*) status in *The Castle*.

42. According to Watt 1979, 173, Conrad thought little of impressionist painting and did not credit the comparison with literature. The fading light and encroaching darkness of the novel's frame narrative is more the literary equivalent of Turner's light-suffused mists and hazes than of Monet or Van Gogh.

43. See the map of Africa Marlow encounters in Brussels, the ultimate form of synoptic visual mastery (Conrad 2003, 73–76). See also Sebald 1998, 117–18, where *Rings of Saturn* intertextualizes this episode of colonialist geography and cartographic imperialism.

44. The phrase is Hell's (2003, 13).

45. "Sebald seems to suggest that writing or the visual arts should become applied arts again . . . in order to alleviate the split between Art and Practice that send Dürer's *Melencolia I* into unproductive brooding, or the related rupture between Scientia and Sapientia, between the narrow, rationalist knowledge of

specialization and the encyclopedic generalism that embraces wide networks of corresponding meanings" (Theisen 2006, 580–81).

46. See also Bond 2004, 40.

47. On Sebald's planar model of memory, see Kilbourn 2004, 140–54.

48. On the significance of the chronotope for Sebald, see chapters 6 and 7 in the present volume.

49. In turn derived from his posthumously published first novel, *Dream of Fair to Middling Women* (1993).

50. At this point in his journey Dante-pilgrim is granted a spectacular view from the lower slopes of Mount Purgatory. As he is taking in the view, he hears a voice and sees Belacqua off to one side sitting listlessly in the shade beneath a large rock. Belacqua doesn't bother climbing since he knows he must spend as long in Purgatory as he lived on earth—unless his stay is cut short by the prayers of a pure woman to intercede on his behalf, ensuring his salvation—i.e., what Dante has in Beatrice.

51. Of the group under consideration here, only two have recourse to the prospect of such "grace": Dante, with Beatrice, and Kurtz, with his "Intended."

52. On the road as literary chronotope, see also Bakhtin 1981, 98.

53. See Sturken and Cartwright 2001, 370.

54. As Jay 1994, 591, argues, "ocular-*ec*centricity, rather than blindness . . . is the antidote to privileging any one visual order or scopic regime. What might be called 'the dialectics of seeing' precludes the reification of scopic regimes" (emphasis in original).

Chapter 2

Portions of this chapter first appeared in Kilbourn 2007.

1. Sebald's personal library, now at the Deutsches Literaturarchiv in Marbach, holds works by all these authors, among many others.

2. Such a view of history as "catastrophe" is of course not unique to Sebald; see, e.g., Hell 2003 regarding Durs Grünbein's "vision of history as catastrophe, as the industrial production of death" (11). In either case the specific history in question is that of Germany in the twentieth century (13).

3. Despite his tenuous relationship with poststructuralist theory (Foucault but not Derrida), in his prose works Sebald is engaged in his own kind of critique of the Western metaphysical tradition.

4. See Kilbourn 2010. On cultural memory, see, e.g., Erll 2011.

5. See also Müller 1984, 123–35. Regarding *Hamletmachine* and Sebald, see Hell 2003, 35n106.

6. See also Jay 1994, 132–33, 315. See Alpers 1983.

7. This is also one of the only images reproduced in the text that I discuss here. This may seem strange given my emphasis on visuality, but, as mentioned, Sebald's prose works manifest an alternative relation of word to image and a radically autocritical way of seeing; in fact, some of the most significant images in Sebald go unreproduced. See, e.g., Albrecht Dürer's 1514 engraving *Melencolia I* (see also Sebald 1998, 9).

8. See also Leder 1990, 142–46.

9. On Foucault's significance for Sebald, see Theisen 2004, 177n37; Long 2006. For another version of Sebald's analysis of the same painting, see Sebald 2003, 178.

10. On Von Trier's film *Melancholia*, see also Bergstrom 2016, 94: "The question of representability in the face of extinction or nothingness is not a new one. In 'Literature and the Right to Death', Maurice Blanchot argues that literature, and by extension all representation, 'is built on top of its own ruins' (2016, 22). In other words, to represent by words or images is to risk the danger of exposing a paradox at the heart of all action. Blanchot anticipates the critique of presence that is taken up later in Derrida (the impossibility of self-presence) and Lacan (the structuring 'void' at the centre of the human psyche). Arguably, extinction and apocalypse become the very structuring possibilities of representation, since 'everything begins from nothing' . . . The danger of capitalism remains. The inability to imagine alternative economic arrangements is the failure of the creative force that resists nothingness."

11. In Buck-Morss's (1989) phrase.

12. See Benjamin 1985, 157–58. See also Jay 1994, 591.

13. See the narrator's conversation with Cornelis de Jong about the long-standing relation in Northern Europe between the sugar trade and the history of art (Sebald 1998, 194). See also Berger 1980. Hell (2003, 15) connects this privileging of vision and the masculine gender in her discussion of German post-Holocaust authorship.

14. See Bal 1991.

15. "The modern science of the individual emerged from the visual penetration of the dead body" (Jay 1994, 395).

16. "The night of time, wrote Thomas Browne in . . . *The Garden of Cyrus*, far surpasseth the day and who knows when was the Aequinox?" Nonbeing always exceeds being, insofar as it is infinite, where being is by definition finite (Sebald 1998, 154).

17. *Eine englische Wallfahrt.*

18. See Lacan 1973, 79–90.

19. For Benjamin the epitome of this transitional figure is Shakespeare's Hamlet, despite the play's non-German provenance; see Benjamin 1985, 157.

20. To quote Bergstrom (2016, 95–96), the "failure of rational, scientific positivism is also linked to the failure of capitalism, each emerging during the Enlightenment as a response to a re-ordering of the human structures of the subject, in terms of perception and economic organization. Capitalism and scientific positivism each prescribe a particular subjective gaze . . . in order to suppress any contradictions or tensions in their systems and which naturalize the paradoxes inherent to their construction."

21. "Wie es eigentlich gewesen" (quoted in Presner 2004, 343).

22. See, e.g., "Max Ferber" in *The Emigrants*, although in this case the relation is one of subject vis-à-vis subjective memory rather than "History" in some putatively objective sense. Sebald often exploits the loss of a clear distinction between these two structures for its creative potential.

23. I thank Sandra Parmegiani for pointing out this passage and its probable significance for Sebald, who possessed a copy of the German translation of Magris's novel *Donau*, now in the Deutsches Literaturarchiv in Marbach, Germany.

24. The "Now" constitutive of the modern (from the Latin *modo*) is the present moment that forever disappears in the gap between sensation and cognition. The perpetual absence of the present moment is a theme in modernity running back

through Benjamin and Heidegger to Bergson and, ultimately, to Saint Augustine, whose meditation on time in his *Confessions* stands behind, e.g., Heidegger's *The Concept of Time*. See Charney 1995.

25. In his preface to the *Lyrical Ballads*, ca. 1800 (Wordsworth and Coleridge 1991).

26. See also "*Il ritorno in patria*," where the narrator, in explaining his belated return to his native Bavarian village, remarks that: "far from becoming clearer, things now appeared to me more incomprehensible than ever. The more images I gathered from the past . . . the more unlikely it seemed to me that the past had actually happened in this or that way, for nothing about it could be called normal: most of it was absurd, and if not absurd, then appalling" (Sebald 1999, 212).

27. Sebald's ambivalence toward remembering vs. forgetting is underscored in the passage he underlined in his copy of Berger's (1980, 58) *About Looking*: "Memory implies a certain act of redemption. What is remembered has been saved from nothingness. What is forgotten has been abandoned."

28. I am grateful to Ben Hutchinson for his help in locating this annotation in Sebald's copy of *Donau*.

29. See Hell 2003, 36; 2004, 361. See also Chandler 2003, 258.

30. This is also the beginning of the shift from the Aristotelian/Ptolemaic conception of the universe as a "finite world" to the early modern idea of an infinite universe. See, e.g., Koyré 1958; Hawking 1988; Harries 2001.

31. See Hell 2003 and 2004 on Sebald's relation to the history of modernity as "catastrophe," particularly in terms of his invocation of Benjamin's angel of history.

32. In his analysis of the work of art in the age of technological reproducibility, Benjamin (2002b, 108) traces the "ultimate re-entrenchment" of aesthetic aura, rapidly giving way before exchange value in the commodified art object, to "the human countenance" as "focal point of early photography." "To have pinpointed this new stage constitutes the incomparable significance of Atget, who, around 1900, took photographs of deserted Paris streets. It has quite justly been said of him that he photographed them like scenes of a crime. The scene of a crime, too, is deserted . . . With Atget, photographs become standard evidence for historical occurrences, and acquire a hidden political significance" (108). With Sebald, to adapt Presner's (2004, 343) reading, the nineteenth-century historical novel's productive relation with photography, with its promise of verisimilitudinous reproduction of historical reality "as it really happened," reaches its apogee and its negation.

33. E.g., the can of "Cherry Coke" the narrator consumes at one point (Sebald 1998, 176), or the scene in which he visits a McDonald's, where he buys "a carton of chips," feeling "like a criminal wanted worldwide as [he] stood at the brightly lit counter" (81).

34. See, e.g., Hell 2003, 28: "What is Sebald's oeuvre all about if not the refusal of realism?"

35. Much of the present tense "action" of *The Rings of Saturn* shares its setting, the coastal heath, with *Lear*; see also Theisen 2006, 576–78. As Theisen points out, Sebald borrows the play's astrological imagery, as well as Lear's saturnine qualities as masculine subject (577–78). *Lear*, as much as *Hamlet*, also informs Müller's *Hamletmachine*.

36. See Crary 2013a, 20. See also Charney 1995. For Judith Ryan (2009, 47–48), *The Rings of Saturn* is a highly modified species of pilgrimage narrative for an extraterritorialized postsecular late modern mind-set.

37. See Crary 2013a, 17–18.

38. On postmemory, see Hirsch 1997, 22; on postmemory in Sebald, see Long 2003; Crownshaw 2004; Anderson 2008.

39. As Dennis Duffy (2010, 202) puts it, "We mutter assurances of love, while the tsunami slams into us in the act of grabbing at the cellphone camera that captures our obliteration." See also Sontag 2001, 18–22.

40. The passage continues a little further on as follows: "Even for Nabokov, recording [the 'visionary moments' of memory] was a very arduous business. A short sequence of words often needed hours of work before the rhythm was right . . . before the gravity of earth had been overcome and the author, now as it were disembodied himself, could reach the opposite bank across his precarious bridge of written characters . . . To set something so beautiful in motion, according to both Nabokov and the messianic theory of salvation, no gaudy show is necessary, only a tiny spiritual movement which releases the ideas that are shut inside our heads and always going around in circles, letting them out into a universe where, as in a good sentence, there is a place for everything and everything in its place" (146–47).

41. See Bloch 1986.

42. It is clear from *Vertigo* and his essay on Peter Weiss, e.g., that Sebald was familiar with the *Divine Comedy*. See "The Remorse of the Heart," in Sebald 2003, 188–89.

43. This is especially true of a work like *Das Schloß*, which can be read as Kafka's modernist rewriting of the *Commedia*. Sebald's invocation of Dante here is in keeping, too, with the subtitle of *The Rings of Saturn: An English Pilgrimage*.

44. See Hawking 1988, 2–3.

45. See also Sebald's essay "The Remorse of the Heart" (Sebald 2003, 173–74) on Peter Weiss: "The concept of catastrophe developed by Weiss in [his] panoramas opens up no eschatological perspective; rather, it denotes a now permanent state of destruction. What is seen, here and now, is already an underworld"; see 188–89 on Weiss's use of a Dantean redemptive structure for his 1965 play *Die Ermittlung* (The investigation), whose thirty-three cantos describe a "period that has left any hope of salvation far behind."

46. This vision of the stars signifies as readily in terms of the *King Lear* intertext outlined above. See also Theisen 2004, who quotes Kent's speech about Lear's daughters: "It is the stars, / The stars above us, govern our conditions . . ." (4.3.33–35).

47. See the scene in *Austerlitz* (Sebald 2001, 32) in which the narrator visits Austerlitz in his book and paper-filled office, near the British Museum in London.

48. See *The Emigrants* (Sebald 1996, 237). See also the opening of *The Rings of Saturn* (Sebald 1998, 3–4), where the narrator recounts his own temporary mental and physical paralysis, during which he "began in [his] thoughts to write these pages."

Chapter 3

Portions of this chapter first appeared in Kilbourn 2006, 2015.

1. Where "intertextuality," as a species of intermediality, is broadly defined as a synonym for "literature" conceived as an endless and boundless process of

recontextualization, rewriting, and dissemination—the interconnectivity among all texts beyond singular acts of artistic intention.

2. Kafka 1971, 226–34; 1936, 102–7. On Sebald as a "bricoleur," see Arthur Williams 1998, 101.

3. See also Sebald's (2003, 189) description of Peter Weiss's 1965 play *Die Ermittlung* as set in "a period that has left any hope of salvation far behind."

4. See Kilbourn 1998.

5. This ironic identification reaches a kind of apogee in section 4 ("*Il ritorno in patria*"), where the Bavarian Wandering Jew elides with the Hunter Gracchus–turned-sailor in a brief interlude in a tiny wooden chapel in the Tyrolean Alps on the way to Wertach im Algäu, the narrator's and, as it happens, Sebald's own *patria*: "Outside, snowflakes were drifting past the small window, and presently it seemed to me as if I were in a boat on a voyage, crossing vast waters" (Sebald 1999, 178–79).

6. In a groundbreaking series of essays, Arthur Williams was among the first to attribute the postmodernist label to Sebald via the foregrounding of specific formal and thematic features of the novels; see, e.g., Arthur Williams 2000, 104; 2001, 74.

7. See Habermas 2001, 1749, on Christianity as already "modern" vis-à-vis a Roman pagan past.

8. See Suchoff 2012, 170.

9. Habermas (2001, 1751) describes "Benjamin's concept of the *Jetztzeit*, of the present as a moment of revelation; a time in which splinters of a messianic presence are enmeshed."

10. Quoted in Benjamin 1969, 116.

11. This metaphysical school, which persists in reading the figure of Nabokov as a kind of "anthropomorphic deity" (de la Durantaye 2008, 443), continues to dominate Nabokov criticism; see, e.g., Alexandrov 1991; Boyd 1990, 1991; Johnson and Boyd 2002; Rutledge 2011; Karen Jacobs 2014. See Wood 1994 for a rare dissenting voice.

12. E.g., "Memory is, really, in itself, a tool, one of the many tools that an artist uses" (Nabokov 1973, 12).

13. "The freshness of the flowers being arranged by the under-gardener in the cool drawing-room of our country house, as I was running downstairs with my butterfly net on a summer day half a century ago: that kind of thing is absolutely permanent, immortal, it can never change, no matter how many times I farm it out to my characters" (Nabokov 1973, 12).

14. I am not the first to apply this terminology to Nabokov's aesthetics. See especially John Burt Foster's (1993) *Nabokov's Art of Memory and European Modernism*, an insightful and comprehensive consideration of "Nabokov's intense absorption with pictorial images fashioned by memory, images that recapture his past so vividly that they seem to transcend time" (182).

16. "The story of the Wandering Jew is one of several important mythical themes developed by Nabokov. According to Western medieval legend, the Wandering Jew . . . refused to allow Christ a short rest on the way to Golgotha. For that reason he was deprived of his own eternal rest. [He] is doomed to wander ceaselessly throughout the ages, awaiting Doomsday, when the curse will be lifted" (Skonechnaia 2002, 186). See Leiser (1974, 157–58) on the Nazi propagandistic appropriation of the myth in the 1941 "documentary" *The Wandering Jew*.

17. See Millington 2006, 50.

18. See Frye 1982, 80–81.

19. In this approach, reading and interpretation play as much of a determining role as writing or authorial intention. See Alexandrov (1991, 177), who propounds an alternative theory of Nabokov's poetics based on an unconvincing analogy with his theories of biological mimicry. See also Wood 1994, 190–91; Frye 1982, 78–101.

20. Note Kafka's statement about there being "an infinite amount of hope—but not for us" (quoted in Benjamin 1969, 116).

21. "When I awoke the next morning from a deep and dreamless sleep, which not even the surging roar of traffic on the Ring had been able to disturb, I felt as if I had crossed a wide stretch of water during the hours of my nocturnal absence. Before I opened my eyes I could see myself descending the gangway of a large ferry, and hardly had I stepped ashore but I resolved to take the evening train to Venice, and before that to spend the day with Ernst Herbeck in Klosterneuburg" (Sebald 1999, 37–38).

22. See Dante (*Inferno* 3.130–36):

> . . . the darkened plain
> quaked so tremendously—the memory
> of terror then, bathes me in sweat again.
> A whirlwind burst out of the tear-drenched earth,
> A wind that crackled with a blood-red light,
> A light that overcame all of my senses;
> And like a man whom sleep has seized, I fell.

23. Arthur Williams (2000, 101) calls this a "Kafkaisierung."

24. According to Zilcosky 2003, 108, "Sebald . . . borrows from Freudian sexual theory, but he also pushes Freud's model beyond its borders. Specifically, Sebald suggests that homosexuality might offer a way out of a system of eternal heterosexual return—not least because homosexuality implies, in both biblical and psychoanalytic jargon, losing one's way."

25. See Casanova's (2005, 235) account: "The word *Tribunal* petrified me utterly, leaving me with only the physical ability to obey."

26. See, e.g., Hutchinson 2009b.

27. See Prager 2006, 118–19, for an insightful exploration of this dimension of Kafka's writings and their fictional appropriation and amplification by Sebald.

28. Here is Casanova's (2005, 235) account of the morning of his arrest: "I dressed myself mechanically, neither hastily nor slowly. I washed and shaved myself . . . combed my hair, and I put on a shirt trimmed in lace and a fine frock-coat, all without thinking about what I was doing, without saying a word, and without [the constable] Messer Grande, who never took his eyes off me, daring to find fault with the fact that I was dressing as if to attend a wedding."

29. "Our reason is like gunpowder, which, while easy to ignite, never ignites unless it is lit; or like a drinking glass, which never breaks unless it is broken" (Casanova 2005, 245).

30. See, e.g., Sebald 1999, 163–67.

31. Certain details in the narrative, such as the fact that the narrator's father comes from the Black Forest (possibly identifying him with the Hunter) (Sebald

1999, 193), not to mention the "primal scene" with Schlag and Romana in the woodshed, accidentally witnessed by the youthful narrator, might encourage a thoroughgoing psychoanalytic reading of *Vertigo*. Sebald's narratives are no more reducible to the Oedipal allegory than the Kafkan texts they remediate, however.

32. On the significance of the German composer to *Vertigo*, see the recurrence of the name Ludwig, whether in reference to the Bavarian emperor, who was Wagner's patron (Sebald 1999, 53), or to the shadowy "Organizzazione Ludwig," an anarcho-terrorist group in part 2 (130).

33. The yellow brimstone, indigenous to Northern Europe, is reputedly the most common butterfly in England, having inspired the Anglo-Saxons to name the insect *buttorfleoge*, after its buttery color.

34. Etymologically, "Gracchus" is a permutation of "jackdaw," or the Czech *kavka*, "blackbird, crow, grackle"; see Wagenbach 1984, 40; see also Koelb 1989, 22; Janouch 1971, 36. Kafka's father's business emblem was a blackbird, in a nod to the Czech version of the family name (Wagenbach 1984, 40). Janouch (1971, 16–17), in one of his reconstructed conversations with the writer, records the following confession: "'I am a quite impossible bird' . . . 'I am a jackdaw—a *kavka* . . . I hop about bewildered among my fellow men. They regard me with deep suspicion. And indeed I am a dangerous bird, a thief, a jackdaw.'" In *Vertigo*, part 2, the narrator is in Vienna, retracing Kafka's movements in 1913, talking to the "jackdaws in the gardens by the city hall, and a white-headed blackbird that shared the jackdaw's interest in [his] grapes" (Sebald 1999, 36).

35. See *The Flying Dutchman*, act 1.

36. See *The Flying Dutchman*, act 1.

37. See Robbins 1991.

38. See Deleuze and Guattari 1986.

39. For Theisen (2006, 572), "Kafka's story elucidates the narrative technique that informs Sebald's interest in mutable identities and metamorphotic [*sic*] identifications." But I would go further: Gregor Samsa wakes up to find his "inner self" expressed externally, in the form of an insectile carapace presumably resistant to all but a metaphorical visualization. Elias Canetti (1974, 27) argues, on the one hand, that for Kafka his room, in which he does his writing, *is* his "outer body," his "forebody," like an outer shell, or carapace. It is the external, but not by any means thick or impermeable, layer protecting him from the world outside, from all the potential threats, real or imagined: food, drink, medicine, the air itself. But above all, it protects him from the proximity of other people, such as the members of his family, whom Kafka could never give up, at least not until he was on the verge of death.

Chapter 4

Portions of this chapter first appeared in Kilbourn 2006.

1. For the latter, see Boyd 1990, 1991. On Sebald's intertextualization of Nabokov, see Ceuppens 2004; Karen Jacobs 2014; Sill 1997; Arthur Williams 1998, 2000, 2001.

3. See also Nabokov 1973, 90.

4. It was here that Nabokov produced the definitive version of *Speak, Memory*, which appeared in 1967.

5. This is a (perhaps intentional) lapse: the dinner scene is set in April 1971 (Sebald 1996, 11), whereas the photo of Nabokov was taken in August of that year; see Boyd 1991, 563–64.

6. In Dante's *Inferno*, canto 5, ll. 100–108, 127–38.

7. See, e.g., Nabokov 1973, 201–3.

8. See Foster 1993, 89–90.

9. On the *Isenheim Altarpiece*, see Sebald 2002, 14–28.

10. In English in the original.

11. See Nabokov 1989, 130; Boyd 1990, 84.

12. See chapter 2 in the present volume.

13. See chapter 2 in the present volume.

14. The very idea of the younger Nabokov voluntarily releasing his specimens flies in the face of everything the elder remembering Nabokov says about his butterfly-hunting mania. Indeed, the episode in Bad Kissingen is related in the midst of a section of *Speak, Memory*, chapter 6, in which the narrator lists the "strange reactions in other creatures" his peculiar passion provokes. Rather than releasing his catches at the end of a day of hunting, Nabokov the lepidopterist enjoys nothing so much as "snuff[ing] out the life of some silver-studded lepidopteron throbbing in [his] net" (Nabokov 1989, 138). The point Boyd (1990, 74) obscures is that to collect butterflies one must kill them.

16. See Wood 1994, 190–91.

17. Arthur Williams (1998, 99) describes the Genewein photo this way: "Its unsettlingly familiar patterns invite an imaginative plumbing of its depths and tell a story which may be in the eye of the reader, or the eye of the author, or the eyes of the subjects whose lives held such promise and whose fate we know."

18. "In Greek religion and mythology, three goddesses who controlled human lives; also called the Moerae or Moirai. They were: Clotho, who spun the web of life; Lachesis, who measured its length; and Atropos, who cut it. The Roman Fates were the Parcae—Nona, Decuma, and Morta" (*Columbia Encyclopedia* 2001).

19. An early *New York Times* review singled out for censure one feature of *The Emigrants*: "the man with the butterfly net, a Nabokovian figure, who keeps appearing and disappearing. I found him blatantly symbolic and literary" (Jefferson 2001, 3). See the positive early responses of critics such as Arthur Williams (1998, 112n20) and Cynthia Ozick (1996, 28).

20. See Arthur Williams (2000, 111n4): "Sebald's works . . . are rich in references to perspective . . . His first-person narrators often overfly areas or stand on high vantage-points, sometimes in dreams, affording them and the reader a bird's eye view of the world, revealing its past and hinting at its future." Like Moses's view of the Promised Land from the top of Mount Nebo, this spatialized view of time allows the past and future to become interchangeable and, in a formulation from *Bend Sinister* (Nabokov's first American novel), for the possibility that escape and return are the same thing (1990, 108). See Deuteronomy 34:1–4.

21. Newton published his *Philosophiae Naturalis Principia Mathematica* in 1687, in which he "postulated a law of universal gravitation according to which each body in the universe was attracted toward every other body by a force that was stronger the more massive the bodies and the closer they were to each other. It was this same force that caused objects to fall to the ground" (Hawking 1988,

4). See *The Rings of Saturn*, part 8, where the narrator engages in a "lengthy conversation concerning Newton's theory of gravity" (Sebald 1998, 209).

22. On Walter Benjamin's intrinsic melancholia, see Sontag 1979, 7–28. This is an excellent introduction to understanding Sebald, written before Sontag had read the German author.

23. Klibansky, Panofsky, and Saxl 1964, quoted in Theisen 2006, 579.

24. "Sebald associates imaginative melancholy's awareness of its inadequate powers of knowledge with Browne, who was born under Saturn in 1605 and believed that nature's oddities and time's variety shows were largely 'still in the Urne unto us'" (Theisen 2006, 580).

25. On Sebald's use of Browne's "quincunx," see Theisen (2006, 579), who also locates this pattern in the "stereometric form" of the "truncated rhomboid" pictured in Dürer's engraving *Melencolia I*.

26. See Browne 1958.

27. For a different but compatible reading of metamorphosis and the possibility of redemption in *The Rings of Saturn*, see Theisen 2006, 572.

28. E.g., the narrator in part 6 compares Somerleyton Hall with Coleridge's poetic dream-vision of the "palace of Kublai Khan, which was built on the site later occupied by Peking at the very time when Dunwich was one of the most important communities in the kingdom of England" (Sebald 1998, 160).

29. See, e.g., "Ashbury" (Sebald 1998, 210) and "Ashburnham" (165)—not to mention "Swinburne"—regarding the punning proliferation throughout the text of "burn" and "ash" in proper names, in English as in German. See also "Ashman" in *Austerlitz* (Sebald 2001, 104).

30. See, e.g., Alexandrov 1991; de la Durantaye 2008.

31. The Leyden jar is the first electrical capacitor, or early battery, invented in the Netherlands in the mid-eighteenth century. It was occasionally used in experiments in galvanism, hence Sebald's image of Swinburne reawakening to new life after lunch, "convulsed with electric energy . . . like a startled moth" (Sebald 1998, 165).

32. Ceuppens 2004, 193, similarly argues that "the butterfly becomes something to be caught and displayed as museum piece, a metaphor of death rather than of transfiguration or life."

33. Such radical defiance of the consumerist ethos is seen most clearly perhaps in the Ashbury family, "ill-equipped for life," "idly sewing and undoing beautiful silk garments from fabric remnants rather than capitalizing on the raising of silk worms" (Theisen 2006, 576).

34. See Kafka 1971, 135–38.

Chapter 5

1. See McCulloh 2003.

2. Originally published in Italian as *Alla cieca*, 2006.

3. For a comprehensive study of the significance of myth for Magris, and in particular the Alcestis myth in *Blindly*, see Parmegiani 2011.

4. As Kafka once said, there is "plenty of hope, an infinite amount of hope—but not for us" (quoted in Benjamin 1969, 116).

5. See, e.g., Prager 2006. See also chapter 6 in the present volume.

6. See also *Diaries* July 6, 1916 (1976, 364).

7. "26 December . . . Do I make my laments here only to find my salvation here? It won't come out of this notebook, it will come when I'm in bed and it will put me on my back so that I will lie there beautiful and light and bluish-white; no other salvation will come" (Kafka 1976, 323).

8. See the conclusion of the "Before the Law" parable in *The Trial*, where just before dying the man from the country learns that the door to the Law, from which he is about to be forever barred, was meant only for him.

9. Kafka 1976, 291–92; emphasis added. This passage is also the intermedial inspiration for the opening scene of American playwright Tony Kushner's 1993 AIDS trilogy *Angels in America: A Gay Fantasia on National Themes*. See Hutcheon and Hutcheon 1999.

10. All biblical quotations are from *New Oxford Annotated Bible* 1977.

11. The letter continues, "Kafka, so I contend, had no answers to these questions. But the form in which they presented themselves to him . . . contains indications of a state of the world in which such questions no longer have a place, because their answers, far from being instructive, make the questions superfluous. Kafka sought—and sometimes glimpsed as in a dream—the structure of this kind of answer that renders the question superfluous" (128).

12. "Heiner Müller's 1958 version shows us a luckless [angel] waiting for history in the petrification of flight, glance, breath": we see this angel as he is buried by the rubble of the past, while the future "explodes his eyeballs" and "strangl[es] him with its breath" (Hell 2004, 363).

13. And of Scholem's poem "Agesilaus Santander," which Benjamin esteemed so highly (Benjamin and Scholem 1992, 128).

14. Quoted in Howe 1992, xii.

15. See the "Anzolo" San Michele in *Microcosms* (1999, 87).

16. In a letter of May 1913, Kafka writes of resuming his diary, despite "the physical impossibility of writing and the inner need for it" (1973, 219). And, immediately preceding the trip to Riva in September of that year—the structuring event in part 3 of *Vertigo*—Kafka asks rhetorically, "Where am I to find salvation?" (231). See also Kafka's letter to Felix Weltsch (from the sanatorium in Riva, September 1913): "Things will not get better, things will never get better for me. Sometimes I think I am no longer in the world but am drifting around in some limbo. If you imagine that I derive some help, some solution from a sense of guilt, you are wrong. The reason why I have this sense of guilt is that it is for me the finest sense of penitence. But one must not look too closely into this matter lest the sense of guilt become merely a form of nostalgia. And once that happens, there immediately rears up, far higher and more threatening than penitence, the feeling of freedom, of redemption, of relative contentment" (1977, 102). See *Vertigo*: "[As] it was Dr. K. who conjured up this tale [of the Hunter Gracchus], it seems to me that the meaning of Gracchus the huntsman's ceaseless journey lies in a penitence for a longing for love, such as invariably besets Dr. K., as he explains in one of his countless *Fledermaus*-letters to Felice, precisely at the point where there is seemingly, and in the natural and lawful order of things, nothing to be enjoyed" (Sebald 1999, 165).

17. See "Dr. K." in Venice (1913): "Perhaps it was the bills, still posted throughout the city, announcing the *spettacoli lirici all'Arena* that August and the word AIDA displayed in large letters which persuaded him that the Veronese show of

carefree togetherness had something of a theatrical performance about it, staged especially to bring home to him, Dr. K., his solitary, eccentric condition—a thought he could not get out of his head and which he was only able to escape by seeking refuge in a cinema" (Sebald 1999, 150). On the significance of the protagonist's demise in Kafka's stories, "Final contortions of this kind, which regularly occur in opera, when, as Dr. K. once wrote, the dying voice aimlessly wanders through the music, did not by any means seem ridiculous to him; rather he believed them to be an expression of our, so to speak, natural misfortune, since after all, as he remarks elsewhere, we lie prostrate on the boards, dying, our whole lives long" (152).

18. Also appropriated in part 1 of Kushner's *Angels in America* (see note 9 above).

19. See, e.g., Sebald 1998, where this theme reinforces the emptiness at the heart of the text, reflective of the narrator's sense of extraterritorial alienation.

20. See especially Sebald 1998, 80–85.

21. Regarding the motif of the inn or hotel room as a sailing ship, see also Sebald 1998, 207–8: "I heard the woodwork of the old half-timber building, which had expanded in the heat of the day and was now contracting fraction by fraction, creaking and groaning. In the gloom of the unfamiliar room, my eyes involuntarily turned in the direction from which the sounds came, looking for the crack that might run along the low ceiling, the spot where the plaster was flaking from the wall or the mortar crumbling behind the paneling. And if I closed my eyes for a while it felt as if I were in a cabin aboard a ship on the high seas, as if the whole building were rising on the swell of a wave, shuddering a little on the crest, and then, with a sigh, subsiding into the depths." See also Sebald 2001, 387.

22. Quoted in Benjamin 1969, 116.

23. See Kafka 1973, 335.

24. On Kafka and tourism, see, e.g., Zilcosky 2003, 15.

25. See Zilcosky 2003, 14–15.

26. On Foucault's influence upon Sebald, see Long 2007, 13–20.

27. On the significance of the Orpheus myth in Magris's oeuvre, see Magris 2011.

28. "Jason is portrayed as the 'great seducer,' the man who knows how to stage the heroic feat of the myth that is at the same time a cheap 'self-advertisement' . . . and who, in order to shine, needs his female victims, first and foremost Medea" (Parmegiani 2011, 114).

29. "Solitary, ancient Medea, unreachable in the mute pain and alienation to which she has been condemned for centuries by Jason's masculine arrogance" (Parmegiani 2011, 114).

30. "Each one of us finds himself in that splendid parable of Borges' about a painter who paints landscapes, seas, rivers, trees only to realise in the end that he has painted his own self-portrait, because his identity is precisely his own way of seeing things" (Magris 2008b).

31. E.g., the "'faint white of the low neck of a blouse', [and] we may conjecture that the erotic aura of such pictures—snapshots . . . so to speak . . . is due to their proximity to death" (156).

32. See, e.g., Friedberg 1994.

33. This final sentence is reputedly a quote from the courtroom testimony of Sadie Mae Glutz (Susan Atkins), on trial for her part in the 1969 Manson family murders of Sharon Tate and others in Los Angeles.

34. See Kilbourn 2010 on "psychokatabasis" as a postmodern narrative genre.

35. See Canetti 1974, 63. Canetti seems justified in reading the whole of *The Trial* in terms of Kafka's relationship with Felice: all the details of K.'s life, public and private, open and intimate, come to be bound up inextricably with his "trial," to the point where it no longer makes sense to distinguish among them; e.g., Felice Bauer; F. B.; Fräulein Burstner; etc. See Canetti 1974, 1–5. Stanley Corngold (2008, 240), by contrast, apropos of Canetti's thesis, is certain that the "intensity of Kafka's relation to literature produced the redemptive expectations of *The Trial* apart from Kafka's relation to his fiancée." For my part, I see no reason not to bring both readings together.

36. See also 225–26.

37. E.g., Hayman 1982, 216–17; Grözinger 1994, 4–5.

38. See Blanchot's (1982, 73) reading of Kafka in this light. Kafka's diary entry for July 28, 1914, reads, "Wenn ich mich nicht in einer Arbeit rette, bin ich verloren" (1990, 663). Where the Greenberg translation reads, "If I can't take refuge in some work, I am lost" (Kafka 1976, 295), Blanchot translates it as "if I don't *save* myself in some work . . ." (1982, 62; emphasis added). Whether a saving of one's self or a need for sanctuary, either way Blanchot's reading is served: there is a special kind of space that only work—for Kafka, writing—provides, a space in which a kind of salvation becomes possible. Kafka's "confidence in his own powers" as a writer allows him to see "what he himself demands of art: no longer that it give reality and coherence to his person, that it save him, that is, from insanity [psychological 'salvation'], but that it save him from perdition [spiritual/moral 'salvation']" (65).

Chapter 6

Portions of this chapter first appeared in Kilbourn 2004.

1. Bakhtin 1981, 84; see also 243.

2. See *Speak, Memory*: "Very lovely, very lonesome. But what am I doing in this stereoscopic dreamland? How did I get here? Somehow, the two sleighs have slipped away, leaving behind a passportless spy standing on the blue-white road in his New England snowboots and stormcoat. The vibration in my ears is no longer their receding bells, but only my old blood singing. All is still, spellbound, enthralled by the moon, fancy's rear-vision mirror. The snow is real, though, and as I bend to it and scoop up a handful, sixty years crumble to glittering frost-dust between my fingers" (1989, 100).

3. See Monteverdi's 1639 opera *Il ritorno in patria d'Ulisse*, which features Tempo, the goddess of time personified, one of three deities who persecute the protagonist in his attempt to return to his homeland.

4. This is apart from sublimated—or otherwise indirectly represented—homosexual or homoerotic relationships. See, e.g., Austerlitz's school friendship with Gerald Fitzpatrick (Sebald 2001, 74–96).

5. With the exception of the noncorrespondence of Marie and Eurydice, in this invocation of the Orpheus myth Austerlitz is much closer to Cocteau's thoroughly ironic modern version than to any of the classical avatars. In fact, my reading of Sebald's version suggests a going beyond Cocteau in that here the hero is made to play the roles of *both* seeker and sought. In this he also ironically recalls Oedipus, albeit in a pre-Freudian sense. For a paradigmatic example of a classical retelling of the Orpheus myth, see book 10 in Ovid 2002.

6. See Barzilai (Long and Whitehead 2004, 203).

7. For a comparable dream about deceased family members, see the opening paragraph in Munro 2006a, 203.

8. From "Whenever in my dreams I see the dead" to "some friend of mine they never knew."

9. "That in some cases the butterfly symbolizes something (*e.g.*, Psyche) lies utterly outside my area of interest" (Nabokov 1973, 168).

10. "My title does not allude to Frances Yates' well-known *The Art of Memory*; Nabokov apparently had no direct contact with the classical and Renaissance memory systems discussed in her book. Rather, the term 'art of memory' proved a convenient and even unavoidable label for one key tendency in Nabokov's memory-writing, his deliberate oscillation between fictive invention and mnemonic truth. This oscillation, when projected onto his choice of narrative modes, corresponds to the intricate interplay between his novels and stories on the one hand, and the different versions of his autobiography on the other" (Foster 1993, x).

11. See Zilcosky 2006, 685–87.

12. A few of these instances are obvious to the attentive reader. See, e.g., the scene in which Austerlitz's description of his dying foster mother's morbid predilection for snowlike face powder explicitly remediates Nabokov's memory of his maternal grandmother's similar habits, which include waking up beneath an open window covered in a blanket of fresh snow (Sebald 2001, 62; Nabokov 1989, 155). Austerlitz tells the narrator that he had been reading "the reminiscences of his childhood and youth by a Russian writer"; the revised edition of *Speak, Memory* first appeared in 1987, while this conversation is set in the early 1990s.

13. Here and throughout, page numbers in round brackets indicate the 1989 Vintage edition, while the numbers in square brackets are for Sebald's copy of *Speak, Memory* (Penguin 1987).

14. See also Wood 1994, 98; see Proust 1996, 1–55.

15. See Draaisma 2000.

16. See Bergson 1988.

17. Note that in *Vertigo*, part 4, "*Il ritorno in patria*," Sebald refers to Germany as *Heimat*, homeland as "fatherland"—ironically underscored in the Italian *patria*, lifted from Monteverdi's *Il ritorno in patria d'Ulisse*.

18. See also Nabokov 1990, 47.

19. See Kilbourn 2010, 93–100.

20. Maximilian is also Sebald's middle name.

21. Among others, Fritz Lang's Siegfried, Ludwig Wittgenstein, Max Aurach (Ferber in English), as well as the subject of an actual BBC radio documentary about the *Kindertransports*, which Austerlitz overhears in Penelope Peacefull's antiquarian bookshop (Sebald 2001, 141).

22. See Kilbourn 2013, 259.

23. See Jaggi 2001, 2.

24. He does, however, unearth memories of elderly women in the parks walking "bad-tempered little dogs," reminiscent of Nabokov's mother, who died in Prague, "on the eve of World War Two" (1989, 48–49). This one example of Sebald's remediation of specific elements in *Speak, Memory* reveals the debt that the Prague sections of *Austerlitz* owe to Nabokov's account of his mother's last years (see especially chapter 2).

25. On Nabokov's attitude toward Freud, see, e.g., Foster 1993, 212.

26. "Through the crystal of my strangely translucent state I vividly visualized her driving away down Morskaya Street" (1989, 37).

27. In a debt to Aristotle, Augustine stresses that "the things which we sense do not enter the memory themselves, but their images are there ready to present themselves to our thoughts when we recall them" (Saint Augustine 1988, 10.8, 215).

28. "Vivid" from the Latin *vivere*, "to live."

29. As Foster 1993, 214, points out, the magic lantern scene that forms the basis for chapter 8 is a "Proustian motif." See Proust 1996, 8–10. See also the magic lantern scene in Ingmar Bergman's 1982 film *Fanny and Alexander*.

30. "And I thought of all I had missed in my country, of the things I would not have omitted to note and treasure, had I suspected before that my life was to veer in such a violent way" (1989, 261).

31. What W. J. T. Mitchell calls word-images (see Foster 1993, 182)—a designation complicated further in Sebald by the presence—or equally conspicuous absence—of photographs and other visual images throughout his novels.

32. The phrase is lifted verbatim from Nabokov's (2008, 82) *The Real Life of Sebastian Knight*: "People liked her because she was quietly attractive with her charming dim face and soft husky voice, somehow remaining in one's memory as if she were subtly endowed with the gift of being remembered: she came out well in one's mind, she was mnemogenic." The latent photographic metaphor in the last lines is also worthy of note.

33. On the significance of the photographs and other images in Sebald's texts, see, e.g., Harris 2001; Long 2003; Crownshaw 2004; Patt 2007.

34. In his reading of Proust, Foster (1993, 209) contends that "in reflecting on involuntary memory" the French novelist "dismisses visual imagery."

35. See, e.g., Proust 1996, 12–13.

36. For the paradigmatic instance of the writer's relationship with his (dead) mother, see Saint Augustine 1988, book 9.12: "O God, who made us both, how could there be any comparison between the honour which I showed to her and the devoted service she had given me? It was because I was now bereft of all the comfort I had had from her that my soul was wounded and my life seemed shattered, for her life and mine had been as one."

37. For a different and much less convincing interpretation of this psychoaffective mechanism, from his usual combined perspective of psychoanalysis and continental philosophy, see Žižek 2000.

38. Crownshaw (2004, 229) argues that the redemption or "resurrection" of the referent via the iconic sign (in a realist aesthetic ideology per se) is negated in the indexical: "For Austerlitz, photographs might seem to resurrect their referent." Iconicity "resurrects" the referent, indexicality leaves it dead; iconicity presents a false redemption of the referent (mimeticism), whereas indexicality is an acknowledgment of its (now) absolute absence. In his reading of Barthes, Crownshaw argues that "the *punctum* calls attention to life that will be (and has already been) lost, and, in so doing, wounds referentiality to the extent that representation can no longer substitute for referent" (229). "Wounded and marked as a sign, the photograph's belated effect is to disrupt the process of historical reference it provokes" (232). In its indexicality as a sign the photo calls attention to itself as a sign, thereby calling attention ("defamiliarizing") its own iconicity;

the absolute absence of the referent is exposed to view within the seeming positivity of the image.

39. Ironically, at the time of the remembered incident Agáta is singing the role of Olympia, the automaton doll in Offenbach's 1881 opera *Tales of Hoffmann* (Sebald 2001, 160).

40. On the past as the "land of the dead," see Kilbourn 2010, 28–35.

41. See Lacan 1995; Elkins 1996, 70.

42. On the nonhuman turn, "OOO," feminist new materialisms, etc., see, e.g., chapters 8 and 9 in Grusin 2015.

43. Quoted in Howe 1992, xii.

44. See Halbwachs 2007.

Chapter 7

1. Like Sebald, claimed by both German- and English-language readers, Alice Munro is as much a North American as a Canadian writer, famously referred to by American critic Cynthia Ozick as "*our* Chekhov" (1996; emphasis added).

2. Munro, born in 1931, moved to Vancouver, B.C., in 1951 after growing up in southwestern Ontario. In 1973 she returned to the region of her childhood, where (in 2017) she still resides.

3. Munro's realism stems "from the tradition of the well-wrought modernist story and the attempt to reproduce a feeling of being by tracking consciousness in all its vagaries," as in, e.g., Joyce's *Dubliners* (McIntyre 1999, 65).

4. Howells (2007, 166) implicitly agrees, pointing out that Munro's "historicizing consciousness [has been] evident in stories published since the 1970s." See also Hancock 1987, 206.

5. See also Duffy (2010, 198), who aligns *Castle Rock* with the tradition of historical fiction, "the kind of novel originating in the work of Sir Walter Scott [in *Waverley* (1814)]. It is a mode of fiction overtly preoccupied with the way in which cultural change works itself out in the lives of obscure individuals." According to Duffy, "Munro had been meditating on history's role in the construction of fiction at least since *Lives of Girls and Women*" in 1971 (199). Moreover, "when successful, the historical novel displays the power to evoke something greater than antiquarianism, or a nostalgia-driven curiosity about how those who came before us managed their lives" (200).

6. Bernstein (2014, 189) positions *Castle Rock* "between historical memoir and fiction," a generic mixture that allows Munro to model a form of diasporic writing that situates the writing subject of the present within a network of complexly (and problematically) nationalized precursors."

7. As Hames (2012, 75) observes (quoting Coleman 2006), "'the conceptual foundation of the Canadian idea of civility' is the deracinated category of Britishness of which the 'Scots, historically, were the primary inventors and promoters'" (see also 81). For Gittings (quoted in Bernstein 2014, 191), Munro's Scottish-themed stories "show a 'Canadian consciousness where a quest for a singular interpretation of individuals becomes just as tyrannical and unsatisfactory as the Calvinist interpretation of the world,'" which, in *Castle Rock* especially, proves a crucial component, ironically, of the narrator's self-formation.

8. See Braidotti 2013.

9. See Sebald's (2004a, 114) notion of "the synoptic view."

10. For Duffy (2010, 198), Munro's "mapping" of what he terms the "Munro Tract transmutes geography and history into an alloy giving them both their due."

11. But not, it should be noted, to literacy. See Munro 2006a, 15.

12. As an unorthodox Marxist critic with Orthodox-mystical leanings writing in Stalinist Russia, Bakhtin privileges the role played by objects—i.e., texts—in the preservation and transmission of social and cultural forms of memory over the individual subject of memory; see, e.g., 1981, 249n17.

13. The figurative connection between place, memory, and writing is a recurring motif in *Speak, Memory* and is often tinged with melancholia: "Alas, these pencils, too, have been distributed among the characters in my books to keep fictitious children busy; they are not quite my own now. Somewhere, in the apartment house of a chapter, in the hired room of a paragraph, I have also placed that tilted mirror, and the lamp, and the chandelier drops. Few things are left, many have been squandered" (1989, 101).

14. See, e.g., Redekop 1999, 22.

15. "Munro tends to construct the nostalgic as grotesque, the better to repudiate it" (38).

16. This in no way contradicts the claims of scholars who read her style as symptomatic of a kind of postmodern rejection of "the artifice inherent in grand narratives as they sweep incidents into neat patterns of beginning, middle, and end, thereby giving events a coherence they lack" (McIntyre 1999, 65).

17. See Kilbourn 2010, 124.

18. See Kilbourn 2010, 28–35.

19. As Redekop (1999, 27) suggests, "Munro's baggage is mainly Scottish."

20. Augustine (1988, 10.8, 214) imagines memory as being "like a great field or a spacious palace, a storehouse for countless images of all kinds which are conveyed to it by the senses. In it are stored away all the thoughts by which we enlarge upon or diminish or modify in any way the perceptions at which we arrive through the senses . . . until such time as these things are swallowed up and buried in forgetfulness." See Kilbourn 2010, 22–23; Yates 1966, 1–28.

21. "This view . . . affirms the [European] traveler's *power* over the foreign world in two ways: it allows him to delineate the exotic lands' borders and . . . to bolster the *singularity* of his perspective. Through this view from above, the traveler can gain a better sense of the land's specificities, his own point-of-view, and, finally, his 'self'" (Zilcosky 2003, 27; emphasis added).

22. See Berger 1980, 87; O'Brien and Szeman 2004, 74; Sturken and Cartwright 2001, 352.

23. "Calvinism . . . is permeated by a sense of the unquiet depths that lie beneath the human surface" (Somacarrera 2015, 88).

24. Published in the United States as *The Beggar Maid*.

25. See, e.g., Duffy (2010, 199), who contends that "the narrative voice behind the *Castle Rock* collection is that of the storyteller rather than of the writer." For Duffy (citing Redekop 1999), Munro's writing is closer to *orature* than literature, "specifically the Scottish oral tradition" (202). Duffy's contention, however, that the "narrative mode" of the story "Meneseteung" represents "a way of story-telling reminiscent of the devices of orality" (202) ignores Munro's mastery of verbal style. See Redekop 1999, 25–26: "It is becoming increasingly obvious that the shapes of Munro's stories cannot be accounted for without some reference

to orality. As her stories get longer and longer, they push at the limits of generic categories. Are they just very long short stories? If they get long enough, can we call them novels? . . . Munro is a storyteller. No matter how long her stories get, she will never be a novelist."

26. By the same token, for Bakhtin (1981, 3) there is no such thing as an oral novel, in terms of the novel as he takes great pains to define it. Determined by language's spoken forms ("speech genres") but intended to be read silently, the novel is therefore irreducibly written.

27. In both texts it is a preacher who gives voice to this most demonstrative dimension of the Presbyterian identity: Elias in *Austerlitz*, whose Sunday-morning sermons manifest rhetorically the apocalyptic eschatology that grounds his identity as much as the brand of Protestant faith he represents. In *Castle Rock* it is the Reverend Thomas Boston, whose credo Munro cites in the opening story.

28. According to Hames (2012, 76), it is in the course of this story that *Castle Rock* shifts from fictionalized microhistorical account of authentic events "into Munro's familiar terrain of small-town secrets and unkindness, and leaves the extravagant longings of its refugees behind." For Howells (2007, 166), Munro's historical fictions are the stories "that lie hidden or forgotten within official histories."

29. See Gittings, quoted in Somacarrera 2015, 94.

Coda

Portions of this chapter first appeared in Kilbourn 2013.

1. This is Bakhtin's point about the role of the novel in contemporary social-political life vis-à-vis the epic in the ancient world.

2. See Crownshaw 2010, vi, on Hirsch's postmemory as "affiliative," which is to say imaginative, rather than "familial" in its operation.

3. Sebald notes in the margin of his copy of *Speak, Memory*: "Trains; City" (1987, 114 [1989, 144]).

4. In this respect Sebald is picking up on the themes of Nabokov's first English-language novel, *The Real Life of Sebastian Knight* (1941).

5. See Boyd 1990, 106.

6. On the former, see, e.g., Edward Fitzgerald in *The Rings of Saturn*, one of many historical writer figures in Sebald whose life is defined by a single, intensely "platonic" relationship with another man (Sebald 1998, 195–207). See also Swinburne's relationship with his "lifetime companion, Watts-Dunton" (163), as well as Henry Selwyn and Johannes Naegeli in *The Emigrants*. On Sebald's interest in the significance of the homoerotic dimension of literary history in connection to the ironic autoerotic-salvific economy at work in these texts, see, in the present volume, chapter 1 concerning *The Rings of Saturn*'s appropriation of Roger Casement's story and chapter 3 on *Vertigo*'s intertextualization of Kafka's diaries of his travels in northern Italy.

7. This quote, which succinctly sums up that aspect of Finch's argument of greatest relevance here, is taken from the publisher's blurb for the book.

8. See also Theisen 2004 on Sebald's intertextualization of Conrad, Casement, Fitzgerald, etc., in *The Rings of Saturn*.

9. As Theisen (2004, 2006) and Finch (2013) differently demonstrate.

10. It also invokes the concluding scene of Fellini's *La Dolce Vita* (1960), in which a group of disaffected revelers watch some fishermen drag an enormous, primordial sea creature onto the beach at Passoscuro, outside Rome.

11. This question puts him in mind of the Borges story, "Tlön, Uqbar, Orbius Tertius," a metafictional "tale which deals with our attempts to invent secondary or tertiary worlds" (Sebald 1998, 69). According to Sebald's citation of the story, the disturbing thing about both copulation and mirrors is that "they multiply the number of human beings" (70).

12. On gender (especially masculinity) in Sebald, see, e.g., Hell 2003. For a more critical reading of this and related themes, see Barzilai (Long and Whitehead 2004).

13. See Kilbourn 2007, 139.

14. See, e.g., Arthur Williams 2001, 68.

15. In French, e.g., "genre and gender . . . are 'one and the same word'" (Duff 2000, 16). Hence Derrida's (1992a, 224; emphasis in original) point that gender is a "biological *genre* . . . the human *genre*, a *genre* of all that is general."

16. See, e.g., Sheppard 2005; Pearson 2008.

17. Part of the collection at the Deutsches Literaturarchiv in Marbach, Germany.

18. See Crownshaw 2004, 215.

19. Notice that Sebald focuses on the Holocaust's significance for literary categorization rather than as the event itself. See Zilcosky 2006, 693–95.

20. Franklin here cites Bryan Cheyette. See also Newton (quoted in Hirsch and Kacandes 2004, 422).

21. See Anderson 2003, 110.

22. See Linda Williams 2001, 10–44. It should also be noted that, in Elsaesser's (1987, 47) words, "The persistence of melodrama might indicate the ways in which popular culture has not only taken note of social crises and the fact that the losers are not always those who deserve it most, but has also resolutely refused to understand social change in other than private contexts and emotional terms."

23. "These images [of concentration camps, etc.] militate against our capacity for discursive thinking . . . and paralyze our moral capacity, and the only way we can approach these things is *obliquely*" (Sebald, as quoted in Schwartz 2007, 80; emphasis added). Trauma studies, insofar as the field developed out of Holocaust studies, is in large part founded on the question or problem of the representation of the traumatic event in memory. This is an enormous constellation of issues that, while relevant to Sebald, cannot be broached in the present study.

24. For a persuasive Levinasian reading of Sebald, see Ribó 2009, 237.

25. See Zilcosky 2006, 695. See also Long 2007, 8, 19.

26. E.g., Long 2003; Crownshaw 2004.

27. "The widow, the orphan, the stranger," in Levinas's phrase.

28. See Zilcosky 2006, 696; Crownshaw 2010, vi. Interestingly, in none of his prose texts does Sebald even attempt to represent or reproduce the perspective or voice of the perpetrator. This perspective is explored in extraordinary depth in Littell 2010.

29. In his review of Zischler 2003, Sebald (2005, 164) remarks of these "mirror-image identities"—the Nazis' appropriation of the Jewish narrative for their own self-fashioning—that "the overriding concept . . . is the myth of the Chosen People, to which Germans blindly subscribed at the time when their ideas of national

emancipation were taking a wrong turn . . . Hitler . . . came to a conclusion which he thought irrefutably justified the annihilation of the Jews: there could not be two Chosen Peoples." Of early twentieth-century German Zionism's relation to German nationalism, Sebald writes, "In the image of themselves that they projected, the two peoples, awakening from long oppression or rousing themselves from alleged neglect, were almost exactly the same, even if their standards and ambitions were different" (163).

30. See, e.g., Sebald 2001, 6–7, 54; Sebald 2005, 27.

31. See Gledhill 1987, 29.

32. See also Sebald 2003, 67–68. See Hell 2004, 362; Presner 2004.

33. See Barzilai's (Long and Whitehead 2004, 212) fascinating analysis of Sebald's gendered representation of a relationship with the Jewish-German past in terms of that between "a living male character" haunted by "the image of an absent, dead or ghostly woman."

34. See Kilbourn 2007, 145. See also Anderson 2003, 119.

35. Martin Klebes (2003) uses this term as well, emphasizing a restitution of memory itself, as opposed to a restitution by means of memory.

36. "Unmoored, trauma demands a new kind of witnessing: the witnessing of the witness who conveys trauma to those who listen . . . Trauma has departed from its origins and arrived in the cultural memory of events not directly witnessed" (Corngold 2008, 236)—i.e., postmemory. This is in line with Richard Crownshaw's (2004) work on photography and trauma in Sebald.

37. See Anderson 2003, 104.

38. I invoke Landsberg's (2003) term "prosthetic memory" somewhat out of its original context.

39. See Sheppard 2005, 424. See also Lubow 2007; Williams 2007, 55 n. 12; Baxter, Henitiuk, and Hutchinson 2013.

40. See Baxter, Henitiuk, and Hutchinson 2013.

41. Andreas Huyssen (2003, 260–61) refers to the Sebaldian prose text as "a unique style of memory narrative, located at the breaking point between documentary and fiction . . . As a German of the postwar generation, he accepts his responsibility to remember while fully acknowledging the difficulty of such remembering across an abyss of violence and pain."

42. As Franklin (2011, 257) remarks of Sebald, "there is also something deeply consoling about his vision of art as capable of offering some sort of recompense."

REFERENCES

Achebe, Chinua. 1988. "An Image of Africa: Racism in Conrad's *Heart of Darkness*." *Massachusetts Review* 18, no. 4 (1977): 782–94. Rpt. In Conrad 1988, 251–61.

Adorno, Theodor. 1981a. *In Search of Wagner*. Translated by Rodney Livingstone. London: Verso.

———. 1981b. "Notes on Kafka." In *Prisms*, translated by Samuel and Shierry Weber, 243–71. Cambridge, Mass.: MIT Press.

———. 1992. *Negative Dialectics*. Translated by E. B. Ashton. New York: Continuum.

Adorno, Theodor, and Max Horkheimer. (1944) 2001. "The Culture Industry: Enlightenment as Mass Deception." In *Dialectic of Enlightenment*, translated by John Herder, 120–67. 1944. Reprint, New York: Continuum.

Albright, Daniel. 1981. *Representation and the Imagination: Beckett, Kafka, Nabokov, and Schönberg*. Chicago: University of Chicago Press.

Alexandrov, Vladimir E. 1991. *Nabokov's Otherworld*. Princeton, N.J.: Princeton University Press.

Alighieri, Dante. 1966. *Le opere di Dante Alighieri*. Edizione nazionale a cura della Società Dantesca Italiana. Verona: Mondadori.

———. 1986. *The Divine Comedy of Dante Alighieri: Inferno, Purgatorio, Paradiso*. Translated by Allen Mandelbaum. New York: Bantam.

Alpers, Svetlana. 1983. *The Art of Describing: Dutch Art in the Seventeenth Century*. Chicago: University of Chicago Press.

Alter, Robert. 1991. *Necessary Angels: Tradition and Modernity in Kafka, Benjamin, and Scholem*. Cambridge, Mass.: Harvard University Press.

Anderson, Mark M. 2003. "The Edge of Darkness: On W. G. Sebald." *October* 106 (Fall): 102–21.

———. 2008. "Documents, Photography, Postmemory: Alexander Kluge, W. G. Sebald, and the German Family." *Poetics Today* 29, no. 1: 129–53.

———. 2011. "Napoleon and the Ethics of Realism: Hebel, Hölderlin, Büchner, Celan." *Journal of European Studies* 41, no. 3–4: 395–412.

Assmann, Jan. 2006. "Invisible Religion and Cultural Memory." In *Religion and Cultural Memory: Ten Studies*, translated by Rodney Livingstone, 37–43. Stanford, Calif.: Stanford University Press.

Bakhtin, Mikhail. 1981. "Forms of Time and of the Chronotope in the Novel." In *The Dialogic Imagination: Four Essays*, edited by Michael Holquist, translated by Caryl Emerson and Michael Holquist, 84–258. Austin: University of Texas Press.

Bal, Mieke. 1991. *Reading Rembrandt: Beyond the Word-Image Opposition*. Cambridge: Cambridge University Press.

————. 1997. *Narratology: Introduction to the Theory of Narrative*. Translated by Christine Van Boheemen. Toronto: University of Toronto Press.

Barrow, John D. 2000. *The Book of Nothing*. London: Cape.

Barthes, Roland. 1981. *Camera Lucida: Reflections on Photography*. Translated by Richard Howard. New York: Hill and Wang.

Barzilai, Maya. 2004. "Facing the Past and the Female Spectre in W. G. Sebald's *The Emigrants*." In *W. G. Sebald: A Critical Companion*, edited by J. J. Long and Anne Whitehead, 203–16. Edinburgh: Edinburgh University Press.

Baudrillard, Jean. 1998. *The Consumer Society: Myths and Structures*. Translated by Chris Turner. London: Sage.

Baxter, Jeanette, Valerie Henitiuk, and Ben Hutchinson, eds. 2013. *A Literature of Restitution: Critical Essays on W. G. Sebald*. Manchester, U.K.: Manchester University Press.

Beckett, Samuel. 1959. *Watt*. New York: Grove Press.

————. 1965. *"Proust" and "Three Dialogues with Georges Duthuit."* London: Calder.

————. 1974. *More Pricks Than Kicks*. New York: Grove Press.

————. 1991. *Three Novels: "Molloy," "Malone Dies," "The Unnamable."* New York: Grove Press.

————. 1993. *Dream of Fair to Middling Women*. Edited by Eoin O'Brien and Edith Fournier. London: Calder.

————. 1995. *Complete Short Prose, 1929–1989*. Edited by S. E. Gontarski. New York: Grove Press.

Benjamin, Walter. 1969. "Theses on the Philosophy of History." In *Illuminations*, edited by Hannah Arendt, translated by Harry Zohn, 253–64. New York: Schocken Books.

————. 1978. *Reflections*. Edited by Peter Demetz, translated by Edmund Jephcott. New York: Harcourt Brace Jovanovich.

————. 1985. *The Origin of German Tragic Drama*. Translated by John Osborne. London: Verso.

————. 2002a. "Paris, the Capital of the Nineteenth Century." In *Selected Writings: Volume 3, 1935–1938*, translated by Edmund Jephcott et al., edited by Howard Eiland and Michael W. Jennings, 32–49. London: Harvard University Press.

————. 2002b. "The Work of Art in the Age of Its Technological Reproducibility." In *Selected Writings: Volume 3, 1935–1938*, translated by Edmund Jephcott et al., edited by Howard Eiland and Michael W. Jennings, 101–33. Cambridge, Mass.: Harvard University Press.

————. 2007a. "On Some Motifs in Baudelaire." In *Illuminations*, edited by Hannah Arendt, 155–200. New York: Random House.

————. 2007b. "Some Reflections on Kafka." In *Illuminations*, edited by Hannah Arendt, 141–46. New York: Random House.

Benjamin, Walter, and Gershom Scholem. 1992. *The Correspondence of Walter Benjamin and Gershom Scholem: 1932–1940*. Edited by Gershom Scholem. Translated by Gary Smith and Andre Lefevere. Cambridge, Mass.: Harvard University Press.

Berger, John. 1980. *About Looking*. New York: Pantheon.

Bergson, Henri. (1896) 1988. *Matter and Memory*. Reprint, New York: Zone Books.

Bergstrom, Anders. 2016. "In Search of Lost Selves: Memory and Subjectivity in Transnational Art Cinema." PhD diss., Wilfrid Laurier University.

Bernstein, Stephen. 2014. "Alice Munro's Scottish Birthright." *ANQ: A Quarterly Journal of Short Articles, Notes, and Reviews* 27, no. 4: 189–93.

Blade Runner. 2006. DVD. Directed by Ridley Scott. Los Angeles: Warner Home Video.

Blanchot, Maurice. 1982. *The Space of Literature.* Translated by Ann Smock. Lincoln: University of Nebraska Press.

———. 1993. *The Writing of the Disaster.* Translated by Ann Smock. Lincoln: University of Nebraska Press.

Bloch, Ernst. 1986. *The Principle of Hope, Volume 3.* Translated by Neville Plaice, Stephen Plaice, and Paul Knight. Cambridge, Mass.: MIT Press.

Bloom, Harold, ed. 1988. *Samuel Beckett's "Molloy," "Malone Dies," "The Unnamable."* New York: Chelsea House.

Blumenberg, Hans. 1979. *Shipwreck with Spectator: Paradigm of a Metaphor for Existence.* Translated by Steven Rendall. Cambridge, Mass.: MIT Press.

———. 1987. *The Genesis of the Copernican World.* Cambridge, Mass.: MIT Press.

Bolter, Jay, and Richard Grusin. 1999. *Remediation: Understanding New Media.* Cambridge, Mass.: MIT Press.

Bond, Greg. 2004. "On the Misery of Nature and the Nature of Misery: W. G. Sebald's Landscapes." In *W. G. Sebald: A Critical Companion,* edited by J. J. Long and Anne Whitehead, 31–44. Edinburgh: Edinburgh University Press.

Borges, Jorge Luis. 1964. Tlön, Uqbar, Orbius Tertius." In *Labyrinths: Selected Stories and Other Writings,* edited by Donald A. Yates and James E. Irby, 3–18. New York: New Directions.

Boyd, Brian. 1990. *Vladimir Nabokov: The Russian Years.* Princeton, N.J.: Princeton University Press.

———. 1991. *Vladimir Nabokov: The American Years.* Princeton, N.J.: Princeton University Press.

Boym, Svetlana. 2001. *The Future of Nostalgia.* New York: Basic Books.

Braidotti, Rosi. 2013. *The Posthuman.* Cambridge: Polity Press.

Brassier, Ray. 2007. *Nihil Unbound: Enlightenment and Extinction.* New York: Palgrave Macmillan.

Brooks, Peter. 1995. *The Melodramatic Imagination: Balzac, Henry James, Melodrama, and the Mode of Excess.* New Haven, Conn.: Yale University Press.

Browne, Thomas. 1958. *"Urne Buriall" and "The Garden of Cyrus."* Edited by John Carter. Cambridge: Cambridge University Press.

Buck-Morss, Susan. 1989. *The Dialectics of Seeing: Walter Benjamin and the Arcades Project.* Cambridge, Mass.: MIT Press.

Budick, Sanford, and Wolfgang Iser, eds. 1989. *Languages of the Unsayable: The Play of Negativity in Literature and Literary Theory.* New York: Columbia University Press.

Bürger, Peter. 1984. *Theory of the Avant-Garde.* Translated by Michael Shaw. Minneapolis: University of Minnesota Press.

Burns, Rob. 2011. "The Calamitous Perspective of Modernity: Sebald's Negative Ontology." *Journal of European Studies* 41, no. 3–4: 341–58.

Burton, Robert. 2001. *The Anatomy of Melancholy.* Edited by Holbrook Jackson. New York: New York Review of Books.

Cacciari, Massimo. 1994. *The Necessary Angel*. Translated by Miguel E. Vatter. Albany: SUNY Press.

Calinescu, Matei. 1987. "On Postmodernism." In *Five Faces of Modernity: Modernism, Avant-Garde, Decadence, Kitsch, Postmodernism*, 265–312. Durham, N.C.: Duke University Press.

Canetti, Elias. 1974. *Kafka's Other Trial: The Letters to Felice*. Translated by Christopher Middleton. New York: Schocken Books.

Casanova, Giacomo. 2005. *The Story of My Life*. Translated by Stephen Sartarelli and Sophie Hawkes. London: Penguin Books.

Catling, Jo, and Richard Hibbitt, eds. 2011. *Saturn's Moons: A W. G. Sebald Handbook*. Oxford: Legenda.

Ceuppens, Jan. 2004. "Seeing Things: Spectres and Angels in W. G. Sebald's Prose Fiction." In *W. G. Sebald: A Critical Companion*, edited by J. J. Long and Anne Whitehead, 190–202. Edinburgh: Edinburgh University Press.

Chandler, James. 2003. "About Loss: W. G. Sebald's Romantic Art of Memory." *South Atlantic Quarterly* 102, no. 1 (Winter): 235–62.

Charman, Caitlin. 2012. "'Secretly Devoted to Nature': Place Sense in Alice Munro's *The View from Castle Rock*." In *Alice Munro: Critical Insights*, edited by Charles E. May, 259–75. Ipswich, Mass.: Salem Press.

Charney, Leo. 1995. "In a Moment: Film and the Philosophy of Modernity." In *Cinema and the Invention of Modern Life*, edited by Leo Charney and Vanessa R. Schwartz, 279–93. Berkeley: University of California Press.

Clark, Katerina, and Michael Holquist. 1984. *Mikhail Bakhtin*. Cambridge, Mass.: Harvard University Press.

Coleman, Daniel. 2006. *White Civility: The Literary Project of English Canada*. Toronto: University of Toronto Press.

The Columbia Encyclopedia. 2001. 6th ed. New York: Columbia University Press. Accessed May 3, 2015. http://www.columbia.edu/~daviss/work/files/_archive /ce_orig.html.

Conrad, Joseph. 1988. *Heart of Darkness: An Authoritative Text*. Edited by Robert Kimbrough. 3rd ed. London: Norton.

———. 2003. *Heart of Darkness*. Edited by D. C. R. A. Goonetilleke. 2nd ed. Peterborough, Ont.: Broadview Press.

Cook, Pam. 2005. *Screening the Past: Memory and Nostalgia in Cinema*. New York: Routledge.

Corngold, Stanley. 2008. "Sebald's Tragedy." In *Rethinking Tragedy*, edited by Rita Felski, 218–40. Baltimore: Johns Hopkins University Press.

Crary, Jonathan. 2013a. *Techniques of the Observer: On Vision and Modernity in the Nineteenth Century*. Cambridge, Mass.: MIT Press.

———. 2013b. *24/7: Late Capitalism and the Ends of Sleep*. London: Verso.

Critchley, Simon, and Peter Dews. 1996. *Deconstructive Subjectivities*. Albany: SUNY Press.

Cronin, Anthony. 1997. *Samuel Beckett: The Last Modernist*. New York: Da Capo Press.

Crownshaw, Richard. 2004. "Reconsidering Postmemory: Photography, the Archive, and Post-Holocaust Memory in W. G. Sebald's *Austerlitz*." *Mosaic* 37, no. 4: 215–36.

———. 2010. *The Afterlife of Holocaust Memory in Contemporary Literature and Culture*. New York: Palgrave Macmillan.

Debord, Guy. 1994. *The Society of the Spectacle*. Translated by Donald Nicholson-Smith. New York: Zone Books.

de Certeau, Michel. 1984. "Walking in the City." In *The Practice of Everyday Life*, translated by Steven F. Rendall, 91–110. Berkeley: University of California Press.

de la Durantaye, Leland. 2008. "The Facts of Fiction, or the Figure of Vladimir Nabokov in W. G. Sebald." *Comparative Literature Studies* 45, no. 4: 425–45.

Deleuze, Gilles. 1986a. *Cinema 1: The Movement-Image*. Translated by Hugh Tomlinson and Barbara Habberjam. Minneapolis: University of Minnesota Press.

———. 1986b. "Postscript on the Societies of Control." *October* 59 (Winter): 3–7.

Deleuze, Gilles, and Félix Guattari. 1986. *Kafka: Toward a Minor Literature*. Translated by Dana Polan. Minneapolis: University of Minnesota Press.

DeLillo, Don. 1986. *White Noise*. New York: Penguin Books.

Derrida, Jacques. 1978. "Violence and Metaphysics: An Essay on the Thought of Emmanuel Levinas." In *Writing and Difference*, translated by Alan Bass, 79–195. Chicago: University of Chicago Press.

———. 1982. "Signature Event Context." In *Margins of Philosophy*, translated by Alan Bass, 307–30. Chicago: University of Chicago Press.

———. 1984. "Of an Apocalyptic Tone Recently Adopted in Philosophy." *Oxford Literary Review* 6, no. 2: 3–37. doi: http://dx.doi.org/10.3366/olr.1984.001.

———. 1992a. *Acts of Literature*. Edited by Derek Attridge. New York: Routledge.

———. 1992b. "How to Avoid Speaking: Denials." In *Derrida and Negative Theology*, edited by Harold Coward and Toby Foshay, 73–142. Albany: SUNY Press.

———. 1993. "Circumfession." In *Jacques Derrida*, by Geoffrey Bennington and Jacques Derrida, 3–315. Translated by Geoffrey Bennington. Chicago: University of Chicago Press.

———. 1996. *Archive Fever: A Freudian Impression*. Chicago: University of Chicago Press.

———. 2001. *The Work of Mourning*. Edited by Pascale-Anne Brault and Michael Naas. Chicago: University of Chicago Press.

Draaisma, Duwe. 2000. *Metaphors of Memory: A History of Ideas about the Mind*. Translated by Paul Vincent. New York: Cambridge University Press.

Duff, David. 2000. *Modern Genre Theory*. Essex, U.K.: Longman.

Duffy, Dennis. 2010. "Too Little Geography; Too Much History: Writing the Balance in 'Meneseteung.'" In *National Plots: Historical Fiction and Changing Ideas of Canada*, edited by Andrea Cabajsky and Brett Josef Grubisic, 197–213. Waterloo, Ont.: Wilfrid Laurier University Press.

Duncan, Isla. 2011. *Alice Munro's Narrative Art*. New York: Palgrave Macmillan.

Eliot, T. S. 2010. *The Wasteland*. New York: Norton.

Elkins, James. 1996. *The Object Stares Back: On the Nature of Seeing*. San Diego: Harcourt.

Elsaesser, Thomas. 1987. "Tales of Sound and Fury: Observations on the Family Melodrama." In *Home Is Where the Heart Is*, edited by Christine Gledhill, 43–69. London: British Film Institute.

———. 2000. *Weimar Cinema and After: Germany's Historical Imaginary*. London: Routledge.

Erll, Astrid. 2011. *Memory in Culture*. Translated by Sara B. Young. New York: Palgrave Macmillan.

Eshel, Amir. 2003. "Against the Power of Time: The Poetics of Suspension in W. G. Sebald's *Austerlitz.*" *New German Critique* 88 (Winter): 71–96.

Fanny and Alexander. 1982. Directed by Ingmar Bergman. Sweden, France, West Germany: Cinematograph AB and Svenska Filminstitutet.

Finch, Helen. 2013. *Sebald's Bachelors: Queer Resistance and the Unconforming Life*. Oxford: Legenda.

Fischer, Gerhard, ed. 2009. *W. G. Sebald: Schreiben ex patria/Expatriate Writing*. Amsterdam: Rodopi.

Foster, John Burt. 1993. *Nabokov's Art of Memory and European Modernism*. Princeton, N.J.: Princeton University Press.

Foucault, Michel. 1971. *The Order of Things: An Archaeology of the Human Sciences*. New York: Vintage.

Franklin, Ruth. 2011. *A Thousand Darknesses: Lies and Truth in Holocaust Fiction*. Oxford: Oxford University Press.

Freccero, John. 1986. *Dante: The Poetics of Conversion*. Edited by Rachel Jacoff. Cambridge, Mass.: Harvard University Press.

Freud, Sigmund. (1917) 1973. "Mourning and Melancholia." In *The Standard Edition of the Complete Psychological Works of Sigmund Freud*, edited by James Strachey, 14: 247–68. 6th ed. London: Hogarth Press.

Frey, Matthias. 2007. "Theorizing Cinema in Sebald and Sebald with Cinema." In *Searching for Sebald: Photography after W. G. Sebald*, edited by Lise Patt with Christel Dillbohner, 226–41. Los Angeles: Institute of Cultural Inquiry.

Friedberg, Anne. 1994. *Window Shopping: Cinema and the Postmodern*. Berkeley: University of California Press.

Frye, Northrop. 1982. *The Great Code: The Bible and Literature*. Toronto: Academic Press Canada.

Fuchs, Anne. 2004. *Die Schmerzensspuren der Geschichte: Zur Poetik der Erinnerung in W. G. Sebalds Prosa*. Vienna: Böhlau.

———. 2006. "W. G. Sebald's Painters: The Function of Fine Art in His Prose Works." *Modern Language Review* 101, no. 1 (January): 167–83.

Fuchs, Anne, and J. J. Long, eds. 2007. *W. G. Sebald and the Writing of History*. Würzburg: Königshausen and Neumann.

The Fuehrer Gives the Jews a City. (1944) [2010]. DVD. Directed by Kurt Gerron. Los Angeles: Seventh Art Releasing.

Fuery, Patrick, and Kelli Fuery, eds. 2003. *Visual Cultures and Critical Theory*. Oxford: Oxford University Press.

Furani, Khaled. 2015. "Is There a Postsecular?" *Journal of the American Academy of Religion* 83, no. 1 (March): 1–26

Furst, Lilian R. 2007. "Memory's Fragile Power in Kazuo Ishiguro's *Remains of the Day* and W. G. Sebald's 'Max Ferber.'" *Contemporary Literature* 48, no. 4 (Winter): 530–53.

Gledhill, Christine. 1987. "Melodrama as Cultural Form." In *Home Is Where the Heart Is*, edited by Christine Gledhill, 28–39. London: British Film Institute.

Gontarski, S. E., ed. 1986. *On Beckett: Essays and Criticism*. New York: Grove Press.

Gray, John. 2003. *Straw Dogs: Thoughts on Humans and Other Animals*. London: Granta.

Grey, Thomas. 2000. *Richard Wagner: "Der fliegende Holländer."* Cambridge: Cambridge University Press.

Grossmith, Bob. 1988. "Nabokov and Self-Divestment." *English Language Notes* 25, no. 3 (March): 73–78.

Grözinger, Karl Erich. 1994. *Kafka and Kabbalah*. Translated by Susan Hecker Ray. New York: Continuum.

Grusin, Richard. 2010. *Premediation: Affect and Mediality after 9/11*. London: Palgrave Macmillan.

———, ed. 2015. *The Nonhuman Turn*. Minneapolis: University of Minnesota Press.

Habermas, Jürgen. 2001. "Modernity: An Incomplete Project." In *The Norton Anthology of Theory and Criticism*, edited by Vincent B. Leitch, 1748–58. New York: Norton.

———. 2003. *The Future of Human Nature*. Cambridge: Polity Press.

———. 2008. "A Post-Secular Society: What Does That Mean?" *Reset: Dialogues on Civilizations*, September 16, 2008. Accessed May 18, 2015. http://www.resetdoc.org/story/a-post-secular-society-what-does-that-mean/.

———. 2010. *An Awareness of What Is Missing: Faith and Reason in a Post-Secular Age*. Cambridge: Polity Press.

Halbwachs, Maurice. 2007. "From *The Collective Memory*." In *Theories of Memory: A Reader*, edited by Michael Rossington and Anne Whitehead, 139–43. Baltimore: Johns Hopkins University Press.

Hames, Scott. 2012. "Diasporic Narcissism: De-sublimating Scotland in Alice Munro and Alistair MacLeod." *Anglistik: International Journal of English Studies* 23, no. 2 (September): 73–82.

Hancock, Geoff. 1987. "Alice Munro." In *Canadian Writers at Work: Interviews with Geoff Hancock*, 187–224. Toronto: Oxford University Press.

Harries, Karsten. 2001. *Infinity and Perspective*. Cambridge, Mass.: MIT Press.

Harris, Stefanie. 2001. "The Return of the Dead: Memory and Photography in W. G. Sebald's *Die Ausgewanderten*." *German Quarterly* 74, no. 4 (Autumn): 379–91.

Hawking, Stephen. 1988. *A Brief History of Time*. Toronto: Bantam Books.

Hayman, Ronald. 1982. *Kafka: A Biography*. Oxford: Oxford University Press.

Heidegger, Martin. 1992. *The Concept of Time*. Translated by William McNeill. Oxford: Blackwell.

Heine, Heinrich. 1967. *Aus den Memoiren des Herren von Schnabelewopski: Mit einem Aufsatz; Heines Fragment eines Schelmenromans von Manfred Windfuhr*. Stuttgart: Reclam.

Hell, Julia. 2003. "Eyes Wide Shut, or German Post-Holocaust Authorship." *New German Critique* 88 (Winter): 9–36.

———. 2004. "The Angel's Enigmatic Eyes, or The Gothic Beauty of Catastrophic History in W. G. Sebald's 'Air War and Literature.'" *Criticism* 46, no. 3 (Summer): 361–92.

Hirsch, Marion. 1997. *Family Frames: Photography, Narrative, and Postmemory*. Cambridge, Mass.: Harvard University Press.

Hirsch, Marion, and Irene Kacandes, eds. 2004. *Teaching the Representation of the Holocaust*. New York: Modern Language Association.

Homer. *The Odyssey*. 1996. Translated by Robert Fagles. New York: Penguin Books.

Houston, Pam. 1992. "A Hopeful Sign: The Making of Metonymic Meaning in Munro's 'Meneseteung.'" *Kenyon Review* 14, no. 4: 79–92.

Howe, Irving. 1992. Introduction to *The Castle*, by Franz Kafka, ix–xxix. Translated by Willa and Edwin Muir. New York: Schocken Books.

Howells, Coral Ann. 2004. "Alice Munro's Heritage Narratives." In *Where Are the Voices Coming From? Canadian Culture and The Legacies of History*, edited by Coral Ann Howells. Amsterdam and New York: Rodopi.

———. 2007. "Writing Family History." *Canadian Literature* 195 (Winter): 166–70.

Hutcheon, Linda. 1988. *A Poetics of Postmodernism: History, Theory, Fiction*. New York and London: Routledge.

———. 2006. *A Theory of Adaptation*. New York and London: Routledge.

———. 2013. *A Theory of Adaptation*. 2nd ed. New York: Routledge.

———, and Michael Hutcheon. 1999. Opera: Desire, Disease, Death. Lincoln: University of Nebraska Press.

Hutcheon, Linda. 1988. A Poetics of Postmodernism: History, Theory, Fiction. New York and London: Routledge.

———. 2006. "Postmodernism." In *The Routledge Companion to Critical Theory*, edited by Simon Malpas and Paul Wake, 115–26. New York: Routledge.

———. 2006. *A Theory of Adaptation*. New York and London: Routledge.

———. 2013. *A Theory of Adaptation*. 2nd ed. New York: Routledge.

———, and Michael Hutcheon. 1999. *Opera: Desire, Disease, Death*. Lincoln: University of Nebraska Press.

Hutchinson, Ben. 2006. "'Egg Boxes Stacked in a Crate': Narrative Status and Its Implications." In *W. G. Sebald: History, Memory, Trauma*, edited by Scott Denham and Mark R. McCulloh, 171–82. Berlin: de Gruyter.

———. 2009a. "'Ein Penelopewerk des Vergessens'? W. G. Sebald's Nietzschean Poetics of Forgetting." *Forum for Modern Language Studies* 45, no. 3: 325–36.

———. 2009b. *W. G. Sebald: Die dialektische Imagination*. Berlin: de Gruyter.

———. 2011. "The Shadow of Resistance: W. G. Sebald and the Frankfurt School." *Journal of European Studies* 41, no. 3–4: 267–84.

Huyssen, Andreas. 2003. *Present Pasts: Urban Palimpsests and the Politics of Memory*. Stanford, Calif.: Stanford University Press.

———. 2010. "Authentic Ruins: Products of Modernity." In *Ruins of Modernity*, edited by Julia Hell and Andreas Schönle, 17–28. Durham, N.C.: Duke University Press.

Jacobs, Carol. 1996. "Walter Benjamin: Topographically Speaking." In *Walter Benjamin: Theoretical Questions*, edited by David S. Ferris, 94–117. Stanford, Calif.: Stanford University Press.

———. 2015. *Sebald's Vision*. New York: Columbia University Press.

Jacobs, Karen. 2014. "Sebald's Apparitional Nabokov." *Twentieth-Century Literature* 61, no. 2 (Summer): 137–68.

Jaggi, Maya. 2001. "Recovered Memories." *The Guardian*, September 21. Accessed January 7, 2011. http://www.guardian.co.uk/books/2001/sep/22/artsandhumanities.highereducation.

Jameson, Frederic. 1999. *Postmodernism; or, The Cultural Logic of Late Capitalism*. Durham, N.C.: Duke University Press.

Janouch, Gustav. 1971. *Conversations with Kafka*. Translated by Goronwy Rees. London: New Directions.

Jay, Martin. 1994. *Downcast Eyes: The Denigration of Vision in Twentieth-Century French Thought*. Berkeley: University of California Press.

Jefferson, Margo. 2001. "Writing in the Shadows." Review of *The Rings of Saturn*, by W. G. Sebald. *New York Times on the Web*. March 18. https://www.nytimes.com/books/01/03/18/bookend/bookend.html.

Johnson, D. Barton, and Brian Boyd. 2002. "Prologue: The Otherworld." In *Nabokov's World, Volume 1: The Shape of Nabokov's World*, edited by Jane Grayson, Arnold McMillin, and Priscilla Meyer, 19–25. Basingstoke, U.K.: Palgrave Macmillan.

Kafka, Franz. 1935. *Erzählungen und kleine Prosa*. Vol. 1 of *Gesammelte Schriften*. Edited by Max Brod. Berlin: Schocken.

———. 1936. *Beschreibung eines Kampfes*. Vol. 5 of *Gesammelte Schriften*. Edited by Max Brod. Prague: Mercy.

———. 1958. *Briefe 1902–1924*. Vol. 7 of *Gesammelte Werke*. Edited by Max Brod. New York: Schocken Books.

———. 1971. *The Complete Stories*. Edited by Nahum N. Glatzer. New York: Schocken Books.

———. 1973. *Letters to Felice*. Edited by Erich Heller and Jürgen Born. Translated by James Stern and Elisabeth Duckworth. New York: Schocken Books.

———. 1974. *Amerika*. Translated by Willa and Edwin Muir. New York: Schocken Books.

———. 1976. *The Diaries of Franz Kafka, 1910–1923*. Edited by Max Brod. New York: Schocken Books.

———. 1977. *Letters to Friends, Family, and Editors*. Translated by Richard and Clara Winston. New York: Schocken Books.

———. 1990. *Tagebücher*. Edited by Hans-Gerd Koch, Michael Müller, and Malcolm Pasley. Frankfurt am Main: S. Fischer Verlag.

———. 1992a. *The Castle*. Translated by Willa and Edwin Muir. New York: Schocken Books.

———. 1992b. *The Trial*. Translated by Willa and Edwin Muir. New York: Schocken Books.

———. 1994. *Collected Aphorisms*. Translated by Malcolm Pasley. London: Penguin Books.

Kempinski, Avi. 2007. "'Quel Roman!': Sebald, Barthes, and the Pursuit of the Mother-Image." In *Searching for Sebald: Photography after W. G. Sebald*, edited by Lisa Patt with Christel Dillbohner, 456–71. Los Angeles: Institute of Cultural Inquiry.

Kilbourn, R. J. A. 1998. "Redemption Revalued in *Tristan and Isolde*: Schopenhauer, Wagner, Nietzsche." *University of Toronto Quarterly* 67, no. 4 (Fall): 781–88.

———. 2004. "Architecture and Cinema: The Representation of Memory in W. G. Sebald's *Austerlitz*." In *W. G. Sebald: A Critical Companion*, edited by J. J. Long and Anne Whitehead, 140–54. Edinburgh: Edinburgh University Press.

———. 2005. "*The Unnamable*: Denegative Dialogue." *European Joyce Studies* 16: 63–89.

———. 2006. "Kafka, Nabokov . . . Sebald: Intertextuality and Narratives of Redemption in *Vertigo* and *The Emigrants*." In *W. G. Sebald: History, Memory, Trauma*, edited by Scott Denham and Mark R. McCulloh, 33–63. Berlin: de Gruyter.

———. 2007. "Catastrophe with Spectator: Subjectivity, Intertextuality and the Representation of History in *The Rings of Saturn*." In *W. G. Sebald and the Writing of History*, edited by Anne Fuchs and J. J. Long, 139–62. Würzburg: Königshausen and Neumann.

———. 2010. *Cinema, Memory, Modernity: The Representation of Memory from the Art Film to Transnational Cinema*. New York: Routledge.

———. 2013. "The Question of Genre in Sebald's Prose (Towards a Post-Memorial Literature of Restitution)." In *A Literature of Restitution: Critical Essays on W. G. Sebald*, edited by Jeanette Baxter, Valerie Henitiuk, and Ben Hutchinson, 247–64. Manchester, U.K.: Manchester University Press.

———. 2015. "Adapting Venice: Intermedial Relations in Visconti, Sebald, and Kafka." *Mosaic* 48, no. 3 (September): 57–74.

Klebes, Martin. 2003. *Remembering Failure: Philosphy and the Form of the Novel*. Dissertation abstract, Northwestern University. Accessed: May 15, 2015. https://philpapers.org/rec/KLERFP.

Klibansky, Raymond, Erwin Panofsky, and Fritz Saxl. 1964. *Saturn and Melancholy: Studies in the History of Natural Philosophy, Religion, and Art*. New York: Basic Books.

Koelb, Clayton. 1989. *Kafka's Rhetoric: The Passion of Reading*. Ithaca, N.Y.: Cornell University Press.

Köhler, Andrea. 1997. "Katastrophe mit Zuschauer." *Neue Zürcher Zeitung*, November 22.

Koyré, Alexandre. 1958. *From the Closed World to the Infinite Universe*. New York: Harper and Row.

Kracauer, Siegfried. 1995. *The Mass Ornament: Weimar Essays*. Edited and translated by Thomas Y. Levin. Cambridge, Mass.: Harvard University Press.

———. 2004. *From Caligari to Hitler*. Princeton, N.J.: Princeton University Press.

Kristeva, Julia. 1986. "Word, Dialogue and Novel." In *The Kristeva Reader*, edited by Toril Moi, 34–61. New York: Columbia University Press.

Kushner, Tony. 2013. *Angels in America: A Gay Fantasia on National Themes*. New York: Theatre Communications Group.

Lacan, Jacques. 1973. "Anamorphosis." In *The Four Fundamental Concepts of Psycho-Analysis* Book XI, edited by Jacques-Alain Miller, translated by Alan Sheridan, 79–90. New York: Norton.

———. 1995. *Reading Seminar XI: Lacan's Four Fundamental Concepts of Psychoanalysis*. Edited by Richard Feldstein, Bruce Fink, and Maire Jaanus. Albany: SUNY Press.

Lambropoulos, Vassilis. 1993. *The Rise of Eurocentrism: Anatomy of Interpretation*. Princeton, N.J.: Princeton University Press.

Landsberg, Alison. 2003. "Prosthetic Memory: The Ethics and Politics of Memory in an Age of Mass Culture." In *Memory and Popular Film*, edited by Paul Grainge, 144–61. New York: Manchester University Press.

Last Year at Marienbad. 1999. DVD. Directed by Alain Resnais. New York: Fox Lorber.

Leder, Drew. 1990. *The Absent Body*. Chicago: University of Chicago Press.

Leiser, Erwin. 1974. *Nazi Cinema*. Translated by Gertrud Mander and David Wilson. London: Secker and Warburg.

Levinas, Emmanuel. 1986. "The Trace of the Other." In *Deconstruction in Context: Literature and Philosophy*, edited by Mark C. Taylor, 345–59. Chicago: University of Chicago Press.

Littell, Jonathan. 2010. *The Kindly Ones*. Toronto: McClelland and Stewart.

Long, Jonathan. 2003. "History, Narrative, and Photography in W. G. Sebald's *Die Ausgewanderten*." *Modern Language Review* 98, no. 1 (January): 117–37.

———. 2006. "Disziplin und Geständnis: Ansätze zu einer Foucaultschen Sebald-Lektüre." In *W. G. Sebald: Politische Archäologie und melancholische Bastelei*, edited by Claudia Öhlschläger and Michael Niehaus, 217–37. Berlin: Schmidt.

———. 2007. *W. G. Sebald: Image, Archive, Modernity*. New York: Columbia University Press.

———. 2011. "In the Contact Zone: W. G. Sebald and the Ethnographic Imagination." *Journal of European Studies* 41, no. 3–4: 413–30.

——— and Anne Whitehead, eds. 2004. *W. G. Sebald: A Critical Companion*. Edinburgh: Edinburgh University Press

Lubow, Arthur. 2007. "Crossing Boundaries." In *The Emergence of Memory: Conversations with W. G. Sebald*, edited by Lynne Sharon Schwartz, 159–73. New York: Seven Stories Press.

Lucretius. 2007. *On the Nature of Things*, translated by A. E. Stallings. London: Penguin Books.

Magris, Claudio. 1999. *Microcosms*. Translated by Iain Halliday. London: Harvill Press.

———. 2001. *Danube*. Translated by Patrick Creagh. London: Harvill Press.

———. 2008a. *Blindly*. Translated by Anne Milano Appel. New Haven, Conn.: Yale University Press.

———. 2008b. "The Self That Writes." Translated by Nick Carter. Almost Island Dialogues, New Delhi, March 8. Accessed May 10, 2009. http://almostisland .com/essay/the_self_that_writes.php.

———. 2011. "You Will Therefore Understand." Translated by Anne Milano Appel. *Quaderni d'italianistica* 32, no. 1: 7–25.

Mars-Jones, Adam. 2006. "Climbing the Family Tree." Review of *The View from Castle Rock*, by Alice Munro. *The Observer*, November 5. Accessed May 15, 2015. https://www.theguardian.com/books/2006/nov/05/fiction.features

Massumi, Brian. 2002. *Parables for the Virtual: Movement, Affect, Sensation*. Durham, N.C.: Duke University Press.

McCulloh, Mark R. 2003. *Understanding W. G. Sebald*. Columbia: University of South Carolina Press.

———. 2006. "Destruction and Transcendence in W. G. Sebald." *Philosophy and Literature* 30, no. 2 (October): 395–409.

McIntyre, Timothy. 1999. "Doing Her Duty and Writing Her Life: Alice Munro's Cultural and Historical Context." In *The Rest of the Story: Critical Essays on Alice Munro*, edited by Robert Thacker, 52–67. Toronto: ECW Press.

McRobbie, Angela. 1994. "The *Passagenwerk* and the Place of Walter Benjamin in Cultural Studies." In *Postmodernism and Popular Culture*, 96–120. London: Routledge.

Melancholia. 2011. DVD. Directed by Lars von Trier. London: Eone Films.

Millington, Barry, ed. 2006. *The New Grove Guide to Wagner and His Operas*. Oxford: Oxford University Press.

Moog-Grünewald, Maria, ed. 2010. *The Reception of Myth and Mythology.* Translated by Duncan Smart. Leiden: Brill.

Morgan, Peter. 2005. "The Sign of Saturn: Melancholy, Homelessness and Apocalypse in W. G. Sebald's Prose Narratives." *German Life and Letters* 58, no. 1 (January): 75–92.

Morson, Gary Saul, and Caryl Emerson. 1990. *Mikhail Bakhtin: Creation of a Prosaics.* Stanford, Calif.: Stanford University Press.

Mosbach, Bettina. 2008. *Figurationen der Katastrophe: Ästhetische Verfahren in W. G. Sebalds "Die Ringe des Saturn" und "Austerlitz."* Bielefeld: Aisthesis.

Müller, Heiner. 1977. "Germania Death in Berlin." In *Explosion of a Memory: Writings,* edited and translated by Carl Weber, 39–87. New York: Performing Arts Journal.

———. 1984. *Hamletmachine and Other Texts for the Stage.* Edited and translated by Carl Weber. New York: Performing Arts Journal.

Munro, Alice. 1994. *Open Secrets.* Toronto: McClelland and Stewart.

———. 1996. *Dance of the Happy Shades.* New York: Vintage.

———. 2006a. *The View from Castle Rock.* Toronto: Penguin Books.

———. 2006b. *Who Do You Think You Are?* Toronto: Penguin Books.

———. 2008. *Lives of Girls and Women.* Toronto: Penguin Books.

———. 2009. *Too Much Happiness.* New York: Vintage.

Nabokov, Vladimir. 1942. "What Faith Means to a Resisting People." *Wellesley Magazine* 26, no. 4: 212.

———. 1973. *Strong Opinions.* New York: McGraw-Hill.

———. 1980. *Lectures on Literature.* Edited by Fredson Bowers. San Diego: Harcourt.

———. 1987. *Speak, Memory: An Autobiography Revisited.* Harmondsworth, U.K.: Penguin Books.

———. 1989. *Speak, Memory: An Autobiography Revisited.* New York: Vintage.

———. 1990. *Bend Sinister.* New York: Vintage.

———. 2008. *The Real Life of Sebastian Knight.* New York: New Directions.

Nancy, Jean-Luc. 1991. Introduction to *Who Comes After the Subject?,* 1–8. Edited by Eduardo Cadava, Peter Conner, and Jean-Luc Nancy. New York: Routledge.

Naremore, James. 2000. *Film Adaptation.* New Brunswick, N.J.: Rutgers University Press.

The New Oxford Annotated Bible with the Apocrypha: Revised Standard Version. 1977. Edited by Herbert G. May and Bruce M. Metzger. New York: Oxford University Press.

O'Brien, Susie, and Imre Szeman. 2004. *Popular Culture: A User's Guide.* Scarborough, Ont.: Thomson-Nelson.

Orpheus. 2000. DVD. Directed by Jean Cocteau. New York: Criterion Collection.

Ovid. 2002. *Metamorphoses.* Translated by Arthur Golding. Edited by Madeleine Forey. London: Penguin Books.

Ozick, Cynthia. 1996. "The Posthumous Sublime." Review of *The Emigrants. New Republic,* December 16, 33–35.

Panofsky, Erwin. 1953. *Early Netherlandish Painting.* Cambridge, Mass.: Harvard University Press.

———. 1997. *Perspective as Symbolic Form.* New York: Zone Books.

Parmegiani, Sandra. 2011. "The Presence of Myth in Claudio Magris's Postmillennial Narrative." *Quaderni d'italianistica* 32, no. 1 (Spring): 111–34.

Patt, Lise. 2007. "Introduction: Searching for Sebald; What I Know for Sure." In *Searching for Sebald: Photography after W. G. Sebald*, edited by Lise Patt with Christel Dillbohner. Los Angeles: Institute of Cultural Inquiry.

Pearson, Ann. 2008. "'Remembrance . . . Is Nothing Other Than a Quotation'": The Intertextual Fictions of W. G. Sebald." *Comparative Literature* 60, no. 3: 261–78.

Prager, Brad. 2006. "Sebald's Kafka." In *W. G. Sebald: History, Memory, Trauma*, edited by Scott Denham and Mark R. McCulloh, 105–26. Berlin: de Gruyter.

Pratt, Mary Louise. 2008. *Imperial Eyes: Travel Writing and Transculturation*. 2nd ed. New York: Routledge.

Presner, Todd Samuel. 2004. "'What a Synoptic and Artificial View Reveals': Extreme History and the Modernism of W. G. Sebald's Realism." *Criticism* (Summer): 341–60.

———. 2010. "Hegel's Philosophy of World History via Sebald's Imaginary of Ruins: A Contrapuntal Critique of the 'New Space' of Modernity." In *Ruins of Modernity*, edited by Julia Hell and Andreas Schönle, 193–211. Durham, N.C.: Duke University Press.

Proust, Marcel. 1996. *In Search of Lost Time, Volume 1: Swann's Way*. Translated by C. K. Scott Moncrieff. London: Vintage.

Redekop, Magdalene. 1999. "Alice Munro and the Scottish National Grotesque." In *The Rest of the Story: Critical Essays on Alice Munro*, edited by Robert Thacker, 21–43. Toronto: ECW Press.

Renfrew, Alastair. 2014. *Mikhail Bakhtin*. Routledge Critical Thinkers. London: Routledge.

Ribó, Ignasi. 2009. "The One-Winged Angel: History and Memory in the Literary Discourse of W. G. Sebald." *Orbis Litterarum* 64, no.3: 222–62.

Rilke, Rainer Maria. 1978. *Duino Elegies*. Translated by David Young. New York: Norton.

Robbins, Jill. 1991. *Prodigal Son/Elder Brother: Interpretation and Alterity in Augustine, Petrarch, Kafka, Levinas*. Chicago: University of Chicago Press.

Rosand, Ellen. 2007. *Monteverdi's Last Operas: A Venetian Trilogy*. Berkeley: University of California Press.

Rosenzweig, Franz. 2005. *The Star of Redemption*. Translated by Barbara E. Galli. Madison: University of Wisconsin Press.

Rutledge, David S. 2011. *Nabokov's Permanent Mystery: The Expression of Metaphysics in His Work*. Jefferson, N.C.: MacFarlane.

Ryan, Judith. 2007. "Fulgurations: Sebald and Surrealism." *Germanic Review* 82, no. 3 (Summer): 227–49.

Said, Edward W. 1994. *Culture and Imperialism*. New York: Vintage.

Saint Augustine. 1988. *Confessions*. Translated by R. S. Pine-Coffin. London: Penguin Books.

Sanders, Julie. 2006. *Adaptation and Appropriation*. London: Routledge.

Schwartz, Lynne Sharon, ed. 2007. *The Emergence of Memory: Conversations with W. G. Sebald*. New York: Seven Stories Press.

Scott, A. O. 2006. "Native Ground." Review of *The View from Castle Rock*. *New York Times*, December 10. Accessed May 15, 2015. https://www.nytimes.com/2006/12/10/books/review/Scott.t.html.

Sebald, W. G. 1972. "The Undiscover'd Country: The Death Motif in Kafka's *Castle*." *Journal of European Studies* 2, no. 1: 22–34.

———. 1976. "The Law of Ignominy: Authority, Messianism and Exile in *Das Schloß*." In *On Kafka: Semi-Centenary Perspectives*, edited by Franz Kuna, 42–58. London: Elek.

———. 1988. "Surveying the Scene: Some Introductory Remarks." In *A Radical Stage: Theatre in Germany in the 1970s and 1980s*, edited by W. G. Sebald, 1–8. Oxford: Berg; New York: St. Martin's Press.

———. 1990. *Schwindel: Gefühle*. Frankfurt am Main: Fischer.

———. 1992. *Die Ausgewanderten: Vier lange Erzählungen*. Frankfurt am Main: Fischer.

———. 1994. *Die Beschreibung des Unglücks: Zur österreichischen Literatur von Stifter bis Handke*. Frankfurt am Main: Fischer.

———. 1995. *Die Ringe des Saturn: Eine englische Wallfahrt*. Frankfurt am Main: Fischer.

———. 1996. *The Emigrants*. Translated by Michael Hulse. New York: New Directions.

———. 1998. *The Rings of Saturn*. Translated by Michael Hulse. New York: New Directions.

———. 1999. *Vertigo*. Translated by Michael Hulse. London: Vintage.

———. 2000. *Austerlitz*. Munich: Hanser.

———. 2001. *Austerlitz*. Translated by Anthea Bell. Toronto: Knopf.

———. 2002. *After Nature*. Translated by Michael Hamburger. New York: Modern Library.

———. 2003. *On the Natural History of Destruction*. Translated by Anthea Bell. New York: Random House.

———. 2004a. "An Attempt at Restitution: A Memory of a German City." *New Yorker*, December 20, 110–14.

———. 2004b. *Unrecounted*. Translated by Michael Hamburger. New York: New Directions.

———. 2005. *Campo Santo*. Translated by Anthea Bell. New York: Random House.

Shakespeare, William. 1997. *King Lear*. Edited by R. A. Foakes. Arden Shakespeare. London: Bloomsbury.

Shaviro, Steven. 2010. *Post-cinematic Affect*. Washington, D.C.: Zero Books.

Sheppard, Richard. 2005. "Dexter—Sinister: Some Observations on Decrypting the Mors Code in the Work of W. G. Sebald." *Journal of European Studies* 35, no. 4: 419–63.

———. 2011. "Guest Editor's Preface." *Journal of European Studies* 41, no. 3–4: 201–2.

Sill, Oliver. 1997. "'Aus dem Jäger ist ein Schmetterling geworden': Textbeziehungen zwischen Werken von W. G. Sebald, Franz Kafka und Vladimir Nabokov." *Poetica* 29, no. 3/4:596–623.

Skonechnaia, Olga. 2002. "The Wandering Jew as a Metaphor for Memory in Nabokov's Poetry and Prose of the 1920s and 1930s." In *Nabokov's World, Volume 1: The Shape of Nabokov's World*, edited by Jane Grayson, Arnold McMillin, and Priscilla Meyer, 186–95. Basingstoke, U.K.: Palgrave Macmillan.

Somacarerra, Pilar. 2015. "'The Unavoidable Collision of Religion and Life': Scots Presbyterianism in Alice Munro's Fiction." *Studies in Canadian Literature* 40, no. 2:88–107.

Sontag, Susan. 1979. Introduction to *One-Way Street*, by Walter Benjamin, 7–28. Translated by Edmund Jephcott and Kingsley Shorter. London: Verso.

———. 1983. *Under the Sign of Saturn*. London: Writers and Readers.

———. 2001. *On Photography*. New York: Picador.

———. 2003. *Regarding the Pain of Others*. New York: Farrar, Straus and Giroux.

Stam, Robert. 2000. *Film Theory: An Introduction*. Oxford: Blackwell.

———. 2005. *Literature through Film: Realism, Magic, and the Art of Adaptation*. Oxford: Blackwell.

Stendhal. (1839) 2000. *The Charterhouse of Parma*. Translated by Richard Howard. New York: Modern Library.

Sterne, Laurence. 1983. *The Life and Opinions of Tristram Shandy, Gentleman*. Oxford: Oxford University Press.

Sturken, Marita. 2008. "Memory, Consumerism, and Media: Reflections on the Emergence of the Field." *Memory Studies* 1, no. 1: 73–78.

Sturken, Marita, and Lisa Cartwright. 2001. *Practices of Looking: An Introduction to Visual Culture*. Oxford: Oxford University Press.

Suchoff, David. 2012. *Kafka's Jewish Languages: The Hidden Openness of Tradition*. Philadelphia: University of Pennsylvania Press.

Taylor, Charles. 1989. *Sources of the Self: The Making of the Modern Identity*. Cambridge, Mass.: Harvard University Press.

———. 2007. *A Secular Age*. Cambridge, Mass.: Belknap Press.

Thacker, Eugene. 2010. *After Life*. Chicago: University of Chicago Press.

Thacker, Robert. 2008. "A 'Booming Tender Sadness': Alice Munro's Irish." In *Canada: Text and Territory*, edited by Máire Áine Ní Mhainnín and Elizabeth Tilley, 132–40. Newcastle, U.K.: Cambridge Scholars.

Theisen, Bianca. 2004. "Prose of the World: Sebald's Literary Travels." *Germanic Review* 79, no. 3: 163–79.

———. 2006. "A Natural History of Destruction: W. G. Sebald's *The Rings of Saturn*." *Modern Language Notes* 121, no. 3 (April): 563–81.

Wagenbach, Klaus. 1984. *Franz Kafka: Pictures of a Life*. Translated by Arthur S. Wensinger. New York: Pantheon.

Ward, Simon. 2004. "Ruins and Poetics in the Works of W. G. Sebald." In *W. G. Sebald: A Critical Companion*, edited by J. J. Long and Anne Whitehead, 58–71. Edinburgh: Edinburgh University Press.

Watt, Ian. 1979. *Conrad in the Nineteenth Century*. Berkeley: University of California Press.

———. 1984. *The Rise of the Novel: Studies in Defoe, Richardson and Fielding*. Berkeley: University of California Press.

Waugh, Patricia. 1996. *Metafiction: The Theory and Practice of Self-Conscious Fiction*. London: Routledge.

Weiss, Peter. 1965. *The Investigation*. Translation Jon Swan and Ulu Grosbard. Woodstock, Ill.: Dramatic Publishing.

Wild Strawberries. 2007. DVD. Directed by Ingmar Bergman. New York: Criterion Collection.

Williams, Arthur. 1998. "The Elusive First-Person Plural: Real Absences in Reiner Kunze, Bernd-Dieter Hüge, and W. G. Sebald." In *"'Whose Story?'": Continuities in Contemporary German-Language Literature*, edited by Arthur Williams, Stuart Parkes, and Julian Preece, 85–113. Bern: Lang.

———. 2000. "W. G. Sebald: A Holistic Approach to Borders, Texts and Perspectives." In *German-Language Literature Today: International and Popular?*, edited by Arthur Williams, Stuart Parkes, and Julian Preece, 99–118. Bern: Lang.

———. 2001. "'Das korsakowsche Syndrom': Remembrance and Responsibility in W. G. Sebald." In *German Culture and the Uncomfortable Past: Representations of National Socialism in Contemporary Germanic Literature*, edited by Helmut Schmitz, 65–86. Aldershot, U.K.: Ashgate.

———. 2007. "Some thoughts On W. G. Sebald: Drawing, Painting, and Music." In *New German Literature: Life Writing and Dialogue Within the Arts*. Edited by Julian Preece, Franklin Finlay, and Ruth J. Owen, 51–74. Bern: Peter Lang.

Williams, Linda. 2001. *Playing the Race Card: Melodramas of Black and White from Uncle Tom to O. J. Simpson*. Princeton, N.J.: Princeton University Press.

Wittgenstein, Ludwig. 1995. *Tractatus Logico-Philosophicus*. Translated by D. F. Pears and B. F. McGuiness. London: Routledge.

Wolfe, Cary. 2010. *What Is Posthumanism?* Minneapolis and London: University of Minnesota.

Wolff, Lynn. 2009. "Literary Historiography: W. G. Sebald's Fiction." In *W. G. Sebald: Schreiben ex patria/Expatriate Writing*, edited by Gerhard Fischer, 317–32. Amsterdam: Rodopi.

Wood, Michael. 1994. *The Magician's Doubts: Nabokov and the Risks of Fiction*. London: Chatto and Windus.

Wordsworth, William, and Samuel Taylor Coleridge. 1991. *Lyrical Ballads*. Edited by R. L. Brett and A. R. Jones. London: Routledge.

Wright, Ronald. 2004. *A Short History of Progress*. Toronto: Anansi.

Yates, Francis A. 1966. *The Art of Memory*. Chicago: University of Chicago Press.

Zilcosky, John. 2003. *Kafka's Travels: Exoticism, Colonialism, and the Traffic of Writing*. New York: Palgrave Macmillan.

———. 2006. "Lost and Found: Disorientation, Nostalgia, and Holocaust Melodrama in Sebald's *Austerlitz*." *Modern Language Notes* 121: 679–98.

Zischler, Hanns. 2003. *Kafka Goes to the Movies*. Translated by Susan H. Gillespie. Chicago: University of Chicago Press.

Zisselsberger, Markus, ed. 2010. *The Undiscover'd Country: W. G. Sebald and the Poetics of Travel*. Rochester, N.Y.: Camden House.

Žižek, Slavoj. 2000. "Melancholy and the Act." *Critical Inquiry* 26, no. 4 (Summer): 657–81.

———. 2010. *Living in the End Times*. London: Verso.

INDEX

Adler, H. G., 154
Adorno, Theodor W., 28, 43, 69, 178n22; Kafka and, 68, 98; on poetry after Auschwitz, 18, 26, 27, 169
affect theory, 4, 148, 149
agency, 4, 5, 65, 96, 107, 111, 134, 159, 168
Albright, Daniel, 179n40
Alpers, Svetlana, 44, 45
angels in modern art and literature, 20, 30, 45, 91–96, 103–4, 189n9; in *Vertigo*, 97–101
appropriation, 5–6, 12, 143, 162, 163, 170, 173
archive (and archival subject), 8, 60, 121, 151
Aristotle, 7, 12, 193n27
Assmann, Jan, 111, 159
Atget, Eugène, 182n32
Augustine, 72, 115, 125, 131, 152, 182n24, 193n27, 193n36, 195n20
autonomy, 4, 57, 162
Ayhenvald, Yuliy, 123

Bakhtin, Mikhail, 3, 5, 7, 9, 146, 172, 195n10, 196n26, 196n1; chronotopes and, 21, 113–14, 140, 143, 145, 152, 154
Barrow, John D., 50
Barthes, Roland, 16, 43, 106, 131, 132, 193n38
Baudrillard, Jean, 36, 51
Bauer, Felice, 62, 68, 92, 101, 110, 191n35
Beckett, Samuel, 23–24, 38–41, 57, 66, 105, 109, 139, 159, 161
Benjamin, Walter, 43, 94; angel of history in, 20, 30, 45, 92, 94–96, 102, 103–4; *flâneur* figure of, 52, 178n20; *Jetztzeit* concept of, 55, 182n24, 184n9; Kafka and, 68, 109; Magris

and, 91; messianism and, 55, 61, 98, 163; "The Work of Art in the Age of Its Technological Reproducibility," 11, 15, 24, 25, 50, 106, 120, 182n32
Bennett, Alan, 51
Berger, John, 77, 182n27
Bergson, Henri, 115, 149, 182n24
Bergstrom, Anders, 15, 181n10, 181n20
Bernhard, Thomas, 33, 139, 169
Bernstein, Stephen, 153, 194n6
Blanchot, Maurice, 39, 112, 179n37, 181n10, 191n38
Bloch, Ernst, 55, 61–62
Blumenberg, Hans, 11, 18, 23, 24–26, 37, 51, 75, 84, 107
Bond, Greg, 51
Borges, Jorge Luis, 23, 70, 190n30, 197n11
Boyd, Brian, 78, 117
Boym, Svetlana, 136, 139, 147–48
Braidotti, Rosi, 14, 142, 175n18
Brecht, Bertolt, 34–35, 162
Brod, Max, 100
Brooks, Peter, 169, 172
Browne, Thomas, 28, 45, 57, 84–86, 181n16, 188n24
Bürger, Peter, 51
Burton, Robert, 43

Calinescu, Matei, 60
Canetti, Elias, 35, 92, 110, 167, 186n39, 191n35
capitalism, 9, 12, 16, 17–18, 24, 37, 41, 43–44, 46, 57, 75, 105–6, 181n10, 181n20; Adorno on, 28
Casanova, Giacomo, 60, 68, 69–71, 111
Casement, Roger, 31–32, 90, 196n6
catastrophe trope, 15, 23, 24–27, 32, 55, 57, 75, 103, 106, 162, 166, 176n4; history as, 10, 17, 18, 43, 163, 180n2; in Klee's *Angelus Novus*, 94